The Masonic Book Club

—————— Vol. 5A ——————

Masonic Membership of the Founding Fathers

Ronald E. Heaton

Westphalia Press
An Imprint of the Policy Studies Organization
Washington, DC

MASONIC MEMBERSHIP OF THE FOUNDING FATHERS

All Rights Reserved © 2025 by Policy Studies Organization

Westphalia Press
An imprint of Policy Studies Organization
1367 Connecticut Avenue NW
Washington, D.C. 20036
info@ipsonet.org

ISBN: 978-1-63723-686-4

Daniel Gutierrez-Sandoval, Executive Director
PSO and Westphalia Press

Updated material and comments on this edition
can be found at the Westphalia Press website:
www.westphaliapress.org

The Masonic Book Club

The *Masonic Book Club* (MBC) was formed in 1970 by two Illinois Masons, Alphonse Cerza, 33°, and Louis L. Williams, 33°. The MBC primarily reprinted out-of-print Masonic books with scholarly introductions; occasionally they would print additional texts as "bonuses" (though none were marked specifically as such on the title pages); sometimes a reprint would be marked "Masonic Book Club Edition"; often an unnumbered bonus was published jointly with the Illinois Lodge of Research or the Supreme Council, 33°, NMJ, USA.

Most of the MBC volumes indicated on the title page, "Volume [*Number*] of the Publications of the Masonic Book Club," some were misnumbered, and some were unnumbered. Indeed, the numbering of the early volumes was inconsistent. For example, *A Serious and Impartial Enquiry* is "Volume Five" (1974) but *Masonic Membership of the Founding Fathers* is "The Masonic Book Club Edition" (1974). Then, *Masonry Dissected* is "Volume Eight" (1977), *The Trestleboard* is "Volume 8A" (1978), and *Anderson's Constitutions of 1738* is "Volume Nine" (1978). If nothing else, MBC books keep bibliophiles on their toes.

The first volumes had deckle-edged paper and pages of slightly different sizes, though eventually the MBC settled into a 6"×9" trimmed-page format for their books. The books were bound in a dark blue fabric with gold lettering. Listed below are the fifty-nine MBC volumes published 1970–2010 with bonuses. N.B.: A number and letter, e.g. "Volume 8A," is a numbering for this reprint series.

The club originally was limited to 333 members, but the number grew to nearly 2,000, with 1,083 members when it dissolved in 2010. In 2017 MW Barry Weer, 33°, the last president of the MBC, transferred the MBC name and assets to the Supreme Council, 33°, SJ, USA. Under the editorship of Arturo de Hoyos, 33°, G∴C∴, and S. Brent Morris, 33°, G∴C∴, the revived Masonic Book Club has the goal of publishing classic Masonic books while supporting Scottish Rite, SJ, USA philanthropies.

Publications of the Masonic Book Club, 1970–2010

1	1970	*The Regius Poem*	Masonic Book Club
2	1971	*The Constitutions of the Free-Masons*	Benjamin Franklin
3	1972	*Ahiman Rezon*	Laurence Dermott
4	1973	*Illustrations of Masonry*	William Preston
5	1974	*A Serious and Impartial Enquiry into the Cause of the Present Decay of Free-Masonry in the Kingdom of Ireland*	Fifield D'Assigny
5A	1974*	*Masonic Membership of the Founding Fathers*	Ronald E. Heaton

6	1975	*The Signers of the Declaration of Independence*	David C. Whitney
7	1976	*The Signers of the Constitution of the United States*	Masonic Book Club
7A	1976*	*Masonic Symbols in American Decorative Art*	Louis L. Williams & Alphonse Cerza
8	1977	*Samuel Prichard's Masonry Dissected, 1730*	Harry Carr
8A	1978*	*Trestle-Board (A facsimile of the original Trestle Board by the Baltimore Masonic Convention of 1843)*	Dwight L. Smith
9	1978	*Anderson's Constitutions of 1738*	Lewis Edward & W. J. Hughan
10	1979	*Sufferings of John Coustos*	Wallace McLeod
11	1980	*The Revelations of a Square*	George Oliver
11A	1980	*Biblical Characters in Freemasonry*	John H. Van Gorden
11B	1980*	*A Masonic Reader's Guide*	*Guide* Alphonse Cerza & Thomas Warden
12	1981	*Three Distinct Knocks and Jachin and Boaz*	Harry Carr
13	1982	*Masonic Almanacs and Anti-Masonic Almanacs*	Plez A. Transou
13A	1982*	*Stephen A. Douglas: Freemason*	Wayne C. Temple
14	1983	*The Beginnings of Freemasonry in America*	Melvin M. Johnson
14A	1983*	*Bespangled, Painted & Embroidered: Decorated Masonic Aprons in America, 1790–1850*	Scottish Rite Masonic Museum & Library
14B	1983*	*Making a Mason at Sight*	Louis L. Williams
15	1984	*Masonic Concordance of the Holy Bible*	Charles Clyde Hunt
15A	1984*	*By Square and Compasses: The Building of Lincoln's Home and Its Saga*	Wayne C. Temple

16	1985	*The Old Gothic Constitutions*	Wallace McLeod
16A	1985*	*Modern Historical Characters in Freemasonry*	John H. Van Gorden
17	1986	*The Rise and Development of Organised Freemasonry*	Roy A. Wells
17A	1986*	*Ancient and Early Medieval Historical Characters in Freemasonry*	John H. Van Gorden
18	1987	*The Lodge in Friendship Village and Other Stories*	P. W. George
18A	1987*	*Masonic Charities*	John H. Van Gorden & Stewart M. L. Pollard
18B	1987*	*Medieval Historical Characters in Freemasonry*	John H. Van Gorden
18C	1987*	*George Washington in New York*	Allan Boudreau & Alexander Bleimann
19	1988	*Records of the Hole Crafte and Fellowship of Masons*	Edward Conder, Jr.
20	1989	*A Candid Disquisition of the Principles and Practices of the Most Ancient and Honourable Society of Free and Accepted Masons*	Wellins Calcott
20A	1989*	*Freemasonry and Nauvoo, 1839–1846*	Robin L. Carr
21	1990	*Masonic Odes and Poems*	Rob Morris
22	1991	*Lessing's Masonic Dialogues*	Gotthold Lessing
22A	1991*	*ABC of Freemasonry: A Book for Beginners*	Delmar D. Darrah
23	1992	*The Folger Manuscript*	S. Brent Morris
24	1993	*Freemasonry and Christianity: Lectures from Two Ages*	T. De Witt Peake & John J. Murchison
25	1994	*The Constitutions of St. John's Lodge*	Robin L. Carr
25A	1994*	*The Mystic Tie and Men of Letters*	Robin L. Carr
26	1995	*Recollections of a Masonic Veteran*	S. Brent Morris

27	1996	The Freemason's Monitor or Illustrations of Masonry in Two Parts	Thomas Smith Webb
28	1997	The Masonic Ladder or the Nine Steps to Ancient Freemasonry	John Sherer
28A	1997*	Freemasonry and Democracy: Its Evolution in North America	Allen E. Roberts & Wallace McLeod
29	1998	The Masonic Harp: Collection of Masonic Odes, Hymns, Songs	George Wingate Chase
30	1999	Symbolic Teachings of Masonry and Its Message	Thomas Milton Stewart
31	2000	Freemasonry Its Meaning and Significance, An Exposition of its Ethics, Religion and Philosophy	Otto Caspari
32	2001	K. R. Cama Masonic Jubilee Volume	Jivanji Jamshedji Modi
33	2002	Caementaria Hibernica	W. J. Chetwode Crawley
34	2003	A Daily Advancement in Masonic Knowledge	Wallace McLeod & S. Brent Morris
35	2004	The Craftsman, and Templar's Textbook and, also, Melodies for the Craft	Cornelius Moore
36	2005	The Text Book of Freemasonry	Retired Member of the Craft
37	2006	Orations of the Illustrious Brother Frederick Dalcho Esq., M.D.	Frederick Dalcho
38	2007	Antiquities of Freemasonry Comprising Illustrations of the Five Grand Periods of Masonry from the Creation of the World to the Dedication of King Solomon's Temple	George Oliver
39	2008	Diogenes' Lamp or an Examination of our Present-Day Morality and Enlightenment	Adam Weishaupt
40	2009	Proofs of Conspiracy Against All the Governments of Europe	John Robison
41	2010	The Evolution of Freemasonry	Delmar Darrah

*indicates a bonus book

Masonic Membership of the Founding Fathers

MASONIC MEMBERSHIP
OF THE
FOUNDING FATHERS

The Masonic Book Club Edition

1974

[This text appeared in the original version]

This Volume is
No. ___407___ *of 888 copies*
specially bound for the members of
The Masonic Book Club
Bloomington, Illinois
1974

PREFACE

Liberty

Running through all the events of the founding of our Nation, the desire for Liberty was the one factor that controlled every thought —that motivated every action. As our Founding Fathers watched the gathering storm and experienced the continuous acts of repression passed and practiced by their British rulers, the need for Freedom— freedom of thought, of speech, of peaceable assembly, of political action—determined every move they made, every step they took.

From the date of its concept in the minds of men, Masonry had stood for freedom, for liberty. Even the name "Freemasonry", no matter how defined, connotes that very thought. So it was completely natural that within the hearts and minds of the Freemasons of the New World, a desire for political freedom, whereby they could work out their own destiny, should become paramount. To translate such thought into action was in the finest tradition of free Englishmen. From the Magna Carta (1215 A.D.) onward, the citizens of England had struggled to throw off the yoke of oppression. The white men who first settled on our shores—the Pilgrims, the Puritans—were in search of religious liberty, a prime factor in the overall panorama of civil, religious, and political freedom.

Our Founding Fathers were not all Freemasons, but all were imbued with the love of Liberty. But many of their outstanding leaders were members of this Fraternity, and the Masonic idea of Liberty, Equality, and Fraternity permeated every action. Brother Heaton has shown this in compiling for us a historical record of our nation's Founders.

The Masonic Book Club is proud to present a copy of this book to its members. Brother Ronald E. Heaton, the author, worked on its contents for many years before its publication in 1965. Even then, it was an idea whose time would not ripen until our Bicentennial years arrived, and now it is most timely. The Masonic Service Association, under the leadership of its very eminent Executive Secretary, Conrad Hahn, first published and distributed this book in 1965. Now, a copy is hard to find so a reprint was needed.

Through the assistance of The Masonic Book Club, arrangements were made by Brother Hahn for the book to be reprinted by the Pantagraph Press of Bloomington, Illinois, a great printing firm here in Central Illinois, of which the Vice-President of our Club, Brother Fred A. Dolan, is Vice-President. Then, through the courtesy of Brother Hahn and with the enthusiastic approval of the author, Brother Ronald E. Heaton, additional copies were printed to allow us to distribute them to our members, as a bonus in tribute to the Bicentennial. These copies for our members have been specially bound in the Club's distinctive binding, and we now place them in your hands for your joy and delight.

Brother Alphonse Cerza, our Secretary, has prepared a special appendix which gives the list of Masonic Presidents and Vice-Presidents, and other valuable statistics, which we hope will make this book an even more valuable reference work. We are intensely proud of our national heritage; and we can be both proud of and thankful for those Masonic forefathers whose Wisdom contrived, whose strength executed, and whose ideals of Beauty adorned our great and glorious Republic, the citadel of Liberty and Freedom.

Louis L. Williams

MASONIC MEMBERSHIP OF THE FOUNDING FATHERS

by
BROTHER RONALD E. HEATON

Member, Charity Lodge No. 190, Norristown, Penna.;
Lehigh Consistory, 32°, A.A.S.R., Allentown, Penna.;
The American Lodge of Research, New York City;
Missouri Lodge of Research; Quatuor Coronati Lodge
No. 2076, London; Society of Blue Friars; Treasurer
and Fellow, The Philalethes Society

THE MASONIC SERVICE ASSOCIATION
8120 FENTON STREET
SILVER SPRING, MD 20910

1974

Copyright, 1965
by The Masonic Service Association of the U. S.
Second Printing, 1974

FOREWORD

This book is an effort on the part of Brother Ronald E. Heaton, of Norristown, Pennsylvania, to search out the answers to questions frequently asked by Masons about the part played by our colonial brethren in the founding of this great nation. The Masonic Service Association is proud to present a work whose thorough scholarship so admirably serves the cause of Masonic Light and Truth.

Originally this material was presented in a series of six Digests which examined the Masonic membership of General Officers of the Continental Army, Washington's Aides and Military Secretaries, Signers of the Articles of Association, Signers of the Declaration of Independence, Signers of the Articles of Confederation, and Signers of the Constitution of the United States. Brother Heaton prepared five of these Digests; the sixth, covering the Declaration of Independence, was prepared by Brother W. Eugene Rice, P. M., of Virginia, and Brother William Moseley Brown, P. G. M., of Virginia.

These military and political leaders are presented in three groupings: I—Membership in the Masonic Fraternity fully documented; II—Membership in the Masonic Fraternity doubtful; III—No evidence of Masonic membership or activity.

The present work combines the material originally presented with much additional information. Its purpose is to bring to the attention of Freemasons the names of 241 individuals who played a prominent part in breaking the ties with Great Britain and setting up our present form of government, and then to establish, when possible from available records, their connection with Freemasonry.

From the convening of the First Continental Congress in Philadelphia on September 5, 1774, until the adoption of the Federal Constitution in the same city on September 17, 1787, a total of 355 representatives from the thirteen colonies sat in the Congresses. There were 74 General Officers in the Continental Army, including General Washington, and another 29 men served as his Aides and Military Secretaries. Many of those in the two Continental Congresses served a short period of time, and many served between the times of great events, like the Declaration of Independence or the adoption of our Constitution.

This present work considers only those who actually signed the documents mentioned previously, plus the military men, a total of 241 individuals. Some appear on more than one list; none appears on all six lists. One man, however, does stand out prominently,—Roger Sherman of Connecticut, who signed all four of the great state papers: the Articles of Association, the Declaration of Independence, the Articles of Confederation, and the Constitution of the United States.

Of these 241 individuals, it is shown that 69 were Masons, 26 of doubtful membership, and 146 not known to be Masons.

It was planned to reproduce a portrait and facsimile signature of all individuals in Group I. Not all the portraits required could be located. If any reader has knowledge of the existence of portraits missing from Group I, the publisher would appreciate being so informed.

Brother Heaton's scholarship provides documentary evidence concerning the Masonic membership of Revolutionary patriots. While it may prove disappointing to some members of the Fraternity because it necessitates a downward revision in the numbers of Masons who were involved in the stirring events of 1770-1790, it in no way lessens the truth or the importance of the statement made forty years ago by Illustrious Melvin M. Johnson, P. G. M. of Massachusetts and Sovereign Grand Commander of the Supreme Council, 33°, A.A.S.R., Northern Jurisdiction, U.S.A., when he wrote in *The Beginnings of Freemasonry in America:*

> "A study of the tremendous influence which Freemasonry had in the Pre-Revolutionary days, in the years of that war, and throughout the formative period of American institutions, will demonstrate that Freemasonry has exercised a greater influence upon the establishment and development of this Government than any other single institution. Neither general historians nor the members of the Fraternity since the days of the first Constitutional Conventions have ever realized how much the United States of America owes to Freemasonry, and how great a part it played in the birth of the nation and the establishment of the Landmarks of that civilization which has given to the citizens of this great land the liberty which they enjoy."

THE EDITOR

BIOGRAPHICAL SOURCES

In the preparation of this work, it has not been the purpose to give complete biographical information on each individual. Many of them have been the subject of biographies over the years. Only a few facts are given for each man, merely to indicate the service rendered to his country during those critical years of our history.

Most of the biographical information on the political leaders has been taken from *The Biographical Directory of the American Congress, 1774-1949,* a Government Printing Office publication, supplemented by information from other sources, principally *The Dictionary of American Biography.* Additional information given is quoted fully in the text.

Francis B. Heitman's work, *Historical Register of Officers of the Continental Army,* Washington, 1914, has been consulted for the military records of those who served in the armed forces during the Revolutionary War.

For the military men, the listing of each officer is according to his rank in the Continental Army and priority of date of appointment, showing period of service in that grade. Service in the Militia of the Colonies is shown in some instances, as well as brevet commissions authorized by Congress.

ACKNOWLEDGMENTS

It is a source of great pleasure for the author to acknowledge with sincere thanks and appreciation the help received from various sources in the preparation of this work. Many have contributed of their specialized knowledge and experience by letter and in person, when requested—so many that it is not possible to mention each by name.

A special word of thanks should be extended to a few in particular for the help given from the beginning of this venture: Brother James R. Case, Grand Historian of the Grand Lodge of Connecticut, for his comments and suggestions from time to time, and for permission to use liberally so much of his own material; Brother Ray Baker Harris (now deceased), P. G. M. (District of Columbia), Librarian of the Supreme Council, Southern Masonic Jurisdiction, Washington, D. C., and his able assistant, Mrs. Inge Baum, for making material available there; Brother William J. Paterson, former Curator and Librarian of the Grand Lodge of Pennsylvania, now retired, whose help was given liberally from the beginning; to his successor, Brother William A. Carpenter, the present Curator and Librarian, and particularly to Brother Charles S. Baker, Jr., who made available some of the vast lore of Masonic information in his care; Mrs. Muriel D. Taylor, Librarian of the Grand Lodge of Massachusetts, who checked much of the original material and supplied the answers to many questions raised, and also made available the records in the Office of the Grand Secretary; Brother Wendell K. Walker, the Librarian of the Grand Lodge of New York, and now the Grand Secretary there, and his assistant, Miss Grace R. Curtis, for providing access to Library and Grand Lodge records there.

To the staffs of the National Archives and the Manuscript Division of the Library of Congress in Washington, D. C., for assistance generously given; and to Brigadier General Herbert H. Vreeland, Jr., Greenwich, Connecticut, for much of the biographical information on the foreign officers who served in the Continental Army.

Brother William Moseley Brown, P. G. M. (Virginia), was generous with his words of encouragement and help from time to time when it was needed most. His inspiration did much to bring this present work to completion; and finally, to the staff of The Masonic Service Association, whose care in editing the manuscripts and seeing that corrections and alterations were properly made and passed on to the printer, a very special word of thanks.

Acknowledgment is made to the Library of Congress, Washington, D. C., The Historical Society of Pennsylvania, Philadelphia, Pennsylvania, the Valley Forge Park Commission, Valley Forge, Pennsylvania, the Yale University Art Gallery, and the Independence National Historical Park (Philadelphia) for making available portraits and documents containing the signatures of patriots illustrated in this work, as well as for permission to reproduce them herein.

R. E. H.

February, 1965

KEY TO THE REFERENCES IN THE TEXT

ALR—American Lodge of Research, *Transactions* for Volume and Number quoted.

APPLETON—*Appleton's Cyclopedia of American Biography.*

BDAC—*Biographical Directory of the American Congress, 1774-1949.*

BOYDEN—William L. Boyden, author of *Masonic Presidents, Vice Presidents, and Signers,* Washington, D. C., 1927.

BROWN—William Moseley Brown, author of *George Washington, Freemason,* Richmond, 1952.

CASE—James R. Case, Grand Historian, Grand Lodge, A. F. & A. M., Connecticut.

DAB—*Dictionary of American Biography.*

DENSLOW—William R. Denslow, author of *10,000 Famous Freemasons.*

GL Proc.—*Proceedings* of the Grand Lodge referred to.

HAYDEN—Sidney Hayden, author of *Washington and his Masonic Compeers,* New York, 1867.

LC—Library of Congress.

LOSSING—Benson J. Lossing, author of *The Pictorial Field-Book of the Revolution,* New York, 1859.

MORSE—Sidney Morse, author of *Freemasonry in the American Revolution,* Washington, D. C., 1924.

OML—Julius F. Sachse, author of *Old Masonic Lodges of Pennsylvania.*

O R—Original records of Lodge referred to.

ROTH—Philip A. Roth, author of *Masonry in the Formation of our Government,* Milwaukee, 1927.

TATSCH—J. Hugo Tatsch, author of *Freemasonry in the Thirteen Colonies,* New York, 1929.

Other sources are quoted fully in the text.

HISTORICAL BACKGROUND

The American Revolution was not a spontaneous event, but rather the result of a pent-up discontent, built up over a period of years.

The French & Indian War, known as the Seven Years' War in Europe, lasted from June 9, 1756, to February 10, 1763, and had cost Great Britain about $560,000,000. The Royal Court and Parliament, looking for some way to pay the bill, decided that since the American colonies would benefit from the results of the war, part if not all of the cost should be borne by them. Determined to maintain absolute jurisdiction over the colonies, oppressive measures were proposed, the most important of which was the Stamp Act.

Such a tax was not new. Benjamin Franklin favored a plan for levying of a stamp duty on all legal writings and instruments; later, Governor Shirley of Massachusetts urged Parliament to adopt a Stamp Tax. Thus a Stamp Act was passed early in 1765, and became effective November 1 of that year. When the news of its enactment reached the colonies, discontent grew. The colonies, instead of being able to pay new taxes, had not yet recovered from the recent war. Men were also raising the question then of the *right* to tax.

The colonies were "up in arms", and a Convention was called to meet in New York City, October 7, 1765. "Nine of the thirteen colonies were represented, and the Assemblies of New Hampshire, Virginia, North Carolina and Georgia wrote that they would agree to whatever was done by the Congress." (Lossing)

The names of the delegates at the organization of the Convention should be recorded; they are truly patriots of the American Revolution.

Massachusetts—James Otis, Oliver Partridge, Timothy Ruggles

New York—Robert R. Livingston, John Cruger, Philip Livingston, William Bayard, Leonard Lispenard

New Jersey—Robert Ogden, Hendrick Fisher, Joseph Borden

Rhode Island—Metcalf Bowler, Henry Ward

Pennsylvania—John Dickinson, John Morton, George Bryan

Delaware—Thomas McKean, Caesar Rodney

Connecticut—Eliphalet Dyer, David Rowland, William S. Johnson

Maryland—William Murdock, Edward Tilghman, Thomas Ringgold

South Carolina—Thomas Lynch, Sr., Christopher Gadsden, John Rutledge

The Convention was in session fourteen days, and adopted a Declaration of Rights, a Petition to the King, and a Memorial to both Houses of Parliament. All of the delegates except Timothy Ruggles, the President, and Robert Ogden signed the proceedings, which reflected "the spirit of men determined to be free." (Lossing)

But thus far no thought of independence was in the minds of the American leaders. Surely negotiation would bring about a satisfactory and a peaceful settlement. Let us present our petition to the King and he will hear us!

While the Stamp Act was in force, the importation of British goods was considerably curtailed. After its repeal, March 22, 1766, Parliament imposed other taxing schemes on the colonists, notably tea. Other events—"The Boston Massacre", the Boston "Tea Party", the quartering of British troops in Boston, closing of American ports—all pointed up the need for unified action on the part of the colonists.

Rhode Island first publicly spoke of the need for a meeting of a general council. Other colonies endorsed the idea, and within the space of sixty-four days, twelve of the thirteen colonies agreed to send delegates, Georgia not taking part in this movement. The Massachusetts Assembly designated the meeting to be held in Philadelphia on September 1, 1774. Accordingly, on September 5, 1774, forty-four delegates from these twelve colonies met in Carpenters' Hall in Philadelphia. Other delegates were to arrive to take part in the sessions before adjournment.

The Congress organized and selected Peyton Randolph of Virginia as President, and Charles Thomson of Pennsylvania as Secretary. Actual sessions began September 6. With the adoption of rules for the order of business on Wednesday, September 7, Lossing comments: "and now, when about to enter upon the general business for which they were convened, the delegates publicly sought Divine aid", when the first prayer in Congress was offered by the Rev. Mr. Duché, an Episcopal clergyman from Philadelphia.

The Congress proceeded to the business at hand, and drew up a Declaration of Colonial Rights, setting forth "grievances complained of, and the inalienable rights of British subjects in every part of the realm." (Lossing) Fourteen articles were agreed to as the basis of an American Association, and engrossed copies of the Articles of Association were signed by fifty-three delegates on October 20, 1774; the First Continental Congress adjourned six days later, October 26, 1774.

On the day it adjourned, the Congress adopted an address to the people of Canada, urging them to join with the colonies in a common resistance. "But its Legislative Assembly made no response, and Congress construed their silence into a negative." (Lossing)

Before adjournment, however, the First Continental Congress had wisely provided for the calling of another Congress if the crisis continued. This action is recorded in the *Journals of Congress*, Vol. 1, p.102: "Saturday, October 22, 1774—Resolved, as the Opinion of this Congress that it will be necessary, that another Congress should be held on the tenth day of May next, unless the redress of grievances, which we have desired, be obtained before that time. And we recommend that the same be held at the city of Philadelphia, and that all the Colonies, in North-America, chuse deputies as soon as possible to attend such Congress."

From the same source, Vol. 1, p. 114: "Wednesday, October 26, 1774—Resolved That the Thanks of this Congress be given to the honourable House of Representatives of the Colony of Pennsylvania for their politeness to the Congress and that the delegates for this Colony to communicate this Resolution to the said hon^ble House . . . The Congress then dissolved itself."

Before another Congress could be convened, actual warfare had started. In April, 1775, the British landed a substantial force to take over military stores accumulated by the colonists in and around Boston. The Massachusetts Minute Men, roused by the midnight rides of Paul Revere, William Dawes, and others, were already assembled on Lexington Green when the British reached there on the morning of April 19. Short but sharp engagements at Lexington and Concord resulted, and the war was on. After the battle of Bunker Hill (actually fought on Breed's Hill) on June 17, 1775, it was evident that the thirteen colonies were prepared to offer resistance to the limit of their resources.

The time for a second Congress was now at hand. On Wednesday, May 10, 1775, forty-eight delegates from eleven of the thirteen colonies met in Philadelphia. Peyton Randolph was unanimously chosen President. After he was seated, Charles Thomson was unanimously chosen Secretary; Andrew McNeare, Doorkeeper; and William Shed, Messenger.

Almost daily thereafter, additional delegates presented their credentials and were admitted to take part in the sessions that followed, so that the colonies were fully represented.

This Congress, destined to endure until finally superseded in 1789 by the government organized under the new Constitution, realized the immediate need for assuming war powers. Hostilities had already begun in New England. The Minute Men were besieging the British in Boston. Munitions of war had to be secured and an army put in the field.

On Monday, May 29, 1775, the Congress addressed a letter "To the Oppressed Inhabitants of Canada", inviting them to join with the Colonists "in resolving to be free, and in rejecting, with disdain, the fetters of slavery, however artfully polished . . . We yet entertain hopes of your uniting with us in the defense of our common liberty."

Washington was appointed Commander in Chief of the Continental Forces on June 15, 1775; he accepted on June 17, and was on his way to Cambridge, Massachusetts, without delay, to take command of the Continental Army there.

After Washington's appointment, the Congress, by successive appointments, created the staff of General Officers of the Continental Army. At the time of Cornwallis' surrender at Yorktown in October, 1781, a total of twenty-nine Major Generals and forty-four Brigadier Generals had been appointed, although not all of these were in the service of the colonies at the conclusion of hostilities. Many of these officers had seen service in the French & Indian War, and this experience in the field was to be especially helpful to the cause of the colonies in the prosecution of the war.

From the very beginning of his service as Commander in Chief, Washington gathered around him young men of exceptional ability to help in the important task of organizing and handling the paper work of the Army. John C. Fitzpatrick, in *The Spirit of The Revolution* (1924), said this about Washington's Aides and Military Secretaries: "George Washington's 'Family', as he called his aides-de-camp during the Revolutionary War, was the most remarkable group of young men to be found in the history of the United States. Washington's well-nigh unerring judgment in appraising men was never better displayed than in the choice of his confidential military assistants. . . ."

Before the war was over, twenty-nine Aides and Secretaries had been appointed, as shown in Heitman's *Historical Register of Officers of the Continental Army*. Many others served for short periods, on a temporary basis, and have not been considered in this present work.

With war a reality, and Washington in active command of the Continental Army, and despite jealousies and sectional differences, Congress kept to the business at hand. The time for memorials and petitions to the King was past. Action was needed now, and gradually there emerged a spirit of unity among the colonies. Possibly some of the delegates remembered Patrick Henry's ringing declaration in the first Congress: "Where are now your boundaries? The distinction between Virginians, Pennsylvanians, New Yorkers, New Englanders are no more. *I am not a Virginian but an American!*"

And Thomas Paine's *Common Sense* spoke of "The Free and Independent States of America."

The war went on, with victories and defeats; Congress debated proposals for union, until on June 7, 1776, Richard Henry Lee, of Virginia, offered this resolution to the Congress: "Resolved, That these United Colonies are, and of right ought to be, free and independent States, that they are absolved from all allegiance to the British Crown, and that all political connection between them and the State of Great Britain is, and ought to be, totally dissolved."

Now it was before the Congress—independence. On Monday, June 10, Congress resolved "That the consideration of the first resolution be postponed to this day, three weeks (July 1st), and in the meanwhile, that no time be lost, in case the Congress agree thereto, that a committee be appointed to prepare a declaration to the effect of the said first resolution . . . "

The next day, Thomas Jefferson, John Adams, Benjamin Franklin, Roger Sherman, and Robert R. Livingston were appointed the committee to draft the Declaration. The story of Jefferson's writing the actual declaration, and the heartaches he suffered as Congress debated the wording, phrase by phrase, and altered his composition, is now well-known to all Americans.

Then, on July 2, as recorded in the *Journals of Congress,* "The Congress resumed the consideration of the resolution agreed to and reported from the committee of the whole; and the same being read, was agreed to as follows:

'Resolved, That these United Colonies are, and of right ought to be free and independent States, that they are absolved from all allegiance to the British Crown, and that all political connection between them, and the State of Great Britain is, and ought to be, totally dissolved.' "

So Lee's resolution was passed, and the Declaration was now on the agenda. John Adams wrote to his wife that same night: "The second day of July, 1776, will be the most memorable epoch in the history of America. I am apt to believe that it will be celebrated by succeeding generations as the great anniversary Festival. It ought to be commemorated, as the day of deliverance, by solemn acts of devotion to God Almighty. It ought to be solemnised with pomp and parade, with shows, games, sports, guns, bells, bonfires, and illumination, from one end of this continent to the other, from this time forward, forevermore."

Two days later the Congress met to discuss and adopt the formal Declaration of Independence reported by the Committee on the second of July. On its adoption, Congress ordered that it be printed and published. John Hancock, President, and Charles Thomson, Secretary, signed it, by order of Congress, so that handbills could be printed, and for publication in the newspapers in the colonies.

A suitably engrossed copy was signed by the members of Congress later. It should be noted that not all members of the Congress present on July 2 and 4 signed the document. Some had voted against independence and refused to sign; others left the Congress before the engrossed copy was ready, and never signed; one delegate, who took his seat on July 4, signed the document although he did not vote for it. Most members signed it in August, 1776, and the rest at a later date. The last to sign was Thomas McKean, in 1781.

After the formal declaration, there were five more long years of war before independence was assured—Long Island, Trenton, Princeton, Brandywine, Germantown,

Saratoga, the winter at Valley Forge, Monmouth, Savannah, Charleston, Camden (South Carolina), Cowpens, and finally Yorktown, October 19, 1781.

Meanwhile, Franklin's efforts to secure aid from France had been successful, and helped greatly in achieving the final victory. The treaty with France was signed February 6, 1778, and celebrated with great rejoicing by the army at Valley Forge on May 6, the day after the news reached there. Secretary of State John Hay, serving in the cabinets of Presidents William McKinley and Theodore Roosevelt, has said of this treaty: "The act of France gave us a standing abroad which we had hitherto lacked . . . Even before 1775 we were a nation; but until our treaties with France the world regarded us as a rebellion."

Lossing's *The Pictorial Field-Book of the Revolution,* states: "It was an easy matter to *declare* the colonies free and independent; it was not so easy to *maintain* that declaration."

Congress had recognized from its beginning the need for an association or union of some kind between the colonies, in order to maintain the declaration, and proposals were presented and debated from time to time. On June 11, 1776, Congress appointed a committee to prepare a form of Confederation. The resolution presented by Richard Henry Lee for independence included the recommendation "That a plan of confederation be prepared and transmitted to the respective Colonies for their consideration and approbation."

A Congressional Committee prepared a draft of a proposed confederation, which was debated in full and then held over until April, 1777, when it was again debated regularly for seven months. The story continues, from the *Journals of Congress* for Saturday, November 15, 1777: "A copy of the Confederation being made out, and sundry small amendments made in the diction, without altering the sense, the same was agreed to, and is as follows:

Articles of Confederation and Perpetual Union, between the States of

New Hampshire	Pennsylvania
Massachusetts Bay	Delaware
Rhode Island and	Maryland
Providence Plantations	Virginia
Connecticut	North Carolina
New York	South Carolina
New Jersey	Georgia

Article I—The stile of this Confederacy shall be The United States of America."

On Thursday, July 9, 1778, "the ratification of the articles of confederation engrossed on a roll of parchment, being laid before Congress, were examined," and signed by delegates from eight of the colonies. Other signatures were added from time to time, until May 5, 1779, when Delaware signed. Maryland was the last colony to ratify the articles. Here again the *Journals of Congress* record the proceedings:

Thursday, February 22, 1781—"The delegates of Maryland having taken their seats in Congress with powers to sign the Articles of Confederation . . . Resolved, that on Thursday next, at twelve o'clock, the final ratification of the Confederation of the United States be announced to the public . . . "

Thursday, March 1, 1781—"According to the order of the day, the hon'ble John Hanson and Daniel Carroll . . . did, in behalf of the said State of Maryland, sign and ratify the said articles, by which act the Confederation of the United States of America was completed, each and every of the Thirteen United States, from New Hampshire to Georgia, both included, having adopted and confirmed, and by their delegates in Congress, ratified the same . . . "

But even before these Articles were formally ratified by all the colonies and became effective, it was seen that there were many weaknesses in them. The main fault was that "each state retains its sovereignty, freedom, and independence . . . " The Congress had no power to enforce its measures. No provision was made for payment of foreign debt. "It was a government of responsibility without power." As a result, most of the war was fought under a gentleman's agreement.

During the war, each state, in maintaining its own sovereignty and freedom, had adopted a constitution and was operating under such an instrument of authority.

The Articles of Confederation had no power to control commerce or raise money. It did have the authority to make requisitions on the states, but could only stand by and hope that the states would respond adequately. It seems they never did.

But in spite of all these shortcomings, the war was fought and finally won. The independence declared by the colonies in 1776 had become a reality in 1781.

With peace in the colonies, it was found that these articles did not provide a suitable form of government for the new nation. The summary of events leading up to the calling of the Constitutional Convention is outlined fully in the National Archives publication, *The Foundation of the Union,* and the reader is referred to this for a step-by-step account of the proceedings. The two quotations which follow are taken from this publication.

"Only 2 years after the Treaty of Paris had been signed, the government under the Articles of Confederation was operating so badly that European nations fully expected the United States to disintegrate. Congress, lacking any power to enforce its orders, was often ignored by the States. Its inability to regulate commerce had resulted in State tariffs so prohibitive that the commerce of some States was close to ruin. When Virginia and Maryland had successfully settled their dispute over navigation and commerce on Chesapeake Bay through an interstate agreement, the Virginia Legislature in 1786 proposed a convention to consider commercial regulations among all the States. This led to the "Annapolis Convention" of September, 1786, which offered the suggestion that Commissioners meet in Philadelphia on the second Monday in May, 1787, to "devise such further provisions as shall appear to them necessary to render the constitution of the Foederal Government adequate to the exigencies of the Union . . . " (p 20)

Congress received and considered the report, and, admitting defects in the Articles of Confederation, resolved on February 21, 1787, that it is "expedient that a Convention of Delegates be held in Philadelphia for the sole and express purpose of revising the Articles of Confederation . . . " (p. 21)

The *Journals of Congress* pick up the story.

The Convention was called for Monday, May 14, 1787, to meet in the State house (Independence Hall) in Philadephia; but it was not until May 25 that a quorum was on hand, ready to take up the business outlined in the Congressional resolution. Washington was the unanimous choice for President of the Convention, and as

Bloom writes, "Thus began the meetings of one of the greatest sessions of wise men in the history of the world."

The meetings, on eighty-seven days, continued from May 25 to September 17, 1787. The Committees completed their work and a draft of the completed constitution was ready for signatures of the deputies on September 17. Fifty-five delegates had attended the sessions, but only forty-one stayed until the end, and three of these refused to sign the document. Accordingly, with thirty-eight deputies signing, and one signature added later, the Constitution "was submitted to the Congress for consideration."

Thursday, September 20, 1787—"Congress assembled, and received 'Report of the Convention to the States'"—the United States Constitution. One week later the Congress authorized transmission to the supreme executive of each State, and the following day, September 28, Congress resolved the Report (Constitution) be sent "to the several legislatures in order to be submitted to a convention of Delegates chosen in each State by the people thereof in conformity to the resolves of the Convention made and provided in that case."

On Friday, October 10, 1788—"Congress assembled, present as before." A footnote gives this added information: "This is the last day on which business was transacted by the Continental Congress."

Monday, November 3, 1788—"Pursuant to the Articles of Confederation only two Gentlemen attended as delegates, namely Mr. (Benjamin) Contee for Maryland, Mr. (Hugh) Williamson for North Carolina." A footnote gives more information: "This is the first day of the federal year 1788-1789. From this date to March 2, 1789, delegates from the various states appeared and presented their credentials, so that it would have been possible at any time that seven states were present for the secretary to have read the credentials and for Congress to have begun its sessions. Because of the organization of the new Government under the Constitution, the Continental Congress for 1788-1789 never transacted any business."

Sol Bloom in his *Formation of the Union under the Constitution* says: "The prelude being over, the curtain rises on the main play. New York City rang down the curtain on the Confederation by a salute of thirteen guns on March 3, 1789 . . ." These articles, born of war-time necessity, had served their purpose. The First Congress of the United States of America was now ready to convene.

From *Debates & Proceedings of the United States Congress,* for Wednesday, March 4, 1789, New York, N. Y., it is recorded: "This being the day for the meeting of the new Congress, the following members of the Senate appeared and took their seats:

From New Hampshire, John Langdon and Paine Wingate

From Massachusetts, Caleb Strong

From Connecticut, William S. Johnson and Oliver Ellsworth

From Pennsylvania, William Maclay and Robert Morris

From Georgia, William Few."

The members present not being a quorum, they adjourned from day to day, until Wednesday, March 11, "It was agreed that a circular should be written the absent members, requesting their immediate attendance."

On Monday, April 6, 1789, a quorum was secured and proceeded "to the choise of a President, for the sole purpose of opening and counting the votes for President of the United States.

"Ordered, that Mr. Ellsworth inform the House of Representatives that a quorum of the Senate is formed; that a President is elected . . . and that the Senate is now ready . . . " . . . "Where it appeared that George Washington, Esquire, was elected President, and John Adams, Esquire, Vice President of the United States of America."

Washington was inaugurated on April 30, 1789, in New York City, and the Government of the United States under the Constitution began actual operation.

THE PRESIDENTS OF THE CONTINENTAL CONGRESS

(dates elected)

Peyton Randolph, of Virginia, September 5, 1774. Resigned, October 22, 1774.

Henry Middleton, of South Carolina, October 22, 1774.

Peyton Randolph, of Virginia, May 10, 1775. Died, October 22, 1775.

John Hancock, of Massachusetts, May 24, 1775.

Henry Laurens, of South Carolina, November 1, 1777.

John Jay, of New York, December 10, 1778.

Samuel Huntington, of Connecticut, September 28, 1779.

Thomas McKean, of Delaware, July 10, 1781.

John Hanson, of Maryland, November 5, 1781.

Elias Boudinot, of New Jersey, November 4, 1782.

Thomas Mifflin, of Pennsylvania, November 3, 1783.

Richard Henry Lee, of Virginia, November 30, 1784.

John Hancock, of Massachusetts, November 23, 1785. Resigned, May 29, 1786, never having served, owing to continued illness.

Nathaniel Gorham, of Massachusetts, June 6, 1786.

Arthur St. Clair, of Pennsylvania, February 2, 1787.

Cyrus Griffin, of Virginia, January 22, 1788.

(Source: *Biographical Directory of the American Congress, 1774-1949.*)

THE CAPITALS OF THE UNITED STATES

Before Washington, D. C., was established as the Capital of the United States, the Continental Congresses met in eight different towns and cities.

> Philadelphia, in Carpenter's Hall, and then in the State House, September 5, 1774, to October 26, 1774; May 10, 1775, to December 12, 1776.
>
> Baltimore, in Henry Fite's House. December 20, 1776, to March 4, 1777.
>
> Philadelphia, in the State House, March 5, 1777, to September 18, 1777.
>
> Lancaster, in the Court House, September 27, 1777 (one day only).
>
> York, in the Court House, September 30, 1777, to June 27, 1778.
>
> Philadelphia, in College Hall, and then in the State House, July 2, 1778, to June 21, 1783.
>
> Princeton, at "Prospect", and then in Nassau Hall, June 30, 1783, to November 4, 1783.
>
> Annapolis, in the State House, November 26, 1783, to June 3, 1784.
>
> Trenton, in the French Arms Tavern, November 1, 1784, to December 24, 1784.
>
> New York City, in the City Hall, and then in Fraunces' Tavern, January 11, 1785, to November 4, 1785; November 7, 1785, to November 3, 1786; November 6, 1786, to October 30, 1787; November 5, 1787, to October 21, 1788; November 3, 1788, to March 2, 1789.
>
> Under the Federal Constitution, two cities served as capitals:
> New York City, from March 4, 1789, to August 12, 1790;
> Philadelphia, from December 6, 1790, to May 14, 1800.

The permanent Capital in Washington, D. C., was established November 17, 1800, at the beginning of the Second Session of the Sixth Congress of the United States.

The First and Second Continental Congresses held sessions as such until March 2, 1781. On March 4, 1781, the Congress became known as the Congress of the Confederation.

The First Session of the First Congress under the Constitution of the United States met in New York City on March 4, 1789, and adjourned on September 29, 1789. George Washington was inaugurated the first President in Federal Hall in New York City on April 30, 1789. The Second Session met from January 4, 1790, to August 12, 1790, in New York City.

The Third Session of the First Congress of the United States met in Congress Hall, in Philadelphia, on December 6, 1790; and Philadelphia remained the temporary seat of the Government until May 14, 1800, the closing of the First Session of the Sixth Congress.

The Congress first met in the Capitol in Washington, D. C., on November 17, 1800, at the opening of the Second Session of the Sixth Congress.

FOUNDING FATHERS IDENTIFIED AS MASONS

SIGNERS OF THE ARTICLES OF ASSOCIATION (10)

Edward Biddle
Richard Caswell
John Dickinson
Joseph Hewes
William Hooper
Charles Humphreys
Robert Treat Paine
Peyton Randolph
John Sullivan
George Washington

SIGNERS OF THE DECLARATION OF INDEPENDENCE (9)

William Ellery
Benjamin Franklin
John Hancock
Joseph Hewes
William Hooper
Robert Treat Paine
Richard Stockton
George Walton
William Whipple

SIGNERS OF THE ARTICLES OF CONFEDERATION (9)

Thomas Adams
Daniel Carroll
John Dickinson
William Ellery
John Hancock
Cornelius Harnett
Henry Laurens
Daniel Roberdeau
Jonathan Bayard Smith

SIGNERS OF THE CONSTITUTION OF THE UNITED STATES (13)

Gunning Bedford, Jr.
John Blair
David Brearley
Jacob Broom
Daniel Carroll
Jonathan Dayton
John Dickinson
Benjamin Franklin
Nicholas Gilman
Rufus King
James McHenry
William Paterson
George Washington

GENERAL OFFICERS IN THE CONTINENTAL ARMY (33)

Benedict Arnold
James Clinton
Elias Dayton
Joseph Frye
Mordecai Gist
John Glover
John Greaton
Edward Hand
James Hogun
Henry Knox
Marquis de Lafayette
Benjamin Lincoln
William Maxwell
Hugh Mercer
Richard Montgomery
John Peter Gabriel Muhlenberg
John Nixon
Samuel Holden Parsons
John Paterson
Israel Putnam
Rufus Putnam
Arthur St. Clair
John Stark
Friedrich W. A. von Steuben
John Sullivan
Jethro Sumner
William Thompson
James Mitchell Varnum
George Washington
George Weedon
Otho Holland Williams
William Woodford
David Wooster

WASHINGTON'S AIDES AND MILITARY SECRETARIES (8)

Hodijah Baylies
Richard Cary
John Fitzgerald
David Humphreys
James McHenry
William Palfrey
Edmund Randolph
John Walker

INDEX

Name	State	Group	Page
Adams, Andrew	Connecticut	III	109
Adams, John	Massachusetts	III	109
Adams, Samuel	Massachusetts	III	109
Adams, Thomas	Virginia	I	1
Alexander, William	New Jersey	II	83
Alsop, John	New York	II	83
Armand, Charles Tuffin (see La Rouërie, Marquis de)	France	III	110
Armstrong, John	Pennsylvania	III	110
Arnold, Benedict	Connecticut	I	2
Baldwin, Abraham	Georgia	III	111
Banister, John	Virginia	III	111
Bartlett, Josiah	New Hampshire	III	111
Bassett, Richard	Delaware	III	112
Baylies, Hodijah	Massachusetts	I	3
Baylor, George	Virginia	III	112
Bedford, Gunning, Jr.	Delaware	I	4
Biddle, Edward	Pennsylvania	I	5
Blair, John	Virginia	I	6
Bland, Richard	Virginia	III	113
Blount, William	North Carolina	III	113
Boerum, Simon	New York	III	113
Braxton, Carter	Virginia	III	114
Brearley, David	New Jersey	I	7
Broom, Jacob	Delaware	I	8
Butler, Pierce	South Carolina	III	114
Carroll, Charles (of Carrollton)	Maryland	III	114
Carroll, Daniel	Maryland	I	9
Cary, Richard	Virginia	I	10
Caswell, Richard	North Carolina	I	11
Chase, Samuel	Maryland	III	115
Clark, Abraham	New Jersey	III	115
Clingan, William	Pennsylvania	III	115
Clinton, George	New York	III	116
Clinton, James	New York	I	12

INDEX - cont.

Name	State	Group	Page
Clymer, George	Pennsylvania	III	116
Cobb, David	Massachusetts	III	116
Collins, John	Rhode Island	III	117
Conway, Thomas	France	III	117
Crane, Stephen	New Jersey	III	117
Cushing, Thomas	Massachusetts	III	118
Dana, Francis	Massachusetts	III	118
Dayton, Elias	New Jersey	I	14
Dayton, Jonathan	New Jersey	I	13
Deane, Silas	Connecticut	III	118
DeBorre, Philippe Hubert de Preudhomme	France	III	119
DeHaas, John Philip	Pennsylvania	III	119
DeHart, John	New Jersey	III	119
DeKalb, Baron Johann	France	II	84
DeWoedtke, Friedrich Wilhelm	Prussia	III	119
Dickinson, John	Penna./Delaware	I	15
Drayton, William Henry	South Carolina	III	120
Duane, James	New York	III	120
DuCoudray, Philippe C. T.	France	III	121
Duer, William	New York	III	121
Duportail, Louis le Bègue	France	III	121
Dyer, Eliphalet	Connecticut	III	122
Ellery, William	Rhode Island	I	16
Fermoy, De La Roche (see La Rochefermoy)	France	III	122
Few, William	Georgia	III	122
Fitzgerald, John	Virginia	I	17
Fitzhugh, Peregrine	Virginia	III	123
FitzSimons, Thomas	Pennsylvania	III	123
Floyd, William	New York	III	123
Folsom, Nathaniel	New Hampshire	III	123
Franklin, Benjamin	Pennsylvania	I	18
Frye, Joseph	Massachusetts	I	20

INDEX - cont.

Name	State	Group	Page
Gadsden, Christopher	South Carolina	III	124
Galloway, Joseph	Pennsylvania	III	124
Gates, Horatio	Virginia	II	85
Gerry, Elbridge	Massachusetts	II	86
Gilman, Nicholas	New Hampshire	I	21
Gist, Mordecai	Maryland	I	22
Glover, John	Massachusetts	I	23
Gorham, Nathaniel	Massachusetts	III	125
Grayson, William	Virginia	III	125
Greaton, John	Massachusetts	I	24
Greene, Nathanael	Rhode Island	II	87
Gwinnett, Button	Georgia	III	125
Hall, Lyman	Georgia	III	126
Hamilton, Alexander	New York	III	126
Hancock, John	Massachusetts	I	25
Hand, Edward	Pennsylvania	I	26
Hanson, Alexander Contee	Maryland	III	127
Hanson, John	Maryland	III	127
Harnett, Cornelius	North Carolina	I	27
Harrison, Benjamin	Virginia	III	127
Harrison, Robert Hanson	Maryland	III	128
Hart, John	New Jersey	III	128
Harvie, John	Virginia	III	129
Heath, William	Massachusetts	III	129
Henry, Patrick	Virginia	II	88
Hewes, Joseph	North Carolina	I	28
Heyward, Thomas, Jr.	South Carolina	III	130
Hogun, James	North Carolina	I	29
Holten, Samuel	Massachusetts	III	130
Hooper, William	North Carolina	I	30
Hopkins, Stephen	Rhode Island	III	130
Hopkinson, Francis	New Jersey	III	131
Hosmer, Titus	Connecticut	III	131
Howe, Robert	North Carolina	II	89
Huger, Isaac	South Carolina	III	131
Humphreys, Charles	Pennsylvania	I	31
Humphreys, David	Connecticut	I	32
Huntington, Jedediah	Connecticut	III	131

INDEX - cont.

Name	State	Group	Page
Huntington, Samuel	Connecticut	III	132
Hutson, Richard	South Carolina	III	132
Ingersoll, Jared	Pennsylvania	III	132
Irvine, William	Pennsylvania	III	133
Jay, John	New York	III	134
Jefferson, Thomas	Virginia	II	90
Jenifer, Daniel of St. Thomas	Maryland	III	134
Johnson, Thomas, Jr.	Maryland	III	135
Johnson, William Samuel	Connecticut	III	135
Johnston, George	Virginia	III	135
King, Rufus	Massachusetts	I	33
Kinsey, James	New Jersey	III	136
Knox, Henry	Massachusetts	I	35
Lafayette, Marquis de	France	I	37
Langdon, John	New Hampshire	II	91
Langworthy, Edward	Georgia	III	136
La Rochefermoy, Matthias A.	France	III	122
La Rouërie, Armand Charles Tuffin, Marquis de (See Armand)	France	III	110
Laurens, Henry	South Carolina	I	39
Laurens, John	South Carolina	III	136
Learned, Ebenezer	Massachusetts	III	137
Lee, Charles	Virginia	III	137
Lee, Francis Lightfoot	Virginia	III	137
Lee, Richard Henry	Virginia	II	92
Lewis, Andrew	Virginia	III	138
Lewis, Francis	New York	III	138
Lincoln, Benjamin	Massachusetts	I	41
Livingston, Philip	New York	II	93
Livingston, William	New Jersey	III	139
Lovell, James	Massachusetts	III	139
Low, Isaac	New York	III	139
Lynch, Thomas, Sr.	South Carolina	III	140
Lynch, Thomas, Jr.	South Carolina	III	140

INDEX - cont.

Name	State	Group	Page
McDougall, Alexander	New York	III	140
McHenry, James	Maryland	I	42
McIntosh, Lachlan	Georgia	III	141
McKean, Thomas	Delaware	II	93
Madison, James	Virginia	III	141
Marchant, Henry	Rhode Island	III	143
Mathews, John	South Carolina	III	143
Maxwell, William	New Jersey	I	43
Meade, Richard Kidder	Virginia	III	143
Mercer, Hugh	Virginia	I	44
Middleton, Arthur	South Carolina	III	144
Middleton, Henry	South Carolina	III	144
Mifflin, Thomas	Pennsylvania	III	144
Montgomery, Richard	New York	I	45
Moore, James	North Carolina	III	145
Morgan, Daniel	Virginia	II	94
Morris, Gouverneur	Penna. New York	III	145
Morris, Lewis	New York	III	146
Morris, Robert	Pennsylvania	II	95
Morton, John	Pennsylvania	III	146
Moultrie, William	South Carolina	III	146
Moylan, Stephen	Pennsylvania	III	147
Muhlenberg, John Peter Gabriel	Virginia	I	46
Nash, Francis	North Carolina	III	147
Nelson, Thomas, Jr.	Virginia	II	96
Nixon, John	Massachusetts	I	47
Paca, William	Maryland	III	147
Paine, Robert Treat	Massachusetts	I	48
Palfrey, William	Massachusetts	I	49
Parsons, Samuel Holden	Connecticut	I	50
Paterson, John	Massachusetts	I	51
Paterson, William	New Jersey	I	52
Pendleton, Edmund	Virginia	III	148
Penn, John	North Carolina	II	97
Pinckney, Charles	South Carolina	III	148
Pinckney, Charles Cotesworth	South Carolina	III	148

INDEX - cont.

Name	State	Group	Page
Poor, Enoch	New Hampshire	III	149
Pulaski, Casimir	Poland	II	98
Putnam, Israel	Connecticut	I	53
Putnam, Rufus	Massachusetts	I	54
Randolph, Edmund	Virginia	I	56
Randolph, Peyton	Virginia	I	57
Read, George	Delaware	III	149
Reed, James	New Hampshire	III	150
Reed, Joseph	Pennsylvania	III	150
Roberdeau, Daniel	Pennsylvania	I	58
Rodney, Caesar	Delaware	III	150
Ross, George	Pennsylvania	III	151
Rush, Benjamin	Pennsylvania	II	99
Rutledge, Edward	South Carolina	III	151
Rutledge, John	South Carolina	III	152
St. Clair, Arthur	Pennsylvania	I	59
Schuyler, Philip	New York	II	99
Scott, Charles	Virginia	III	152
Scudder, Nathaniel	New Jersey	III	152
Sherman, Roger	Connecticut	II	100
Smallwood, William	Maryland	II	101
Smith, James	Pennsylvania	II	102
Smith, Jonathan Bayard	Pennsylvania	I	60
Smith, Richard	New Jersey	III	153
Smith, William Stephens	New York	III	153
Spaight, Richard Dobbs	North Carolina	III	153
Spencer, Joseph	Connecticut	III	154
Stark, John	New Hampshire	I	61
Stephen, Adam	Virginia	III	154
Steuben, Fred. W. A. von	Prussia	I	62
Stirling, Earl of (see Alexander, William)	New Jersey	II	83
Stockton, Richard	New Jersey	I	64
Stone, Thomas	Maryland	III	154
Sullivan, John	New Hampshire	I	65
Sumner, Jethro	North Carolina	I	66

INDEX - cont.

Name	State	Group	Page
Taylor, George	Pennsylvania	III	154
Telfair, Edward	Georgia	III	155
Thomas, John	Massachusetts	III	155
Thompson, William	Pennsylvania	I	67
Thornton, Matthew	New Hampshire	III	155
Thornton, Presley Peter	Virginia	III	156
Tilghman, Matthew	Maryland	III	157
Tilghman, Tench	Pennsylvania	III	157
Tronson, du Coudray (see du Coudray, Philippe C. T.)	France	III	121
Trumbull, John	Connecticut	III	157
Trumbull, Jonathan, Jr.	Connecticut	III	158
Van Dyke, Nicholas	Delaware	III	158
Varick, Richard	New York	III	158
Varnum, James Mitchell	Rhode Island	I	68
Walker, Benjamin	New York	III	159
Walker, John	Virginia	I	69
Walton, George	Georgia	I	71
Walton, John	Georgia	III	159
Ward, Artemas	Massachusetts	III	160
Ward, Samuel	Rhode Island	III	160
Washington, George	Virginia	I	73
Wayne, Anthony	Pennsylvania	II	103
Webb, Samuel Blatchley	Connecticut	II	104
Weedon, George	Virginia	I	75
Wentworth, John, Jr.	New Hampshire	III	160
Whipple, William	New Hampshire	I	76
Williams, John	North Carolina	III	161
Williams, Otho Holland	Maryland	I	77
Williams, William	Connecticut	III	161
Williamson, Hugh	North Carolina	III	161
Wilson, James	Pennsylvania	III	162
Wisner, Henry	New York	III	162
Witherspoon, John	New Jersey	II	105
Wolcott, Oliver	Connecticut	III	163
Woodford, William	Virginia	I	78
Wooster, David	Connecticut	I	79
Wythe, George	Virginia	III	163

MASONIC MEMBERSHIP OF THE FOUNDING FATHERS

GROUP I
Membership in the Masonic Fraternity Accepted

(69)

THOMAS ADAMS
VIRGINIA

Born 1730, in New Kent County, Virginia.

Died in August, 1788, on his estate "Cowpasture", Augusta County, Virginia.

Buried, presumably on his estate. (Virginia State Library, April 11, 1961)

SIGNER OF THE ARTICLES OF CONFEDERATION

The Historical Society of Pennsylvania

BIOGRAPHICAL

Attended common schools in Virginia; served as Clerk of Henrico County. Business interests took him to England in 1762, where he remained until shortly before the Revolutionary War.

Member, Continental Congress, 1778-1780.

Member of Virginia House of Burgesses, and Chairman of New Kent County Committee of Safety in 1774. Member, Virginia State Senate, 1783-86.

MASONIC

Member, Fredericksburg Lodge, Fredericksburg, Virginia. Ballotted for, made member and admitted to the Lodge, May 29, 1756.

BENEDICT ARNOLD
CONNECTICUT

Born January 14, 1741, in Norwich, Connecticut.

Died June 14, 1801, in London, England.

"Buried in a crypt at Battersea, on the south bank of the Thames, three thousand miles from his birthplace, Arnold had few obituaries." (Cornel Lengyel's *I, Benedict Arnold, The Anatomy of Treason.*)

GENERAL OFFICER IN THE CONTINENTAL ARMY

BIOGRAPHICAL

In business in early life as a trader in the West Indies.

Captain in Lexington Alarm, April 1775; Colonel, Continental Army, September 1, 1775; wounded at Quebec, December 31, 1775; Colonel, 20th Continental Infantry, January 1, 1776, effective from September 1, 1775; Brigadier General, Continental Army, January 10, 1776; and Major General, February 17, 1777.

Deserted to the enemy, September 25, 1780, and his name dropped from the rolls of the army, by order of Congress, October 4, 1780.

While in command at West Point in 1780, he arranged to surrender that key position to the British. The capture of Major John André on September 23, 1780, uncovered the plot, and Arnold fled to the British. Received a commission as Brigadier General in the British Army, and substantial monetary compensation for his losses. Later he led British expeditions into Virginia and Connecticut.

MASONIC

Affiliate of Hiram Lodge No. 1, New Haven, Connecticut. His name appears on membership list of this lodge as of April 10, 1765.

A letter of October 15, 1926, by Robert I. Clegg of The Masonic History Company, states: " . . . I find on page 20 (*History of Hiram Lodge*) a paragraph to the effect that 'The first record in Book II states that Bro. Benedict Arnold is by R. W. Nathan Whiting proposed to be made a member (i.e., an affiliate of this R. W. Lodge) and is accordingly made a Member of this Lodge.' Arnold is recorded as being present as a visiting brother. . . . Evidently Arnold had already been made a Mason but I do not find any record among my papers as to where he was initiated."

"June 12, 1771—meeting of the Lodge." (Solomon Lodge No. 1, Poughkeepsie, N. Y.) Benedict Arnold is listed as a visitor. On either side of the name is pasted in capital letters "N" and "B". This comment from McClenachan, vol. 1, p. 280, is pertinent: "The name of Benedict Arnold is very heavily crossed and recrossed, but readily discernible between the crossed lines. This has every appearance of having been done a long period ago, the ink having the same dingy-brown aged look and color.

The large letters N B are on a small piece of paper wafered on and the B is much larger type than the N".

"May 16, 1781—Ordered that the Name of Benedict Arnold be considered as obliterated from the Minutes of this Lodge, a Traitor." On either side of this entry appears pasted in capital letters "N" and "B", with a hand pointing to the word traitor. (*O R*, Solomon Lodge No. 1, Poughkeepsie, N. Y.)

HODIJAH BAYLIES

MASSACHUSETTS

Born September 17, 1756, in Uxbridge, Massachusetts.

Died April 26, 1843, in Dighton, Massachusetts.

Buried (probably) in Old Cemetery, Dighton, Massachusetts. (Massachusetts Historical Society records).

LIEUTENANT COLONEL AND AIDE-DE-CAMP TO GENERAL WASHINGTON

No Likeness Available

BIOGRAPHICAL

Harvard graduate, 1777. Married a daughter of General Benjamin Lincoln.

Lieutenant Colonel and Aide-de-Camp to General Washington from May 13, 1782, to December 23, 1783; First Lieutenant, Henry Jackson's Continental Regiment, March 1, 1777; Major and Aide-de-Camp to General Benjamin Lincoln, November, 1777; taken prisoner at Charleston, May 12, 1780.

Member, Society of the Cincinnati; Judge of Probate Court, 1804-1835.

MASONIC

Card in the Library of the Grand Lodge of Massachusetts indicates he was initiated in Lodge of St. Andrew, July 10, 1777, and then received the second and third degrees in 1777 in Masters Lodge No. 2, Albany, New York. The Parker Index of the *Grand Lodge of Massachusetts Proceedings, 1773-1804*, indicates he received all three degrees in Masters Lodge No. 2, in Albany.

Brother Wendell K. Walker, Grand Secretary of the Grand Lodge of New York, advises they have a roster dated beginning in 1768 and including names entered in 1857. The name, "Major Hodijah Baylies," appears in this list under date of 1777.

This list, covering the period from 1768 to 1824, is printed in McClenachan's *History of Freemasonry in New York*, Volume 1, pp. 258-63.

See also "Roster of Brethren belonging to lodges in New York State who fought on the side of liberty and independence in the war of the Revolution . . . Baylies, Hodijah (Major) Masters #2". (*GL Proc.*, New York, 1912, p. 301)

GUNNING BEDFORD, JR.
DELAWARE

Born 1747, in Philadelphia, Pennsylvania.

Died March 30, 1812, in Wilmington, Delaware.

Buried in graveyard of the Presbyterian Church in Wilmington.

Reinterred on the grounds of the Masonic Home of Delaware in Wilmington.

**SIGNER OF THE
CONSTITUTION OF THE UNITED STATES**

BIOGRAPHICAL

Graduate of the College of New Jersey (now Princeton University) in 1771; studied law, admitted to the Delaware bar, and practiced in Dover and Wilmington.

Member, Continental Congress, 1783-85. Delegate to the Federal Constitutional Convention of 1787, and a leader in having Delaware the first state to ratify the Constitution on December 7, 1787. United States Judge for District of Delaware, September 26, 1789, and served until his death. Presidential elector in 1789, when George Washington was the unanimous choice for President, and again in 1793.

Attorney General of Delaware, April 26, 1784, and served to September 26, 1789. State Senator in 1788.

MASONIC

Member of Lodge No. 14 at Christiana Ferry, Delaware, receiving his degrees: EA, March 21, 1782; FC, July 10, 1782; MM, September 11, 1782. Elected first Grand Master of Delaware, June 7, 1806; installed on August 4, 1806; re-elected June 24-25, 1807, and again, June 24-25, 1808. (*History of the Grand Lodge of A. F. & A. M. of Delaware*, by Charles E. Green, Grand Historian of the Grand Lodge of Delaware.)

EDWARD BIDDLE

PENNSYLVANIA

Born 1738, in Philadelphia, Pennsylvania.

Died September 5, 1779, at Chatsworth, near Baltimore, Maryland.

Buried in St. Paul's Churchyard, Baltimore, Maryland.

SIGNER OF THE ARTICLES OF ASSOCIATION

No Likeness Available

BIOGRAPHICAL

Studied law, admitted to the bar, and commenced practice in Reading, Pennsylvania.

Pre-Revolutionary leader, serving in provincial army until 1763, attaining the rank of Captain. Member, Continental Congress, 1774-76, 1778, and 1779.

Member, State Assembly in 1767-1775, and Speaker in 1774; member, provincial convention in Philadelphia, 1775, and re-elected to State Assembly in 1778.

MASONIC

Member of Lodge No. 2, Philadelphia, March 29, 1763, as shown in *Old Masonic Lodges of Pennsylvania*, Sachse, Volume 1, page 70.

JOHN BLAIR

VIRGINIA

Born 1732, in Williamsburg, Virginia.

Died August 31, 1800, in Williamsburg, Virginia.

Buried in Bruton Parish Churchyard, Williamsburg, Virginia.

SIGNER OF THE
CONSTITUTION OF THE UNITED STATES

BIOGRAPHICAL

Attended the College of William & Mary, Williamsburg, Virginia, and later studied law at the Middle Temple, London.

Delegate to the Federal Constitutional Convention in 1787. One of the first Associate Justices of the Supreme Court of the United States, September 30, 1789; resigned, 1796.

Member of the Virginia House of Burgesses, 1766 to 1770. Judge of Court of Appeals in Virginia in 1777; later Chief Justice, and in 1780, Judge of the High Court of Chancery.

MASONIC

Initiated, December 21, 1762, in a lodge at the "Crown Tavern." Charter member, Williamsburg Lodge No. 6 under the new English charter of 1773. Original Minutes of this lodge show that he received degrees of FC and MM on December 23, 1773. Succeeded Peyton Randolph as Master of Williamsburg Lodge, June 7, 1774, and is shown presiding as Master on St. John the Baptist Day, 1774. Signed the by-laws of this lodge, July 6, 1773.

"Elected first Grand Master of Masons of Virginia, October 13, 1778, and served until 1784." (*Early Freemasonry in Williamsburg, Virginia,* by George Eldridge Kidd, Past Master, Williamsburg Lodge, No. 6.)

DAVID BREARLEY

NEW JERSEY

Born June 11, 1745, in Spring Grove, New Jersey.

Died August 16, 1790, in Trenton, New Jersey.

Buried in St. Michael's Churchyard, Trenton, New Jersey, in the Masonic form and ceremonies peculiar to the Ancient Craft.

**SIGNER OF THE
CONSTITUTION OF THE UNITED STATES**

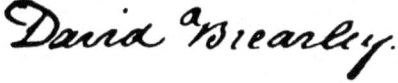

Grand Lodge of New Jersey

BIOGRAPHICAL

Delegate to the Federal Constitutional Convention from New Jersey; United States District Judge.

Captain, 2nd New Jersey, October 28, 1775, to November, 1776; Lieutenant Colonel, 4th New Jersey, November 28, 1776; Lieutenant Colonel, 1st New Jersey, January 1, 1777; resigned, August 4, 1779. Served also as Colonel of New Jersey Militia.

Lawyer; Chief Justice of New Jersey.

MASONIC

"He stood high in Masonic circles." (DAB)

"We have good reason to believe, short of the actual records, that he was made a Mason in Military Lodge No. 19 of Pennsylvania," from *The History of Freemasonry in New Jersey, 1787-1937*, p. 76, by David McGregor, Grand Historian, Grand Lodge of New Jersey. Again, p. 140, same reference: "Three of the four Jerseymen who signed the Federal Constitution were Freemasons, viz: David Brearley of Trenton, William Paterson of New Brunswick, and Jonathan Dayton of Elizabethtown."

First Grand Master of Masons in New Jersey, from 1786 until his death in 1790. "New Brunswick, December 18, 1786, call to form Grand Lodge . . . do hereby unanimously nominate and elect the following Master Masons to the several offices following, to wit: The Hon. David Brearley, Esq., Chief Justice of New Jersey, Right Worshipful Grand Master." (*GL Proc.*, New Jersey, 1786-1857, p. 1.)

JACOB BROOM

DELAWARE

No Likeness Available

Born 1752, in Wilmington, Delaware.

Died April 25, 1810, in Philadelphia, Pennsylvania.

Buried in Christ Churchyard, Philadelphia, Pennsylvania.

SIGNER OF THE CONSTITUTION OF THE UNITED STATES

BIOGRAPHICAL

Member of the Delaware delegation to the Federal Constitutional Convention in 1787. "Held many offices of public honor and trust." (Appleton)

Member of State Legislature, 1784-5-6, and 1788. An original incorporator and first Treasurer of the first library incorporated in Wilmington, 1788. First Postmaster of Wilmington, 1790-92. One of the original promoters and stockholders of the Delaware (now National) Bank. "Sandwiched among these things and part of them he was . . . busy, among the first in laying a foundation for the permanent prosperity of Wilmington. . . . After diligent search no essay, oration, or printed portrait, not even a silhouette of Jacob Broom is discoverable. His work follows him. It is an enduring memorial." (*Delaware Historical Papers, No. 51,* for 1909.)

MASONIC

"Early member of Lodge No. 14, Christiana Ferry, (Wilmington) under Provincial Grand Lodge of Pennsylvania." (*History of the Grand Lodge of A. F. & A. M. of Delaware,* Charles E. Green.)

Old Masonic Lodges in Pennsylvania, Sachse, Vol. 1, p. 307: "Jacob Broome elected Secretary and Treasurer, June 24, 1780; elected Junior Warden on June 25, 1781, and Treasurer, December 18, 1783." (Note spelling of last name.)

DANIEL CARROLL

MARYLAND

Born July 22, 1730, at Carroll Manor, in Upper Marlborough, Prince Georges County, Maryland.

Died May 7, 1796, at Rock Creek (Forest Glen) near Washington, D. C.

Buried, presumably in Forest Glen Cemetery, adjoining St. John's Church in Forest Glen, Maryland.

SIGNER OF THE ARTICLES OF CONFEDERATION AND THE CONSTITUTION OF THE UNITED STATES

BIOGRAPHICAL

Educated at the Jesuit School at Bohemia Manor, Maryland, and at St. Omer's College, France; returned to Maryland in 1748.

Member, Continental Congress, 1780-84; active state legislator.

Member of the Federal Constitutional Convention in 1787. Member, First United States Congress, March 4, 1789, to March 3, 1791. Active in fixing the seat of the Government of the United States; appointed by President Washington, January 22, 1791, one of the Commissioners to locate the District of Columbia and the Federal City, and served until July 25, 1795, when he resigned.

MASONIC

For Carroll's Masonic record, see "The List of Forfeits for Non-Attendance of the members of Lodge No. 16, Baltimore, 1733-1780" in the Library of the Maryland Historical Society, showing degrees received: EA, May 9, 1780; FC, July 11, 1780; MM, May 8, 1781.

See also *Daniel Carroll, a Framer of the Constitution*, by Sister Mary Virginia Geiger, Washington, 1943, p. 179: "The cornerstone of the Capital was laid on April 15, 1791, at Jones' Point, just south of Alexandria, the ceremony being conducted by the Masonic Lodge of that district. Daniel Carroll, as a Freemason and a Commissioner, was one of the officials in attendance at the celebration. Carroll was initiated into Lodge No. 16 on May 9, 1780, passed the requirement for his admittance on July 11, 1780, and was raised to the degree of Master Mason on May 8, 1781. At the laying of another cornerstone on September 18, 1793, Carroll was one of the participants with George Washington. The several lodges of Maryland and of Alexandria were in charge of the ceremony and the three Commissioners were among the distinguished guests." Then follows a statement about Catholics and Masons, and this: "Carroll's membership as a Catholic in the Society was not unusual in that period, due no doubt, as has been previously stated, to the lack of knowledge concerning the Society . . . "

See also Arthur Preuss, *A Study in American Freemasonry*, St. Louis, 1908, *passim*; and also Wilhelmus Bryan, *National Capitol*, New York, 1914.

*This was the laying of the cornerstone of the National Capitol.

RICHARD CARY

VIRGINIA

Mrs. Arthur Osgood Choate, Pleasantville, New York

Born January 13, 1747, in Charlestown, Massachusetts.

Died December 13, 1806, in Cooperstown, New York. (Gravestone shows date to be December 15, 1806.)

Buried in Christ Episcopal Church Cemetery, Cooperstown, New York.

LIEUTENANT COLONEL AND AIDE-DE-CAMP TO GENERAL WASHINGTON

BIOGRAPHICAL

Harvard graduate, 1763, with A.B. degree; received A.M. degree in 1766.

Lieutenant Colonel and Aide-de-Camp to General Washington, June 21, 1776, to December 17, 1776. Brigade Major, August 15, 1775.

Washington's opinion of Cary: "Colonel Richard Cary was the greatest gentleman in the American Army."

Cary's business interests took him to Baltimore in 1773; back to Boston in 1774, and south again in 1775, probably accounting for his being listed as a Virginian. After the war he had business interests in St. Croix and New York City. In January, 1797, he was settled at "Head of Lake Otsego" (Springfield, New York). He suffered severe reverses of fortune and was "put on the limits" as the penalty for unpaid debts.

MASONIC

"September 20, 5796 - Br. Cary having been Initiated & passed previous to his becoming a Member of this Lodge; was now raised to the Sublime Degree of Master Mason." (*O R*. Otsego Lodge No. 138, Cooperstown, New York). These records also show Cary in attendance as a visitor on June 21 and 22, 1796, and as a member, March 7 and July 4, 1797. Cary probably received the first two degrees in a Military Lodge while attached to Washington's staff.

RICHARD CASWELL

NORTH CAROLINA

Born August 3, 1729, in Harford, (now Baltimore County), Maryland.

Died November 10, 1789, in Fayetteville, North Carolina.

Buried in the family cemetery on his estate near Kinston, Lenoir County, North Carolina.

SIGNER OF THE ARTICLES OF ASSOCIATION

No Likeness Available

BIOGRAPHICAL

Moved to North Carolina in 1746. Studied law, admitted to the bar in 1754, and practiced in Hillsboro, North Carolina.

Member, Continental Congress, 1774-76.

Appointed delegate from North Carolina to the convention that framed the Constitution of the United States in 1787, but did not attend.

Colonel, North Carolina Partisan Rangers, 1776-77; Major General, State Militia, 1780, to end of the war.

Deputy Surveyor of the Colony, 1750; Clerk of Court in Orange County, North Carolina, in 1753. Member of Colony Assembly from Johnston County, 1754 to 1771. Governor of North Carolina, 1776-1780, and again, 1785-88. Comptroller General of the State, 1782; State Senator, 1782-84, and served as Speaker. Member and Speaker of the State House of Commons in 1789, and served until his death.

No authentic picture, print or portrait is known to be available of Caswell. (Wm. S. Powell, North Carolina Collection Library, University of North Carolina, Chapel Hill, N. C.)

MASONIC

See the *North Carolina Lodge of Research Bulletin*, Vol. IV, part 2, p. 150: "St. John's Lodge No. 1, New Bern, N. C. At a Lodge on Monday, Decem. 28, A. L. 5773 (sic 5772)—The Lodge being opened in due form—Bro. Cogdell (R. Cogdell, Pro. Mr.) moved that Bro. Richd. Caswell might take the obligation again, having passed the different degrees of Masonry formerly tho not in a regular Constituted Lodge. Assented to that he be admitted on taking the Obligation, which he accordingly did."

See also Vol. VII, p. 141, same source, showing Caswell's election as Deputy Grand Master.

Vol. VII, p. 159, same source, shows him serving as Grand Master of Masons in North Carolina, June 24, 1789.

JAMES CLINTON
NEW YORK

Born August 9, 1733, in Little Britain, New York.

Died December 22, 1812, in Little Britain, New York.

Buried on Christmas Day in the Clinton family private burying ground, Little Britain, New York. Later reinterred in Woodlawn Cemetery, near Newburgh, New York, in the town of New Windsor.

GENERAL OFFICER IN THE CONTINENTAL ARMY

BIOGRAPHICAL

Served in French and Indian War; Colonel, 3rd New York, June 30, 1775, to January, 1776; Colonel, 2nd New York, March 8, 1776. Brigadier General, Continental Army, August 9, 1776; wounded at Fort Montgomery, October 6, 1777; Brevet Major General, September 30, 1783, and served to close of the war.

General Clinton served on the court-martial at the trial of Major John André. He was the father of DeWitt Clinton, Governor of New York and Grand Master of Masons in New York from 1806 until 1819. Member of the Society of the Cincinnati.

MASONIC

"James Clinton was a member of Warren Lodge No. 17, New York." (Roth, p. 71.)

"General James Clinton is often confused with his son, DeWitt Clinton. Both were Masons." (Brown, p. 168.)

JONATHAN DAYTON

NEW JERSEY

Born October 16, 1760, in Elizabethtown (now Elizabeth), New Jersey.

Died October 9, 1824, in Elizabethtown, New Jersey.

Buried in a vault in St. John's Churchyard, Elizabeth, New Jersey.

**SIGNER OF THE
CONSTITUTION OF THE UNITED STATES**

BIOGRAPHICAL

Graduate of the College of New Jersey (now Princeton University), 1776. Then studied law and admitted to the bar.

Elected to the Continental Congress to fill vacancy caused by the declination of William Paterson; re-elected, 1788, serving from November 6, 1787, to March 3, 1789. The youngest member of the Federal Constitutional Convention in 1787. On November 25, 1788, he was chosen to the First Congress under the Constitution, but declined to serve.

Member, Second, Third, Fourth, and Fifth United States Congresses, March 4, 1791, to March 3, 1799, serving as Speaker during the fourth and fifth sessions. United States Senator, March 4, 1799, to March 3, 1805.

" . . . was arrested in 1807 on charge of conspiring with Aaron Burr in treasonable projects; gave bail and was subsequently released, but never brought to trial." (BDAC, p. 1067)

Ensign, 3rd New Jersey, February 7, 1776; Regimental Paymaster, August 26, 1776; 1st Lieutenant, January 1, 1777; Captain Lieutenant, April 7, 1779; Aide-de-Camp to General Sullivan, May 1, 1779; Captain, 3rd New Jersey, March 30, 1780; taken prisoner at Elizabethtown, October 5, 1780; exchanged—; transferred to 2nd New Jersey, January 1, 1781; retained in Consolidated New Jersey Regiment in April, 1783, and served to November 3, 1783. Served with his father through much of the Revolution.

Member, New Jersey State Assembly, 1786, 1787, and 1790, serving as Speaker in 1790.

MASONIC

See *History of Freemasonry in New Jersey, 1787-1937*, p. 140, by David McGregor, Grand Historian of the Grand Lodge of New Jersey: "Three of the four Jerseymen who signed the Federal Constitution were Freemasons, viz: David Brearley of Trenton, William Paterson of New Brunswick, and Jonathan Dayton of Elizabethtown."

"Probably a member of Temple Lodge No. 1, at Elizabethtown, and was present at the Grand Lodge of New Jersey on December 30, 1788." (Denslow)

The Proceedings of the Grand Lodge of New Jersey for this date (1788), covering a meeting held at Newark, list "Hon. Jona. Dayton, Esq., No. 1 Lodge."

ELIAS DAYTON

NEW JERSEY

Born May 1, 1737, in Elizabethtown, New Jersey.

Died July 17, 1807, in Elizabethtown, New Jersey.

Buried in First Presbyterian Churchyard Cemetery, Elizabeth, New Jersey.

GENERAL OFFICER IN THE CONTINENTAL ARMY

Elias Dayton

BIOGRAPHICAL

Colonel, 3rd New Jersey, January 18, 1776; transferred to 2nd New Jersey, January 1, 1781; Brigadier General, Continental Army, January 7, 1783, and served to the close of the war. Served in the British Army, under General Wolfe at Quebec.

Member Committee of Safety at Elizabethtown; Trustee of Presbyterian Church there. Served in the New Jersey Legislature, 1791-92, and 1794-96.

One of the original members of the Society of the Cincinnati, and the first President of the New Jersey Society.

MASONIC

"Member Military Lodge No. 19, A. Y. M., under Pennsylvania warrant, 1780." (Case)

Dayton is shown as a member of Pennsylvania Lodge No. 19. (*GL Proc. New Jersey* 1936-37, Vol. 39-40, p. 122)

JOHN DICKINSON
DELAWARE - PENNSYLVANIA

Born November 8, 1732, on his father's estate, "Crosiadoré", near Trappe, Talbot County, Maryland.

Died February 14, 1808, in Wilmington, Delaware.

Buried in Friends Burial Ground, Fourth and West Streets, Wilmington, Delaware.

SIGNER OF THE ARTICLES OF ASSOCIATION, THE ARTICLES OF CONFEDERATION, AND THE CONSTITUTION OF THE UNITED STATES

BIOGRAPHICAL

Dickinson represented two colonies during the formative years of the Republic. He signed the Articles of Association as a representative from Pennsylvania; he signed both the Articles of Confederation and the Constitution of the United States while representing Delaware. (He was not present at the actual signing of the Constitution; his signature was added, at his request, by George Read, of Delaware.)

Studied law in Philadelphia, and later at the Middle Temple in London. Returned to America, admitted to the bar in 1757, and commenced practice in Philadelphia.

Married Mary Norris, daughter of Isaac Norris, July 19, 1770.

Member of the Continental Congress from Pennsylvania, 1774-76, and from Delaware, 1776-77, 1779, and 1780. Represented Delaware in the Federal Constitutional Convention of 1787.

Colonel of first battalion raised in Philadelphia; Brigadier General, Pennsylvania Militia, 1777. Dickinson favored peaceful means of settlement in differences with England, and voted against the Declaration of Independence, believing this to be his duty; but when it came to fighting, he and McKean were the only two members of Congress who took up arms in defense of the measures they had been advocating.

Member of Pennsylvania Assembly in 1764, and a representative from Pennsylvania in the "Stamp Act Congress" in 1765.

President of the State of Delaware, 1781; returned to Pennsylvania and was its President from 1782-85.

Founder of Dickinson College, Carlisle, Pennsylvania.

MASONIC

See Sachse, *Old Masonic Lodges in Pennsylvania*, Volume 1, p. 351, re Lodge No. 18, A. Y. M., Dover, Delaware: "Meeting January 11, 1780, in Lodge Room, Dover—'Petitions signed by John Dikinson . . . being handed up to the Chair and read were ordered to lay over until next Meeting'." On page 358, same reference, is a list of members, showing John Dickinson "Entered, January 11, 1780," followed by this notation: "Never since Appeared in Lodge."

The original Lodge Records of Lodge No. 18, Dover, Delaware, in the Library of the Grand Lodge of Pennsylvania, also show this information. Brother Charles E. Green's *History of the Grand Lodge of A. F. & A. M. of Delaware* mentions that Dickinson was raised on January 11, 1780, in Lodge No. 18, Dover, Delaware, of the Provincial Grand Lodge of Pennsylvania.

WILLIAM ELLERY

RHODE ISLAND

Born, December 22, 1727, in Newport, Rhode Island.

Died, February 15, 1820, in Newport, Rhode Island.

Buried in the graveyard next to Island Cemetery, Newport, Rhode Island.

SIGNER OF THE DECLARATION OF INDEPENDENCE AND THE ARTICLES OF CONFEDERATION

BIOGRAPHICAL

Privately educated; Harvard graduate, 1747; studied law, admitted to the bar, 1770, and practiced in Newport. Member, Continental Congress, May 14, 1776, to 1781; and from 1783 to 1785. Member, Board of Admiralty, 1779; Chief Justice of Rhode Island, 1785.

MASONIC

"He was a member of the First Lodge of Boston, October 25, 1748." (Roth, p. 157)

Proceedings of the Grand Lodge of Massachusetts, 1733-1792, Appendix, p. 397: "Copy of a paper in the handwriting of Charles Pelham, Secretary of the First or Royal Exchange Lodge, written in 1751—'a General List of the Brethren made in the First Lodge of Free and Accepted Masons in Boston, N. England, Also those accepted Members in it; with the Time when made or Admitted, from the First Foundation A.M. 5733.'" Then follows the list of names, a William Ellery is shown on p. 400, under date of October 25, 1748. Apparently this same man is the visitor recorded on p. 28 of the same *Proceedings*, at the Feast of St. John the Evangelist, Thursday, December 27, 1753, in Boston.

"In Sibley's *Harvard Graduates* I find that after graduation in 1747 William Ellery of Rhode Island remained in Boston for a year or two and joined St. John's Lodge. Mention of the fact appears in one of his letters cited." (Case)

JOHN FITZGERALD

VIRGINIA

Born, probably in Ireland (Virginia State Library).

Died December 3, 1799, in Alexandria, Virginia.

Buried in the Catholic Cemetery at the south end of Washington Street, Alexandria, Virginia.

LIEUTENANT COLONEL AND AIDE-DE-CAMP TO GENERAL WASHINGTON

No Likeness Available

BIOGRAPHICAL

Lieutenant Colonel and Aide-de-Camp to General Washington from October/November, 1776, to July 6, 1778; Captain, 3rd Virginia, February 8, 1776; Major, 3rd Virginia, October 3, 1776; Major, 9th Virginia, January 28, 1777; wounded at Monmouth, June 28, 1778; resigned, July 6, 1778.

See *The History of Old Alexandria* (Virginia), Mary G. Powell, Richmond, 1928, p. 114: "Colonel John Fitzgerald came from Ireland before the Revolution. He became an intimate friend of General Washington and Aide to him during the Revolution. He settled in Alexandria as a merchant and at one time was Mayor of the town. He was President of the Patowmack Company and served Alexandria in many ways. He was an ardent Catholic and besides founding that Church here, left the impress of his name on a Catholic institution, Fitzgerald Lodge." Same reference, p. 161: "John Fitzgerald was one of the Aldermen of Alexandria when municipal government went into operation March 9, 1780." On page 363 of the same book Colonel Fitzgerald is listed in a group of officers from Alexandria.

Member of the Society of the Cincinnati.

MASONIC

Member, Williamsburg Lodge No. 6, Virginia. Initiated September 4, 1778. (*O R*, Williamsburg Lodge No. 6)

BENJAMIN FRANKLIN

PENNSYLVANIA

Born January 17, 1706, in Milk Street, Boston, Massachusetts.

Died April 17, 1790, in Philadelphia, Pennsylvania.

Buried in Christ Church Burial Ground, Philadelphia, Pennsylvania.

SIGNER OF THE DECLARATION OF INDEPENDENCE AND THE CONSTITUTION OF THE UNITED STATES

BIOGRAPHICAL

"There is no greater American." (Case)

Member, Continental Congress, 1775-76, member of the Committee appointed to draft the Declaration of Independence, and delegate to the Federal Constitutional Convention in 1787. One of the three Commissioners sent to France to solicit aid for the colonies in the Revolution. Minister to France, 1776-1785. One of the negotiators of the treaty of peace with Great Britain in 1781. Returned to Philadelphia in September, 1785.

Clerk of the Pennsylvania General Assembly, 1736-1750; member of Provincial Assembly, 1744-1754. Deputy Postmaster General of the British North American Colonies, 1753-1774. Governor of Pennsylvania, 1785-88. President of the Trustees of the University of Pennsylvania.

Printer, publisher, inventor, scientist, politician, diplomat and statesman. Elected a member of the Royal Society because of his scientific discoveries. A friend of Voltaire, and assisted in raising him, April 7, 1778.

MASONIC

"Early in the year 1731, we find that the young printer was Entered, Passed, and Raised to the Sublime Degree of a Master Mason in St. John's Lodge, held at the Tun Tavern in Water St., Philadelphia. The cost of his entrance fee was three pounds sterling . . . " (*Benjamin Franklin, the Freemason*, by Brother William J. Paterson, former Librarian and Curator, Grand Lodge of Pennsylvania, December, 1955). Note: *American Lodge of Research Transactions*. Vol. 6, No. 1, p. 65, says this date is June 24, 1731.

"5734 June 24. Being the anniversary of St. John the Baptist the Brethren Celebrated the Feast in due manner and Form, and chose our Rt. Worshl. Bro: Mr. Frederick Hamilton Master of the Lodge. About this time Our Worshl Bro. Mr. Benja Franklin from Philadelphia became acquainted with Our Rt Worsl Grand Master Mr. Price, who further Instructed him in the Royal Art, and said Franklin on his Return to Philadelphia call'd the Brethren there together, who pettition'd Our Rt. Worshl Grand Master for a Constitution to hold a Lodge, and Our Rt Worshl Grand Master having this Year Recd Orders from the Grand Lodge in England to Establish Masonry in all North America did send a Deputation to Philadelphia, appointing the Rt Worshl Mr. Benja Franklin first Master; which is the begining of Masonry there." (*GL Proc. Mass., 1733-1792*, p. 4)

"Friday, October 11, 1754. At a Quarterly Communication of Grand Lodge Holden at Concert Hall, Boston, Present . . . Bro. Benjamin Franklin." (*GL Proc. Mass. 1733-1792*, p. 34)

See also *Franklin's Bi-Centenary Celebration, Memorial Volume, Grand Lodge of Pennsylvania*, Philadelphia, 1906, p. 50: "The Masonic career of Benjamin Franklin extends over a period of almost sixty years, during which time he was accorded the highest Masonic honors at home and abroad."

"Record as a Freemason well documented." (Case)

Franklin was made a member of Loge des Neuf Soeurs, sometimes called the Lodge of the Nine Muses, in Paris, in 1777, and was elected Venerable (Worshipful Master) in May, 1779, and re-elected the following year.

A brief summary of Franklin's Masonic career follows: February 1730-1: Initiated in St. John's Lodge, Philadelphia. (See *Liber B* in collection of The Historical Society of Pennsylvania, and also *An Account of St. John's Lodge, Philadelphia*.) June 24, 1732 - elected Junior Grand Warden.

June 24, 1734 - elected Grand Master of Pennsylvania.

1734/5: according to tradition, Masonic and family, the cornerstone of Independence Hall, Philadelphia, was laid by Franklin and Brethren of St. John's Lodge.

June 10, 1749 - appointed Provincial Grand Master by Thomas Oxnard, of Boston. (The first native born American to hold such office.)

March 13, 1750 - deposed as Provincial Grand Master, but immediately appointed Deputy Grand Master by William Allen, Provincial Grand Master.

November 17, 1760 - present at Grand Lodge of England, London, and entered on the minutes as "Provincial Grand Master".

JOSEPH FRYE

MASSACHUSETTS

Born March 19, 1712, in Andover, Massachusetts.
Died July 25, 1794, in Fryeburg, Maine.
Buried in Pine Grove Cemetery, Fryeburg, Maine.

GENERAL OFFICER IN THE CONTINENTAL ARMY

No Likeness Available

BIOGRAPHICAL

Major General, Massachusetts Militia, June 21, 1775; Brigadier General, Continental Army, January 10, 1776; resigned, April 23, 1776, on account of infirmity.

MASONIC

Card in the office of the Grand Secretary of the Grand Lodge of Massachusetts does not show where or when he got his degrees. The card does show, however, that he was a Major General, and was included in the list of Masons invited to attend the Feast of St. John, December 27, 1760, and also that he was a bearer at General Joseph Warren's funeral (reinterment) on April 8, 1776. This was a public service, and names of bearers do not necessarily indicate they were Masons.

These same two references can also be found in *The Proceedings of the Grand Lodge of Massachusetts, 1733-1792*, pp. 407 and 431.

NICHOLAS GILMAN

NEW HAMPSHIRE

Born August 3, 1755, in Exeter, New Hampshire.

Died May 2, 1814, in Philadelphia, Pennsylvania.

Buried in Exeter Cemetery, Exeter, New Hampshire.

SIGNER OF THE CONSTITUTION OF THE UNITED STATES

BIOGRAPHICAL

Member, Continental Congress, 1786-88. Member of the first four Congresses of the United States, from March 4, 1789, to March 3, 1797, but declined to be candidate for re-election in 1796. Presidential elector in 1793 and 1797. Served as United States Senator from March 4, 1805, until his death.

Member, Federal Constitutional Convention in 1787.

Captain in the New Hampshire Line at the outbreak of the war. Transferred to the staff of the Adjutant General and served until the close of the war.

MASONIC

From the Library of the House of the Temple, Supreme Council, A. A. S. R., Southern Masonic Jurisdiction, Washington, D. C.: The by-laws and list of officers of St. John's Lodge No. 1, Portsmouth, New Hampshire, examined, and Gilman is shown as a member of this lodge on March 20, 1777.

"He became a member of St. John's Lodge No. 1, Portsmouth, N. H., March 20, 1777." (Denslow)

MORDECAI GIST

MARYLAND

Born February 22, 1742, in Baltimore, Maryland.

Died August 2, 1792, in Charleston, South Carolina.

Buried in the graveyard of St. Michael's Protestant Episcopal Church, Charleston, South Carolina.

GENERAL OFFICER IN THE CONTINENTAL ARMY

BIOGRAPHICAL

Educated for business life and was a Baltimore merchant when the Revolutionary War began.

Captain, Baltimore Independent Company, July, 1775; Major of Smallwood's Maryland Regiment, January 14, 1776; Colonel, 3rd Maryland, December 10, 1776; Brigadier General, Continental Army, January 9, 1779, and served to close of the war.

Member of the Society of the Cincinnati.

MASONIC

Freemasonry in Maryland, Schultz, Vol. 1, p. 92, states that Gist was a member of Lodge No. 16, Baltimore, Maryland. He received the degrees as follows:

    Entered Apprentice, March 14, 1775.
    Fellowcraft, April 11, 1775.
    Master Mason, April 25, 1775.

He was appointed first Worshipful Master of Army Lodge No. 27, chartered by the Grand Lodge of Pennsylvania, for Masons in the Maryland Line of the Continental Army, warranted April 4, 1780.

It was General Gist who presented the petition for a National Grand Lodge, with George Washington as General Grand Master, at the Morristown, New Jersey, meeting of American Union Lodge in 1779.

Served as Deputy Grand Master of Masons in South Carolina in 1787. Elected Grand Master in 1790, and held that office for two years.

In 1791 he was Grand Master of Masons in South Carolina at the time of Washington's tour of the southern states.

JOHN GLOVER

MASSACHUSETTS

Born November 5, 1732, in Salem, Massachusetts.

Died January 30, 1797, in Marblehead, Massachusetts.

Buried in the Old Burial Hill Cemetery, Marblehead, Massachusetts. (Marblehead Historical Society).

GENERAL OFFICER IN THE CONTINENTAL ARMY

(Valley Forge Park Commission)

BIOGRAPHICAL

Colonel of a Massachusetts Regiment, May 19 to December, 1775; Colonel, 14th Continental Infantry, January 1, 1776; Brigadier General, Continental Army, February 21, 1777; retired on half-pay, July 22, 1782, on account of ill health. General Glover's men took Washington across the Delaware on that eventful Christmas night in 1776, and the same men took Washington's forces off Long Island after the defeat there.

A shoemaker and soldier by trade. Served in State House of Representatives, May, 1788 to March, 1790. A Town Selectman for many years and had the privilege of welcoming President Washington to Marblehead on the Presidential tour in the fall of 1789.

The *Salem Gazette,* January 31, 1797, shows date of death to be January 30, 1796 (should be 1797), "of an Hepatick disease." See also the account of Dr. John Drury to Estate of John Glover, Esq., Item 3610, Marblehead Historical Society.

MASONIC

Mrs. Muriel D. Taylor, Librarian in the Grand Lodge of Massachusetts, wrote on March 14, 1957: "Actually a Charter Member of Philanthropic Lodge, March 25, 1760." (*Proceedings of the Grand Lodge of Massachusetts,* 1900, p. 46)

The same *Proceedings* quotes a letter of April 10, 5760, from Dr. John Lowell, Marblehead: "A list of Brothers before the opening of a Lodge in Marblehead and belonging to the same town". These twelve men were:

"Samuel Glover
    Senior Warden
John Roades,
    Secretary
Henery Saunders
John Glover
Edward Middlesex Walker
John Peirce

Andrew Tucker
    Junior Warden
Jonathan Glover,
    Treasurer
Samuel Reed
George Stacey
Andrew Tucker, Jr.
John Reed, Jr."

JOHN GREATON

MASSACHUSETTS

(Free Library of Philadelphia)

Born March 10, 1741, in Roxbury, Massachusetts.

Died December 16, 1783, in Roxbury, Massachusetts.

Buried in Old Burying Ground, Eustis and Washington Streets, Roxbury, Massachusetts, but no stone marks his resting place. (Fellowes Athaenaeum)

GENERAL OFFICER IN THE CONTINENTAL ARMY

BIOGRAPHICAL

Lieutenant Colonel, Heath's Massachusetts Regiment, May 19, 1775; Colonel, July 1, 1775; Colonel, 24th Continental Infantry, January 1, 1776; Colonel, 3rd Massachusetts, November 1, 1776; Brigadier General, Continental Army, January 7, 1783, and served to the close of the war.

An innkeeper in Roxbury and an officer in the State Militia before the Revolutionary War.

MASONIC

Mrs. Muriel D. Taylor, Librarian of the Grand Lodge of Massachusetts, advises: "The card in the Grand Secretary's file does not show where or when he got his degrees. Original records of Washington Lodge No. 10 (Army) in our Archives indicate he was an officer of that Lodge."

Greaton is listed as a visitor at American Union Lodge (Army) at its meeting of June 24, 1779, at West Point, New York, the Festival of St. John the Baptist. He was included among the Master Masons. This meeting was opened at Nelson's Point, but the festival was held at West Point.

In the Washington Lodge, Roxbury, Massachusetts, centennial anniversary of 1896, Roxbury is mentioned as the home of Brother and General Greaton (p. 171).

He signed the by-laws of Masters Lodge, Albany, 1777, and was installed as first Junior Warden of Washington Lodge No. 10, 1779. (From the original minutes of November 11, 1779, in the archives of the Grand Lodge of Massachusetts.)

JOHN HANCOCK

MASSACHUSETTS

Born January 12, 1737, in Braintree (now Quincy), Massachusetts.

Died October 8, 1793, in Quincy, Massachusetts.

Buried in Old Granary Burying Ground, Boston, Massachusetts.

SIGNER OF THE DECLARATION OF INDEPENDENCE AND THE ARTICLES OF CONFEDERATION

BIOGRAPHICAL

Harvard graduate, 1754; successful merchant. Later received honorary degrees from Harvard, Yale, Brown, and Princeton Universities. Treasurer of Harvard University.

Member, Continental Congress, 1775-1780, 1785, and 1786, serving as President from May 24, 1775, to October, 1777. He was President of the Congress when the Declaration of Independence was adopted. Its first signer, with signature boldly written "so that King George III may read it without putting on his glasses." Again re-elected President of the Continental Congress, November 23, 1785, but resigned, May 29, 1786, not having served on account of illness.

Major General, Massachusetts Militia, 1776.

Served in the State House of Representatives in 1766, in which Samuel Adams, James Otis, and Thomas Cushing also served; member of the Provincial Congress at Concord, and President of that body, 1774. First Governor of Massachusetts, 1780-85, and again from 1787 until his death.

MASONIC

Member of Merchants Lodge No. 277, Quebec, January 26, 1762; affiliated with St. Andrews Lodge, Boston, October 14, 1762. (Roth, p. 41)

"Record as a Freemason well documented." (Case)

Mrs. Muriel D. Taylor, Librarian of the Grand Lodge of Massachusetts, writes on March 14, 1957: "card in the Grand Secretary's file records degrees as taken in Merchants Lodge No. 277, Quebec, Canada, 1762. Affiliated with St. Andrews Lodge, Boston, October 14, 1762."

EDWARD HAND

PENNSYLVANIA

Born December 31, 1744, in Clyduff, Kings County, Province of Leinster, Ireland.

Died September 3, 1802, at "Rockford", Lancaster County, Pennsylvania.

Buried in St. James' Episcopal Cemetery, Lancaster, Pennsylvania.

GENERAL OFFICER IN THE CONTINENTAL ARMY

BIOGRAPHICAL

Studied medicine at Trinity College, Dublin. Emigrated to Philadelphia in 1767 with the 48th Royal Irish Regiment as Surgeon's Mate. Resumed practice of medicine in Lancaster, Pennsylvania, after the war.

Lieutenant Colonel, Thompson's Pennsylvania Rifle Battalion, June 25, 1775; Lieutenant Colonel, 1st Continental Infantry, January 1, 1776; Colonel, March 7 to Demember 31, 1776; Colonel, 1st Pennsylvania, January 1, 1777, to rank from March 7, 1776; Brigadier General, Continental Army, April 1, 1777; Adjutant General, Continental Army, January 8, 1781, to November 3, 1783; Brevet Major General, September 30, 1783; Major General, United States Army, July 19, 1798; honorably discharged, June 15, 1800. Member of the court-martial which tried and condemned the British spy, Major John André.

Appointed by President Washington, March 21, 1791, as Inspector of the Revenue for Survey No. 3 in the District of Pennsylvania.

Member, Continental Congress, 1784-85, and of the Pennsylvania Assembly, 1785-86. Also served as Burgess of Lancaster in 1787 and 1788.

Named Lay Deputy at the Diocesan Convention of the Episcopal Church in Philadelphia. At Washington's visit to Lancaster, July 4, 1791, Hand headed the reception committee, and Washington recorded, "Took Tea with Mrs. Hand."

President of the Pennsylvania Society of the Cincinnati, 1799.

MASONIC

"Quite possible he was made a Mason in a British Regimental Lodge even before he came to America." (Case)

"He was Worshipful Master of Military Lodge No. 19." (Roth, p. 88) Brother James R. Case and the Grand Lodge of Iowa confirm this information.

The History of Lodge 61, Wilkes-Barre, Pennsylvania, by O. J. Harvey, P. M., pp. 26 and 494, asserts that General Hand succeeded Colonel Procter as Master of

Montgomery Lodge No. 19 (now at Philadelphia) in 1781, then in the Pennsylvania Lines. Brother Sachse, in *Old Masonic Lodges in Pennsylvania,* Vol. 2, p. 16, states that "this probably is an error, as no record substantiating this statement can be found."

Tatsch says "after Procter's resignation, the lodge was in charge of Major Isaac Craig, Senior Warden, who subsequently become Master."

CORNELIUS HARNETT

NORTH CAROLINA

Born April 20, 1723, probably in Chowan County, near Edenton, North Carolina. Lossing says, "native of England. The precise time when he came to America is not known."

Died April 20, 1781, in Wilmington, North Carolina, as a prisoner on parole.

Buried in St. James' Churchyard, Wilmington, North Carolina.

SIGNER OF THE ARTICLES OF CONFEDERATION

No Likeness Available

BIOGRAPHICAL

Appointed Justice of the Peace for New Hanover County in April, 1750; served eleven years as Town Commissioner. Chairman of the Sons of Liberty of North Carolina and member of Committee of Correspondence.

Member of Continental Congress, 1777-1780. Captured by the British at the occupation of Wilmington, North Carolina, in January, 1781, and died as a prisoner in Wilmington, April 20, 1781.

Harnett served in four Provincial Congresses and succeeded Richard Caswell as President of the Congress in November, 1776. Governor of North Carolina, 1775-76. Hailed in 1773 as "the Samuel Adams of North Carolina." (Josiah Quincy, *Memoir of the Life of Josiah Quincy, Jr., of Mass.,* 1825, p. 120)

No authentic picture, print, or portrait is known to be available of Harnett. (William S. Powell, North Carolina Collection Librarian, University of North Carolina, Chapel Hill, N. C.)

MASONIC

"Harnett himself held high rank as a Mason, and though a deist in religion, he served for many years as Vestryman of St. James Parish in Wilmington." (DAB, Vol. 8, p. 280.)

Served as North Carolina District Provincial Grand Master under Joseph Montfort. (ALR, Vol. VI, No. 1)

See *North Carolina Lodge of Research*, Vol. II, Part 1, 1932, p. 18: "Milner's successor, as Deputy Provincial Grand Master for America, was Cornelius Harnett, Master of St. John's Lodge No. 1, of Wilmington. Harnett was an outstanding figure, and one of the foremost statesmen of his time."

JOSEPH HEWES

NORTH CAROLINA

Independence National Historical Park Collections

Born January 23, 1730, near Kingston, New Jersey.

Died November 10, 1779, in Philadelphia, Pennsylvania.

Buried in Christ Church Cemetery, Philadelphia, Pennsylvania.

SIGNER OF THE ARTICLES OF ASSOCIATION AND THE DECLARATION OF INDEPENDENCE

BIOGRAPHICAL

Attended Princeton College; moved to Edenton, North Carolina, in 1756. (W. Eugene Rice, in *Masonic Membership of the Signers of the Declaration of Independence*, gives the date as 1760.)

Member of the First and Second Continental Congresses, 1774-77, and 1779 until his death.

Prominent state legislator; member, State House of Commons, 1766-1775, and again in 1778 and 1779.

"Member of the Committee on the Marine and was in effect our first Secretary of the Navy." (Case)

MASONIC

"He was probably raised in Philadelphia." (Roth, p. 154)

"Hewes is recorded as a visiting Brother at a meeting of Unanimity Lodge in Edenton on St. John' the Evangelist Day, December 27, 1776, just after his return from the Continental Congress in Philadelphia. He was probably made a Mason in the latter city." (*GL Proc. North Carolina.* 1912, p. 75).

Brother G. W. Baird, PGM, says he "was a member of a Masonic lodge in North Carolina."

See also the *Edenton Daily News,* Edenton, North Carolina, for April 25, 1932, quoting excerpts from *The Colonial History of Unanimity Lodge No. 7, A. F. & A. M.,* written by E. W. Spires, on the 155th anniversary (November 9, 1930): "Perhaps the most interesting entry in the old records from a historical viewpoint is found in the minutes of the meeting of December 27, 1776, wherein Joseph Hewes is recorded as visitor . . . While listed as a visitor of the Lodge, he, not unlike many others, doubtless transferred his membership here at a later date, but some of the records of the later date were lost."

JAMES HOGUN

NORTH CAROLINA

Born in Ireland, the year and place not known.

Died January 4, 1781, at Haddrell's Point, South Carolina, in captivity, "where he fills an unmarked grave of a hero."

(*Biographical History of North Carolina,* Vol. IV, edited by Samuel A. Ashe, Greensboro, 1906.)

GENERAL OFFICER IN THE CONTINENTAL ARMY

No Likeness Available

BIOGRAPHICAL

Major, Georgia Militia in 1776; Colonel, 7th North Carolina, November 26, 1776; transferred to 3rd North Carolina, June 1, 1778; Brigadier General, Continental Army, January 9, 1779; taken prisoner at Charleston, May 12, 1780, and died in captivity, January 4, 1781.

Member, Committee of Safety in December, 1774. Member, Assembly in Halifax, August 21, 1775, and again, April 4, 1776.

MASONIC

Member of Royal Arch Lodge No. 3, Philadelphia. He signed the by-laws as "James Hogun", although the minutes refer to him as "James Hogan."

Original Minutes of the Lodge: "Royal Arch Lodge No. 3, dated April 13, 1779, and marked Lodge of Emergency: Brigadier General Peter Muhlenberg and Brig. General James Hogan were Ballotted for unanimously approved and Initiated in Virtue of a Dispensation granted them for that purpose by the Right Worshipful Grand Master they paid their Lodge Dues $60 Dollars to the Treas."

Later entries show that he received the Fellowcraft degree on April 15, 1779, and became a Master Mason on April 17, 1779, the same dates on which these degrees were conferred on General Muhlenberg. (*O R. Royal Arch Lodge No. 3*)

Douglas Southall Freeman's *Life of Washington*, V. 5, p. 101, states: "On March 19, (1779) Arnold was to write Washington that he had transferred the Philadelphia post to Brig. Gen. James Hogun", evidence that Hogun was in Philadelphia at the time mentioned.

WILLIAM HOOPER
NORTH CAROLINA

Independence National Historical Park Collections

Born June 17, 1742, in Boston, Massachusetts.

Died October 14, 1790, in Hillsboro, North Carolina.

Buried in the Hooper family cemetery (now part of the historic Old Town Cemetery) in Hillsboro, North Carolina. On April 25, 1894, Hooper's remains were disinterred and taken to Greensboro to be reburied with those of John Penn at the Guilford Courthouse National Military Park. (Greensboro, N. C. *Daily News* for July 1, 1962).

SIGNER OF THE ARTICLES OF ASSOCIATION AND THE DECLARATION OF INDEPENDENCE

BIOGRAPHICAL

Attended the Boston Latin School and was graduated from Harvard College in 1760; studied law under James Otis, admitted to the bar, and moved to Wilmington, North Carolina, in 1767, where he began the practice of law.

Member, Continental Congress, 1774-77.

Member, Colonial Assembly of North Carolina, 1773-76; published a series of articles against the Crown, arousing the people to the issues involved, and was disbarred for one year. Prominent in Revolutionary movements. Member, State Assembly in 1777 and 1778. Served as a member of a commission to settle a boundary dispute between Massachusetts and New York in 1786.

MASONIC

A statement that he was a member of Hanover Lodge in Masonborough, North Carolina, prior to 1787 is in the *Proceedings of the Grand Lodge of North Carolina* for 1912, p. 74.

"Member of Hanover Lodge, Masonborough, N. C., about 1780." (Case)

"Member of Hanover Lodge, Masonborough, N. C., which ceased to exist in 1787." (Boyden)

CHARLES HUMPHREYS

PENNSYLVANIA

Born September 19, 1714, in Haverford, Delaware County, Pennsylvania.

Died March 11, 1786, in Haverford, Delaware County, Pennsylvania.

Buried in Old Haverford Meeting House Cemetery, Haverford, Delaware County, Pennsylvania.

SIGNER OF THE ARTICLES OF ASSOCIATION

No Likeness Available

BIOGRAPHICAL

Member, Continental Congress, 1774-76.

A Quaker, he opposed war, and voted against the Declaration of Independence.

Member of Provincial Congress, 1764-1774.

MASONIC

See *Old Masonic Lodges of Pennsylvania*, Sachse, Vol. 1, p. 102, showing him to be a member of Tun Tavern Lodge No. 3 of the Moderns in Philadelphia, April 11, 1750.

The same reference, page 46, shows Humphreys subscribed £15 to the Freemason's Hall Fund on March 13, 1754.

DAVID HUMPHREYS
CONNECTICUT

Gilbert Stuart: "General David Humphreys" (detail), Yale University Art Gallery

Born July 10, 1752, in Derby, Connecticut.

Died February 21, 1818, in New Haven, Connecticut.

Buried in Grove Street Cemetery, New Haven, Connecticut.

LIEUTENANT COLONEL AND AIDE-DE-CAMP TO GENERAL WASHINGTON

BIOGRAPHICAL

Yale graduate, 1771; M. A. degree in 1774.

Captain, 6th Connecticut, January 1, 1777; Brigade Major to General Parsons, March 29, 1777; Major and Aide-de-Camp to General Israel Putnam, December 18, 1778; Aide-de-Camp to General Nathanael Greene, May, 1780; Lieutenant Colonel and Aide-de-Camp to General Washington, June 23, 1780, to April 1, 1783; transferred to 4th Connecticut, January 1, 1781; transferred to 2nd Connecticut, January 1, 1783.

In May, 1784, appointed secretary of commission for negotiating treaties of commerce with foreign powers; member of commission to treat with Creek Indians on frontiers of southern states in 1789. Appointed first United States Minister to Portugal in February, 1791; appointed United States Minister to Spain in May, 1796, and remained there until November, 1801.

Between 1802 and 1812, he devoted himself to agriculture and manufacturing in his native state, importing the finest breeds of horses and sheep. Brother James R. Case, Grand Historian of the Grand Lodge of Connecticut, is authority for the statement that Humphreys introduced Merino sheep into America.

He established a woolen and cotton mill in Seymour, Connecticut, in 1803, and a paper mill in 1805. Later served in the War of 1812 as Brigadier General of the State Militia.

Member, Society of the Cincinnati. Received honorary degree of LL.D. from Brown University in 1802, and similar honor from Dartmouth College in 1804.

Member of Royal Society of London in June, 1807.

MASONIC

"Among the names appearing on the minutes of St. Paul's Lodge in Litchfield, Connecticut, during 1781-2-3, are several which are familiar in American history and Masonic annals - Moses Cleaveland, 'founder' of the city in Ohio; Ephraim Kirby, first General Grand High Priest of Royal Arch Masons; William Judd, later Grand Master of Masons in Connecticut; and D. Humphreys, Esq., aide to Washington, and later diplomat and pioneer in the Merino wool industry in America. They were apparently fellow students in the Litchfield Law School as well as wartime buddies. Cleaveland and Humphreys were in Yale together." (Case)

RUFUS KING

MASSACHUSETTS

Born March 24, 1755, in Scarboro, Maine (then part of Massachusetts).

Died April 29, 1827, in Jamaica, Long Island, New York.

Buried in the Cemetery of Grace Church, Jamaica, Long Island, New York.

SIGNER OF THE CONSTITUTION OF THE UNITED STATES

BIOGRAPHICAL

Attended Governor Dummer Academy, near Newburyport, Massachusetts; graduated from Harvard College in 1777. Studied law in Newburyport, admitted to the bar, and commenced practice in 1780.

Member of the Massachusetts House of Representatives in 1782.

Member, Continental Congress, 1784-87; United States Senator from New York, July 16, 1789, to May 23, 1796, when he resigned. Re-elected, February 4, 1813, and served to March 3, 1825. Delegate to the Federal Constitutional Convention of 1787.

Appointed Captain and Aide-de-Camp to General Glover, August 16, 1778, and served to July, 1782.

Moved to New York in 1788 and served that State as a prominent legislator. Minister Plenipotentiary to Great Britain, succeeding Thomas Pinckney, from May 20, 1796 to May 18, 1803, and from May 5. 1825 to June 16, 1826.

Unsuccessful candidate for Vice President of the United States in 1804; for Governor of New York in 1815; and for President of the United States in 1816.

MASONIC

"He is thought to have been a member of a lodge in Newburyport, Mass., but no proof is available. His brother, William King, was first governor of Maine and first Grand Master of Maine." (Denslow)

A search of the records of St. John's Lodge, Newburyport, Massachusetts, by Brother William F. Mahoney during 1961 would now indicate that King was a member of that Lodge. The record of one Rufus King in this Lodge shows he became a member prior to 1781, with this additional information:

Present at Lodge December 27, 1781, September 25, 1782, and January 29, 1783. Filled these offices: May 29, 1782, acting as Treasurer, and again on June 24, 1782. March 30, 1783, and March 31, 1784, acting as Junior Warden. December 27, 1783, fined three shillings for being absent without permission of the Worshipful Master, John Tracy.

There is recorded in the by-laws a note that he died in New York City, but no date is given.

An article in long hand in the lodge records lists one Rufus King as a lawyer and Minister Plenipotentiary to the Court of Saint James (8 years).

A letter from Brother Mahoney dated January 22, 1961, states: "As far as our records go, we are content to believe that RUFUS KING was a member of this Lodge and we are prepared to prove the same. We believe that our records are proof of his membership."

With a letter of October 15, 1961, from Brother Mahoney was sent a tracing of King's signature on the by-laws of the Lodge, which compared favorably with signature shown on the Constitution. We feel that this evidence, which Brother Mahoney has carefully searched for, is sufficient to verify the membership in the Masonic Fraternity of Rufus King, signer of the Constitution.

A Rufus King installed the Wardens at the constitution of United Lodge, Topsham, Maine, September 28, 1805. (*GL Proc. Massachusetts,* 1792-1815, p. 315.)

HENRY KNOX

MASSACHUSETTS

Born July 25, 1750, in Boston, Massachusetts.

Died October 25, 1806, in Thomaston, Maine.

Buried: "The remains of Knox and his family rest in a lot about 12 x 15 feet in the village cemetery." (Thomaston, Maine)

See *General Knox, His Family, His Manor House, and his Guests,* by Lewis Frederick Starrett, 1902, p. 28.

GENERAL OFFICER IN THE CONTINENTAL ARMY

BIOGRAPHICAL

Educated in common schools, and commenced business as a bookseller in Boston before the war.

Served as a volunteer at Bunker Hill in June, 1775; Colonel, Continental Regiment of Artillery, November 17, 1775; Brigadier General and Chief of Artillery, Continental Army, December 27, 1776; Major General, March 22, 1782, to rank from November 15, 1781; Commander in Chief of the Army, December 23, 1783, to June 20, 1784; Secretary of War, March 2, 1785.

Member of the court-martial which tried Major John André in 1780. A close friend and trusted advisor of Washington.

The first Secretary of War under the Federal Government in Washington's administration, September 12, 1789, to December 31, 1794.

First Secretary-General of the Society of the Cincinnati, from 1783 to 1799, and Vice President in 1805.

MASONIC

Knox is mentioned as "Brother Henry Knox, a member of the First Lodge of Boston". (Morse, p. 78)

"Knox visited St. John's Lodge in Boston in 1800 . . . we are not sure where or when he became a member of the Mystic Tie." (Hayden)

Grand Lodge of Massachusetts: a copy of the records of St. John's Lodge, Boston (February, 1784-December, 1806), in the Library, indicates that Brother Henry Knox visited the Lodge on November 26, 1800.

An examination of the Knox papers in the Library of the Massachusetts Historical Society would establish that Knox was in Boston at the time of the Grand Lodge meeting of November 26, 1800:

Knox wrote *from* Boston on November 20 to Benjamin Horner about a threatened suit;

gave a promissory note to Jonathan Wright on November 24;

notice to settlers concerning deeds for his Maine lands on November 24;

certain instructions to Jackson Durant on November 29.

The next letter is dated December 20, 1800, from Thomaston, Maine; the first one prior to the November 20th date is dated November 5, 1800, and contains instructions to John Gleason.

There exist other references, unverified or traditional. *The Masonic Eclectic*, Vol. III, No. 1, of January, 1879, quotes from the article, "An Old Masonic Chair and its Historical Association," p. 113: "The membership of the Lodge (Williamsburg Lodge No. 6, Virginia) has been most distinguished, and it was doubtless during its session held in the period of our struggle for independence, honored with the presence of General Washington, LaFayette, Count D'Estaing, Generals Knox and Hamilton, and other distinguished patriots who are known to have been members of the Masonic Fraternity."

The following remarks by R. W. Brother Sereno D. Nickerson are quoted from *The Proceedings of the Grand Lodge of Massachusetts, 1906*, p. 208: "Another portrait was that of General Knox, who was a good Mason, and a most active soldier in the Revolutionary War."

The Proceedings of the Grand Lodge of Georgia, 1880, pp. 24 and 25, report as follows on the Yorktown Centennial: "Alluding to the fact that the Continental Congress had, one hundred years before, ordered a monument to be erected at Yorktown, the brother graphically portrayed the scene and the Masonic Fraternity then assembled to lay the cornerstone. At that communicaion of the Grand Lodge of Virginia, could have been found . . . Massachusetts, her Henry Knox . . . "

MARIE-JOSEPH PAUL YVES ROCH GILBERT du MOTIER de LA FAYETTE

FRANCE

Born September 6, 1757, in the Parish of Chavaniac, Diocese of Saint Flour, Auvergne, France

Died May 20, 1834, at his town house, Rue d'Anjou, Paris, France.

Buried in Picpus Cemetery, Paris, France. His grave was covered with earth from Bunker Hill.

GENERAL OFFICER IN THE CONTINENTAL ARMY

BIOGRAPHICAL

Lafayette landed in America for the first time on June 13, 1777, and was commissioned a Major General in the Continental Army on July 31, 1777, holding that commission until November 3, 1783. Wounded at Brandywine, September 11, 1777; served at Valley Forge during the winter of 1777-78. Sailed for France, January 11, 1779, and returned to the United States April 27, 1780. Again returned to France December 22, 1781, returning to this country in 1784.

A member of the court-martial that tried Major John André in 1780. The last surviving General Officer of the Revolutionary War.

Became a member of the French National Assembly in 1789, but fell a victim of the French Revolution. Imprisoned by the Austrians from 1792 to 1797. Returned to France in 1799, and served his country again from 1818 to 1824.

Returned to America again in 1824, for a triumphal tour from Maine to Georgia, from Missouri to Louisiana. Received unprecedented honors, Masonic and otherwise, on this trip.

Lafayette never asked payment for any of his services, but claimed citizenship in America on account of his commission in the Continental Army. Congress never declared him an American citizen, but the General Assembly of Maryland did, decreeing that "the marquis de la Fayette, and his heirs male forever, shall be, and they and such of them are hereby deemed, adjudged, and taken to be, natural born citizens of this State". On December 28, 1824, Congress granted him $200,000 and one township of land for his services and sacrifices in the Revolutionary War.

A founding member of the Society of the Cincinnati.

MASONIC

No documentary evidence has yet been uncovered which will give positive proof of the time and place of Lafayette's initiation into the Fraternity.

"Revisited the United States in 1824-25 and wherever he travelled was the recipient of Masonic honors such as no man ever received before or since . . . On record as a Freemason in Paris as early as 1775, when he was a visiting brother at the institution of the Lodge of St. John de la Candeur." (Case)

Lafayette himself said this about his membership, quoted from *A Pilgrimage of Liberty,* a contemporary account of the triumphal tour of General Lafayette in 1825, by Edgar Ewing Brandon, published by The Lawhead Press, Athens, Ohio, 1944:

At a reception and banquet at Nashville, as reported in the *Nashville Whig* of May 7 and 14, 1825, Brother Wilkins Tannehill, Grand Master, welcomed Lafayette, and the General replied in substance as follows:

" . . . He had, he said, been long a member of the order, having been initiated, young as he was, even before he entered the service of our country in the revolutionary war . . . He had never for a moment ceased to love and venerate the institution, and was therefore peculiarly delighted to see that it had spread its genial influence thus far to the west, and that his brethren here were not only comfortably but brilliantly accommodated. He considered the order as peculiarly valuable in this country, where it not only fostered the principles of civil and religious liberty, but was eminently calculated to link the extremities of this wide republic together, and to perpetuate, by its fraternizing influence, the union of the states."

The History of Bro. Gen. LaFayette's Fraternal Connections with the Right Worshipful Grand Lodge F. & A. M. of Pennsylvania, by Julius F. Sachse, Philadelphia, 1916, says: "No original documentary evidence is known to be in existence which records the initiation of General LaFayette in the Masonic Fraternity, nor in what Lodge, or when this took place."

There is a tradition in Masonic circles that General Lafayette was made a Mason in one of the Military Lodges at Morristown, New Jersey, where a Festal Lodge was held December 27, 1779. However, Lafayette was in Paris at this time. Another tradition holds that he was made a Mason in a Military Lodge which met at Valley Forge during the winter of 1777-78, but no documentary evidence of such action has thus far been discovered.

These two claims received principal attention over the years, although the first one was wholly discarded when evidence was produced to show that Lafayette was not in America at that time.

This uncertainty led to the resolution of September 6, 1824, in the Grand Lodge of Pennsylvania, and the appointment of a Committee to satisfy themselves that General Lafayette was an Ancient York Mason. The Committee was satisfied with its investigation and with subsequent action of the Grand Lodge of Pennsylvania in enrolling Lafayette an Honorary Member. However, the information which the Committee based its decision on has not come down to us.

An article by Most Worshipful Brother Ray Baker Harris, Librarian, Supreme Council, 33°, Southern Jurisdiction, in *The New Age* for July, 1941, entitled *LaFayette a Mason in 1775,* offers the latest and most authoritative evidence of Lafayette's Masonic membership. Extracts from the article follow, quoted by permission of Brother Harris:

"The Library of the Supreme Council recently acquired four rare 18th century Masonic publications. These were secured from France just prior to the occupation of Paris.

"One of these described in detail the several meetings and the inauguration ceremonies connected with the formation of the Loge de Saint Jean de la Candeur, Paris, in December of 1775. This Lodge had invited to the inauguration ceremonies 'the Honorary, Regular and Subordinate Officers, and Deputies, of all Lodges composing the Grand Orient of France to assist in this ceremony, and also all Brethren who could be recommended as regular Masons' . . . Then follows a Tableau of one hundred 'Les Chers Freres Visiteurs.' Considering the statement regarding invitations, as well as the fact that this was a ceremony *in lodge,* it may be concluded that all these visitors were Regular Masons under the Grand Orient. In the list appear not only the name of the Marquis de LaFayette, but also those of Comte de Rochambeau and such known friends and relatives of LaFayette as . . .

"While this seems to establish conclusively that LaFayette was a Mason in 1775, prior to coming to America, it leaves unsolved the mystery of his Mother Lodge. It seems logical to conclude . . . that he was made a Mason in one of the Lodges composed in whole or in large part by the members of his regiment, either when he was with the Black Musketeers Regiment or later with the Noailles Regiment of Dragoons . . . This must be a subject for future research, and it is useless to speculate now on the several possible Lodges in which he might have received his degrees."

HENRY LAURENS

SOUTH CAROLINA

Born March 6, 1724, in Charleston, South Carolina.

Died December 8, 1792, at "Mepkin", on the Cooper River, thirty miles above Charleston.

Buried: His remains were cremated - the first white cremation on record in America - and his ashes interred on his estate, "Mepkin".

SIGNER OF THE ARTICLES OF CONFEDERATION

BIOGRAPHICAL

Received early education in Charleston; went to England in 1744 to further his education, and on his return to America in 1747, established successful business in Charleston.

Member, Continental Congress, January 10, 1777, and served as President from November 1, 1777, to December 9, 1778. Elected Minister to Holland by Continental

Congress, October 21, 1779, and sailed early in 1780. He was captured on the voyage and held prisoner in the Tower of London for fifteen months; released, December 31, 1781, in exchange for Lord Cornwallis.

Appointed one of the peace commissioners and signed the preliminary Treaty of Paris, November 30, 1782. Returned to America August 3, 1784, and retired to his plantation.

Subsequently elected to the Continental Congress, the State Legislature, and to the Federal Constitutional Convention in 1787, all of which offices he declined.

Prominent State legislator, 1757 to 1777. Member, American Philosophical Society in Philadelphia, 1772-1792.

MASONIC

Member, Solomon's Lodge No. 1, Charleston, South Carolina, serving as Treasurer in 1755, and Grand Steward in 1754.

See Albert G. Mackey, *History of Freemasonry in South Carolina*, p. 29, re the re-establishment of the Provincial Grand Lodge: "On the 5th of December, 1754, he (Peter Leigh) caused the following notice to be issued, which, as it is the very first instance of the notice of a Masonic meeting that was ever published in South Carolina, will perhaps on that account be viewed as a curiosity. It was inserted in Timothy's *South Carolina Gazette* for the 5th of December, 1754, and was headed

'By order of the Grand Master

The Grand Annual Feast and General Communication of the Free and Accepted Masons, is to be holden in Charleston, on Friday, the 27th of December, instant, being St. John the Evangelist's Day.'

"In the meantime the Hon. Peter Leigh had constituted a Provincial Grand Lodge, with the following officers . . .

Charles Pinckney, Henry Laurens,
Provincial Grand Stewards.

Then, Friday, the 27th of December, 1754, the members of Solomon's Lodge, having met, elected the following officers . . . Mr. Henry Laurens, Treasurer."

BENJAMIN LINCOLN

MASSACHUSETTS

Born January 24, 1733, at Hingham, Massachusetts.

Died May 9, 1810, at Hingham, Massachusetts.

Buried in the Hingham Cemetery, Hingham, Massachusetts.

GENERAL OFFICER IN THE CONTINENTAL ARMY

BIOGRAPHICAL

Major General, Continental Army, February 19, 1777; wounded at Saratoga, October 7, 1777. Surrendered at Charleston, May 12, 1780; prisoner of war until exchanged November, 1780; Secretary of War, October 30, 1781; resigned October 29, 1783, but requested by Congress to perform the duties thereof to November 12, 1783.

Active in the affairs of his community; a deacon in his Church for many years. Lossing says of him: "General Lincoln was temperate and religious. No profane word was ever heard uttered by his lips."

Present at the surrender of Cornwallis at Yorktown, October 19, 1781, and appointed to receive the sword of the British Commander.

President of the Massachusetts Society of the Cincinnati, 1783.

In 1786-87 he commanded Massachusetts Militia in suppressing Shay's Rebellion. Lieutenant Governor of Massachusetts in 1787. Appointed Collector of the Port of Boston in 1789, and served for twenty years.

MASONIC

In the *125th Anniversary - Lodge of St. Andrew, 1756-1906*, Boston, 1907, Lincoln's name appears on the membership list, with this record:

> Entered Apprentice - December 25, 1780
> Fellowcraft - January 11, 1781
> Master Mason - May 4, 1781

This information also appears in the records of the Grand Secretary of the Grand Lodge of Massachusetts.

The Proceedings of the Grand Lodge of Massachusetts, 1733-1792 p. 286, also record a Grand Lodge Meeting in Boston, Wednesday, December 27, 1780. Among those present was "Honorable Gen. Lincoln." On page 325 is recorded another Grand Lodge Meeting on June 24, 1785, with Benjamin Lincoln present, representing Rising Sun Lodge.

Vol. 3 of the 1924 edition of *Little Masonic Library*, p. 304, states: "General Lincoln, having been paroled and exchanged, rejoined the Army in the spring of 1781, and was made a Mason in Massachusetts Lodge, Boston, the same year." The Librarian of the Grand Lodge of Massachusetts writes: "If this refers to *the* Massachusetts Lodge, it is not correct, as Lincoln's name does not appear in the list of members of that Lodge. If it is a Lodge in Massachusetts, then it is definitely The Lodge of St. Andrew."

JAMES McHENRY

MARYLAND

Historical Society of Pennsylvania

Born November 16, 1753, in Ballymena, County Antrim, Ireland.

Died May 3, 1816, at "Fayetteville", his estate near Baltimore, Maryland.

Buried in Westminster Presbyterian Churchyard, Baltimore, Maryland.

ASSISTANT SECRETARY TO GENERAL WASHINGTON, AND SIGNER OF THE CONSTITUTION OF THE UNITED STATES

BIOGRAPHICAL

Educated in Dublin; came to the Colonies in 1771 and studied at Newark Academy in Delaware; apprentice to Dr. Benjamin Rush in 1771.

Assistant Secretary to General Washington, May 15, 1778, to August 30 (presumably), 1780; Surgeon, 5th Pennsylvania Battalion, August 10, 1778; taken prisoner at Fort Washington, November 16, 1776; prisoner of war on parole until exchanged, May 6, 1778; Major, Continental Army, May 25, 1781, to rank from October 30, 1780. Aide-de-Camp to General Lafayette, August 30 (presumably), 1780, to November 6, 1781. Served throughout the Virginia and Yorktown campaigns.

Member, Continental Congress, 1783-86. Member Constitutional Convention in 1787.

Secretary of War in Washington's Cabinet, January 28, 1796, to May 13, 1800, in the administration of President John Adams.

Member, State Senate, 1781-86. Original member of the Society of the Cincinnati.

MASONIC

Information from the Grand Lodge of Maryland states that he was a member of Spiritual Lodge No. 23, Maryland, receiving his degrees as follows:

>Entered Apprentice, May 21, 1806
>Fellowcraft, June 18, 1806
>Master Mason, July 30, 1806
>Remarks: "Struck off, 1809".

Vol. VI, No. 1, of American Lodge of Research *Transactions* also gives the same information.

WILLIAM MAXWELL

NEW JERSEY

Born, 1733, in County Tyrone, Ireland.

Died, November 4, 1796, at Lansdown, Hunterdon County, New Jersey.

Buried in the graveyard adjoining the Old Stone Church, Greenwich Township, Warren County, New Jersey.

GENERAL OFFICER IN THE CONTINENTAL ARMY

No Likeness Available

BIOGRAPHICAL

Entered colonial service in 1758, serving in French & Indian War.

Colonel, 2nd New Jersey, November 8, 1775; Brigadier General, Continental Army, October 23, 1776; served with the Army at Valley Forge during the winter of 1777-78; resigned, July 25, 1780.

Biographical data on Maxwell is scarce. He never married, and no likeness of him has been found. Washington said of him: "I believe him to be an honest man, a warm friend to his country, and firmly attached to its interests." "Little is known of his personal history." (Appleton)

Member, New Jersey Provincial Congress in 1775. Member of New Jersey Assembly for a short time after the war.

MASONIC

Member of Military Lodge No. 19, A. Y. M., under Pennsylvania warrant. (Case)

The same information appears in *The Proceedings of the Grand Lodge of New Jersey, 1936-37*, Vol. 39-40, p. 122, and in Sachse's *Old Masonic Lodges of Pennsylvania*, Vol. 2, p. 18.

HUGH MERCER
VIRGINIA

Born in 1725 in Aberdeenshire, Scotland.

Died January 12, 1777, in Princeton, New Jersey.

Buried in Christ Churchyard, Philadelphia, Pennsylvania. His remains were transferred to Laurel Hill Cemetery, Philadelphia, November 26, 1840; monument to his memory dedicated by the St. Andrews Society.

GENERAL OFFICER IN THE CONTINENTAL ARMY

Hugh Mercer

BIOGRAPHICAL

Studied medicine at Marischall College, University of Aberdeen. Emigrated to Philadelphia early in 1747, and practiced medicine there. Served in the French & Indian War. Settled in Fredericksburg and resumed practice of medicine.

Colonel, 3rd Virginia, February 13, 1776; Brigadier General, Continental Army, June 5, 1776; died, January 12, 1777, of wounds received at Princeton, January 3, 1777.

Crossed the Delaware, December 25, 1776, with his troops, and fought at the battle of Trenton. An active supporter of Virgina's opposition to English oppression.

MASONIC

Member of Fredericksburg Lodge No. 4, Virginia. Mercer petitioned for membership, December 26, 1761, and was initiated Entered Apprentice; passed Fellowcraft on January 19, 1767; and raised to degree of Master Mason on February 14, 1767. (*O R*)

Mercer later served as Worshipful Master of this Lodge.

RICHARD MONTGOMERY

NEW YORK

Born December 2, 1738, in Swords, County Dublin, Ireland.

Died December 31, 1775, in Quebec, Canada.

Buried in Quebec, with military funeral and burial by courtesy of Carleton, the commanding general of the British forces there. In 1818 his remains were moved to St. Paul's Churchyard, New York City, and interred there on July 8.

GENERAL OFFICER IN THE CONTINENTAL ARMY

BIOGRAPHICAL

Educated at Trinity College, Dublin, Ireland.

An officer in the British Army at 18; his regiment came to Halifax in 1757, and took part in the Louisburg campaign. He returned to Europe after the French & Indian War, and returned to New York in 1774; married eldest daughter of Robert R. Livingston.

Brigadier General, Continental Army, June 22, 1775; Major General, December 9, 1775, but the news of this promotion did not reach him before he was killed at Quebec on December 31, 1775.

A member of the First Provincial Convention in New York in April, 1775.

MASONIC

Accepted by his contemporaries as a Freemason and never doubted since. (Case)

"The names of Warren, Montgomery, and Wooster became a standing Masonic toast during the war, commemorative of their virtues as patriot Masons who fell early in their Country's defense." (Hayden, p. 317)

One presumption is that he was a member of Lodge of Unity, No. 18, under Irish Registry in the 17th Regiment of Foot.

JOHN PETER GABRIEL MUHLENBERG

VIRGINIA

Born October 1, 1746, in Trappe, Montgomery County, Pennsylvania.

Died October 1, 1807, in Trappe, Montgomery County, Pennsylvania.

Buried in Augustus Lutheran Churchyard, Trappe, Montgomery County, Pennsylvania.

GENERAL OFFICER IN THE CONTINENTAL ARMY

BIOGRAPHICAL

Studied at Philadelphia Academy (later the University of Pennsylvania), and at the University of Halle, Germany; served in a German regiment of dragoons; returned to Philadelphia in 1766. Ordained by ministerium of Pennsylvania, 1768. Ordained to Episcopal priesthood, April 23, 1772, by the Bishop of London.

Colonel, 8th Virginia, March 1, 1776; Brigadier General, Continental Army, February 21, 1777, and served to close of war. Brevet Major General, September 30, 1783. Returned to Pennsylvania, and settled in Montgomery County.

Member, First, Third, and Sixth Congresses of the United States. (March 4, 1789-March 3, 1791; March 4, 1793-March 3, 1795; March 4, 1799-March 3, 1801). Member, United States Senate, and served from March 4, 1801, until his resignation, June 30, 1801.

Appointed Collector of the Port of Philadelphia in 1802 by President Jefferson, and served in that post until his death.

Member, Virginia House of Burgesses, 1774. Vice President of Pennsylvania, 1785-88.

Member, Society of the Cincinnati.

MASONIC

Member of Royal Arch Lodge No. 3, Philadelphia. His name appears as a member in printed by-laws, under date of April 13, 1779.

From the Original Minutes of the Lodge: "Royal Arch Lodge No. 3, dated April 13, 1779, and marked Lodge of Emergency: 'Brigadier General Peter Muhlenberg and Brig. General James Hogan were Ballotted for and unanimously approved and Initiated in Virtue of a Dispensation granted them for that purpose by the Right Worshipful Grand Master they paid their Lodge Dues $60 Dollars to the Treas.'"

Later entries show Fellowcraft degree on April 15, 1779, and Master Mason on April 17, 1779. (*O R*, Royal Arch Lodge No. 3)

JOHN NIXON

MASSACHUSETTS

Born March 1, 1727, in Framingham, Massachusetts.

Died March 24, 1815, in Middlebury, Vermont.

Buried: *Proceedings of the American Antiquarian Society,* Vol. 36, Part 1, pp 38-70, by John W. Merriam, closes by saying: "But beyond this fact (Government pension of $150. per year) I have found nothing of his later life, and have not located his place of burial."

GENERAL OFFICER IN THE CONTINENTAL ARMY

BIOGRAPHICAL

Took part in the siege of Louisbourg in 1745, and was a Captain of provincial troops under General Abercrombie at Ticonderoga.

Captain of Company of Minute Men at Lexington, April 19, 1775; Colonel of a Massachusetts Regiment, April 24 to December, 1775; wounded at Bunker Hill, June 17, 1775; Colonel, 4th Continental Infantry, January 1, 1776; Brigadier General, Continental Army, August 9, 1776; resigned, September 12, 1780, on account of infirmity arising from his wounds.

Member of Congregational Church for many years. Moved to Middlebury in 1803 and spent the remainder of his life with his family there.

MASONIC

A Grand Lodge Meeting of June 24, 1764, mentions application for a Warrant dated March 5, 1762, from Lodge No. 7 of New York, to hold a lodge at Crown Point, or in the colony of Connecticut. "The Warrant may be enclosed by way of a Packet, seal'd and directed to Capt. John Nixon, commanding the Massachusetts troops at Crown Point." (*GL Proc. Mass. 1733-1792,* p. 91). (Benson Lossing, in his *Pictorial Field Book of the Revolution,* says Nixon was a Captain at Ticonderoga.)

Photostat in the Library of the Grand Lodge of New York, dated June 24, 1779, shows Brother Nixon listed as Visitor (Master Mason) at festival of St. John the Baptist, at a meeting of American Union Military Lodge held at West Point, New York.

Visitor to American Union Lodge as a Master Mason, June 24, 1779. (Case)

Card in Office of Grand Secretary of the Grand Lodge of Massachusetts does not show where or when he got degrees.

ROBERT TREAT PAINE

MASSACHUSETTS

Independence National Historical Park Collections

Born March 11, 1731, in Boston, Massachusetts.

Died May 12, 1814, in Boston, Massachusetts.

Buried in Old Granary Burial Ground, Boston, Massachusetts.

SIGNER OF THE ARTICLES OF ASSOCIATION AND THE DECLARATION OF INDEPENDENCE

BIOGRAPHICAL

Attended the Boston Public Latin School, and was graduated from Harvard College in 1749; studied theology and was Chaplain of troops on the northern frontier in 1755. Studied law; admitted to the bar in 1757, and practiced in Boston.

Member, Continental Congress, 1774-78.

Member, State House of Representatives, 1777; Attorney-General of Massachusetts, 1777-1790; member, Governor's Council in 1779 and 1780. Judge, Massachusetts Supreme Court, 1790-1804. A founder of the American Academy of Arts and Sciences.

MASONIC

"His connection with Freemasonry not doubted, although the lodge in which he was made is not discovered as yet. He may have been made in a British regimental lodge during one of the campaigns against the French." (Case)

"Meeting of Grand Lodge, Tuesday, 26th June 5759 . . . St. John the Baptist day being a Sunday, Our Right Worshipfull Brother Jeremy Gridley Esqr Grand Master notified the Brethren in the Publick Prints that he should Celebrate the Feast of St. John the Baptist at the House of Mr. John Gratons at the Grey Hound Tavern in Roxbury where the Deputy Grand Master Held a Grand Lodge (the Grand Master being at Portsmouth) and the day was Celebrated as usual the Following Brethren Present . . ." Then follows a list of forty-seven names, including that of Robert Treat Paine. (*GL Proc. Mass. 1733-1792*, pp. 63-4)

Mrs. Muriel D. Taylor, Librarian of the Grand Lodge of Massachusetts, advised on March 14, 1957, that the card in the Grand Secretary's file does not record where or when he took the degrees.

WILLIAM PALFREY

MASSACHUSETTS

Born February 24, 1741, in Boston, Massachusetts.

Died: Lost at sea in December, 1780, while on special business to France by order of the Continental Congress.

LIEUTENANT COLONEL AND AIDE-DE-CAMP

TO GENERAL WASHINGTON

Independence National Historical Park Collections

BIOGRAPHICAL

Major and Aide-de-Camp to General Lee, July 16, 1775; Aide-de-Camp to General Washington, March 6, 1776, to April 27, 1776; Paymaster General, April 27, 1776, with rank of Lieutenant Colonel from July 9, 1776; appointed United States Consul to France, November 4, 1780; vessel on which he sailed was lost at sea in December, 1780.

MASONIC

Member, St. Andrew's Lodge at Boston: EA, December 5, 1760; FC, December 18, 1760; MM, January 27, 1761, and later served as Junior Warden and Senior Warden of this Lodge.

Palfrey, with seven others, petitioned the Massachusetts Grand Lodge on May 11, 1770, for new lodge under the title of The Massachusetts Lodge. The charter was granted May 13, 1770, and Palfrey's name is the second one on the charter. He is on record as Senior Warden of this lodge on June 1, 1770; elected Worshipful Master December 3, 1770, and again, December 18, 1778.

Elected Grand Secretary of the Massachusetts Grand Lodge December 4, 1778. "It was in all probability through the influence of William Palfrey, Grand Secretary, that the charter (The Massachusetts Lodge) was granted." (p. 61 of *Celebration of the 125th Anniversary of The Massachusetts Lodge, 1770 - May 17, 1895.* Boston, 1896)

SAMUEL HOLDEN PARSONS

CONNECTICUT

(The Historical Society of Pennsylvania)

Born May 14, 1737, in Lyme, Connecticut.

Died November 17, 1789. Drowned in Big Beaver River, Pennsylvania. His body was recovered and given burial, but river bank has since washed away. (Case)

GENERAL OFFICER IN THE CONTINENTAL ARMY

BIOGRAPHICAL

Harvard graduate, 1756; a fellow-student with Joseph Warren (martyred at Bunker Hill). Studied law; admitted to the bar, and practiced in Lyme. King's Attorney in 1773.

Colonel in the Lexington Alarm, April, 1775; Colonel, 6th Connecticut, May 1 to December 10, 1775; Colonel, 10th Continental Infantry, January 1, 1776; Brigadier General, Continental Army, August 9, 1776; Major General, October 23, 1780. Retired, July 22, 1782. Drowned, November 17, 1789.

Served on the court-martial that tried Major John André.

President of the Connecticut Society of the Cincinnati, 1784.

MASONIC

One of the original members of American Military Union Lodge No. 1 in the Connecticut Line.

Brother James R. Case makes this information available from his notes:
"Entered in St. John's Lodge No. 2, Middletown, May 18, 1763.
Fellowcraft in Hiram Lodge No. 1, New Haven, October 23, 1765, while the General Assembly was in session.
Charter Member, American Union Lodge.
Served as Treasurer of American Union Lodge, February 13, 1776.
Master Mason in American Union Lodge, February 27, 1776.
Worshipful Master, American Union Lodge, February 15, 1779.
Worshipful Master, St. John's Lodge No. 2, Middletown, February 18, 1783.
Royal Arch Mason, Middletown, September 19, 1783.
Emissary to New York, November, 1783, to ascertain means of obtaining authority for a Grand Lodge in Connecticut."

Parsons is listed as being present at the Masonic convention in Morristown, New Jersey, during the Revolutionary War (December 27, 1779).

JOHN PATERSON

MASSACHUSETTS

Born in 1744, in Newington Parish, Wethersfield (now New Britain), Connecticut.

Died July 19, 1808, in Lisle, New York.

Buried in the Church-on-the-Hill Cemetery, Lenox, Massachusetts.

GENERAL OFFICER IN THE CONTINENTAL ARMY

(*Valley Forge Park Commission*)

BIOGRAPHICAL

Attended common schools; graduate of Yale College, 1762; studied law; admitted to the bar and practiced in New Britain, Connecticut, and Lenox, Massachusetts.

Colonel of a Massachusetts Regiment, April to December, 1775; Colonel, 15th Continental Infantry, January 1, 1776; Brigadier General, Continental Army, February 21, 1777, and served to close of war; Brevet Major General, September 30, 1783.

Member, Provincial Congress of Massachusetts, 1774-75.

Practiced law in Lenox, Massachusetts, after the war, and was active in local political affairs. Moved to New York in 1791; was active in public service in Broome County. Member New York State legislature, 1792-93, and the State Constitutional Convention, 1801.

Represented New York in the Eighth United States Congress, March 4, 1803, to March 3, 1805.

Commanded the Massachusetts troops at the time of Shay's Rebellion. A splendid monument erected to his memory in Lenox, Massachusetts, where he was a resident. Member, Society of the Cincinnati.

MASONIC

Mrs. Muriel D. Taylor, Librarian of the Grand Lodge of Massachusetts, furnished this information under date of March 14, 1957:

"A petitioner and charter member of Berkshire No. 5 Lodge in Stockbridge, Mass., March 8, 1777. (*1 Mass.-260-1, 1920 Mass. 233, 1870 Mass. 26*). Visited American Union Lodge, June 24, 1779, per Plumb, *History of American Union Lodge No. 1, Free and Accepted Masons of Ohio, 1776 to 1933.* Washington Lodge No. 10, 1877, p. 64: Charter Master, Washington (Military) Lodge No. 10, Nov. 11, 1779 (Original minutes, November 11, 1779)."

Freemasonry in the Thirteen Colonies, Tatsch, p. 211, states that "Massachusetts Grand Lodge chartered Washington Lodge No. 10 in the Revolutionary Army. A dispensation for the Military Lodge was granted by the Massachusetts Grand Lodge to Gen. John Paterson . . . as Master under the title of 'Washington Lodge' to make Masons, pass Fellowcrafts, and raise Masters, in this state, or in any of the United States where there is no Grand Lodge." The Charter was granted October 6, 1779.

The Grand Lodge meeting of October 6, 1779, records that "in answer to a petition for charter to hold a Travelling Lodge . . . Having nominated Gen. John Paterson, Col. Benj. Tupper, S. W., and Major Wm. Hull, J. W., voted, a Charter be Granted them, for holding Regular Lodges, make Masons, pass and Raise, in this State or any of the United States of America, where no other Grand Master presides. But in any other where there is a Grand Master, Constituted by the Brethren of these United States, they are to Inform Him, and Receive his sanction." (*GL Proc. Mass. 1733-1792*, p. 277)

WILLIAM PATERSON

NEW JERSEY

Born December 24, 1745, in Antrim, Ireland.

Died September 9, 1806, in Albany, New York.

Buried in Van Rensselaer Manor House vault, near Albany, New York.

SIGNER OF THE CONSTITUTION OF THE UNITED STATES

BIOGRAPHICAL

Emigrated to the Colonies in 1747 and settled in New Castle, Pennsylvania. Attended private schools; graduated from Princeton College in 1763; studied law; admitted to the bar in 1768, and practiced in New Bromly, New Jersey.

Elected delegate to Continental Congress in 1780, but did not serve on account of duties as Attorney General of New Jersey. Delegate to the Federal Constitutional Convention of 1787, and sponsored "the Paterson Plan" for United States Constitution.

Member, United States Senate, March 4, 1789, to November 13, 1790, but resigned, having been elected Governor of New Jersey. Re-elected Governor and served from October 30, 1790, to March 30, 1793, when he resigned to become an Associate Justice of the Supreme Court of the United States, serving from March 30, 1793, until his death.

State Senator, 1776-77. Attorney General of New Jersey from September 4, 1776, to June 13, 1783, when he resigned. Governor of New Jersey, succeeding William Livingston, August 1, 1790.

MASONIC

Member, Trenton Lodge No. 5, New Jersey, receiving EA and FC degrees on May 17, 1791, and MM degree on November 7 of same year. *The History of Trenton Lodge No. 5*, p. 17, gives this same information.

See *History of Freemasonry in New Jersey, 1787-1937*, p. 140, by David McGregor, Grand Historian of the Grand Lodge of New Jersey: "Three of the four Jerseymen who signed the Federal Constitution were Freemasons, viz: David Brearley, of Trenton, William Paterson, of New Brunswick, and Jonathan Dayton of Elizabethtown."

ISRAEL PUTNAM

CONNECTICUT

Born January 7, 1718, in Salem Village, now Danvers, Massachusetts.

Died May 29, 1790, in Brooklyn, Connecticut.

Buried in South Cemetery, Brooklyn, Connecticut, with Masonic honors. Later re-interred under a monument erected by the Putnam Phalanx, near the center of the town.

GENERAL OFFICER IN THE CONTINENTAL ARMY

BIOGRAPHICAL

Lieutenant Colonel in the Lexington Alarm, April, 1775; Colonel, 3rd Connecticut, May 1, 1775; Major General, Continental Army, June 19, 1775; retired, June 3, 1783. One of the first four Major Generals appointed, and the only one of this grade to serve throughout the war.

MASONIC

Made a Mason at Crown Point in a Military Lodge in 1758, during the French & Indian War. Visitor to the lodges in New Haven and Hartford; guest of American Union Lodge at Redding, April, 1779. Buried with Masonic honors. (Case)

An Early History of St. John's Lodge No. 4, A. F. & A. M., Hartford, Connecticut, 1762-1937, p. 53, states that "The first name that appears on the records as a visiting Brother is that of Israel Putnam, on May 11, 1763." The General was a frequent visitor to this Lodge.

The Masonic Casket, Vol. 1, No. 5, published May 1, 1861, p. 37, notes that "Israel Putnam was a Mason, as will be seen by reading the following record . . . 'At a Lodge of Free Masons, held at the Fountain Tavern, New Haven, October 28, 1766, present: . . . Colonel Israel Putnam'."

A Grand Lodge of Iowa advice, written June 30, 1958, states: "The card in our 'Famous Masons' file states that Israel Putnam received his degrees in a Military Lodge at Crown Point, New York, June 7, 1758, but fails to state where this information was obtained."

RUFUS PUTNAM

MASSACHUSETTS

Independence National Historical Park Collections

Born April 9, 1738, in Sutton, Massachusetts.

Died May 24, 1824, presumably at his home in Marietta, Ohio.

Buried in Mound Cemetery, Marietta, Ohio.

GENERAL OFFICER IN THE CONTINENTAL ARMY

BIOGRAPHICAL

Largely self-educated. Served in the French & Indian War.

Lieutenant Colonel, Brewer's Massachusetts Regiment, May 19 to December, 1775; Lieutenant Colonel, 22nd Continental Infantry, January 1, 1776; Colonel Engineer, August 5, 1776; Colonel, 5th Massachusetts, November 1, 1776, to rank from August 5, 1776; Brigadier General, Continental Army, January 7, 1783, and served to close of the war.

The last surviving General Officer of the Revolutionary War, except for Lafayette.

After the Revolutionary War, he organized the Ohio Company of Associates, in Northwest Territory, and founded the city of Marietta, the first permanent settlement in the territory.

Judge of the territory in 1790, general of militia, and Surveyor General of the United States. Concluded peace treaty with the Indians in 1793, and presided at the Ohio Constitutional Convention in 1802. All this service earned him the title of "Father of Ohio." Member of the Society of the Cincinnati.

MASONIC

The record in the office of the Grand Secretary, Grand Lodge of Massachusetts, shows degrees received in American Union Lodge (Army) as follows: First degree—July 26, 1779; Second degree—August 26, 1779; Third degree—September 9, 1779.

He served as Worshipful Master of the Lodge in 1794.

The original records of Washington Lodge No. 10 (Army) in the Archives of the Grand Lodge of Massachusetts, Minutes of 1790, December 7, contain a list of "members initiated since 24 June 1780", and Colonel Rufus Putnam's name is included.

He is also on record as Royal Arch Mason in Philadelphia, 1792.

He attended American Union Lodge at Marietta, Ohio, at its re-organization, June 28, 1790, as Junior Warden. He was elected first Grand Master of Masons in Ohio, January 8, 1808, but did not serve because of illness.

In Vol. 1 of W. M. Cunningham's *History of Freemasonry in Ohio,* pp. 41-3, is quoted this letter from Putnam, dated Marietta, Ohio, December 26, 1808, and submitted to the Grand Lodge of Ohio on January 5, 1809, acknowledging his election as Grand Master, but declining the appointment. "My sun is far past the meridian; it is almost set . . . " (Yet he lived another fifteen years!)

EDMUND RANDOLPH

VIRGINIA

Independence National Historical Park Collections

Born August 10, 1753, at "Tazewell Hall", Williamsburg, Virginia.

Died September 12, 1813, in Clarke County, Virginia.

Buried in Old Chapel Cemetery, Millwood, Virginia.

AIDE-DE-CAMP TO GENERAL WASHINGTON

BIOGRAPHICAL

Graduate of the College of William and Mary, Williamsburg, Virginia; studied law; admitted to the bar and practiced in Williamsburg. Aide-de-Camp to General Washington, August 15, 1775, to March 25, 1776.

Member, Continental Congress, 1779-1782. Deputy Mustermaster General, Southern Department, March 25, 1776; resigned, April 26, 1776.

Member of the Federal Constitutional Convention in 1787. Member of President Washington's first Cabinet, as Attorney General, September 26, 1789.

The last Attorney General of Virginia under Royal Government. Governor of Virginia, 1786, but resigned in 1788 to serve in State House of Delegates so he could participate in the codification of the laws of Virginia in 1788 and 1789.

In 1794 he succeeded Jefferson as Secretary of State, but resigned in 1796 because of a misunderstanding with Washington. Served as counsel for Aaron Burr in his trial for treason at Richmond.

MASONIC

See *Early Freemasonry in Williamsburg, Virginia,* by Brother George Eldridge Kidd, Richmond, 1957. Member of Williamsburg Lodge No. 6. Proposed for membership, March 1, 1774; ballotted for and accepted, March 29, 1774. Received EA degree, March 29, 1774; FC degree, April 2, 1774; and MM degree, May 28, 1774.

In the minutes headed "On the Feast of St. John the Baptist 1777", there is an entry: "Brother Edmund Randolph discontinued himself a member of this Lodge." (*O R,* Williamsburg Lodge No. 6)

Charter Master of Jerusalem Lodge No. 54, Richmond, Virginia, November 29, 1797. Richmond-Randolph Lodge No. 19, Richmond, Virginia, was named in his honor. Second Deputy Grand Master of Masons in Virginia, 1784-85; the third Grand Master of Masons in Virginia, 1786-87-88, and as such, signed the charter of Alexandria Lodge No. 22.

PEYTON RANDOLPH

VIRGINIA

Born September, 1721, at "Tazewell Hall", Williamsburg, Virginia.

Died October 22, 1775, in Philadelphia, Pennsylvania.

Buried in Chapel of the College of William and Mary, Williamsburg, Virginia.

SIGNER OF THE ARTICLES OF ASSOCIATION

BIOGRAPHICAL

Educated by private tutors; graduate of College of William and Mary, Williamsburg; studied law in the Inner Temple, London.

Member of the First Continental Congress, and elected its first President, September 5, 1774, but resigned October 22, 1774, to attend the State legislature. Re-elected to the Continental Congress in 1775, but forced to resign on account of ill health.

King's Attorney for Virginia, 1748; Speaker of the House of Burgesses, 1766. A member of that body from 1764 to 1775.

MASONIC

"1774—Provincial Grand Master in the Masonic order in Williamsburg." (DAB)

See *Early Freemasonry in Williamsburg, Virginia*, by Brother George Eldridge Kidd, Richmond, 1957. Randolph is referred to as Grand Master in the Treasurer's Book in the Lodge held in the Crown Tavern in 1762; first Master of the Lodge under the English charter of 1773; referred to as Provincial Grand Master in Minutes of 1774. He was the last Provincial Grand Master of Virginia.

Received warrant from Lord Petre, Grand Master of England, constituting him Master of the Lodge in Williamsburg. This warrant dated at London, November 6, 1773, and Registry No. 457. (Hayden)

From *American Archives*, 5th Series, Vol. 3, p. 902: "Williamsburg, Nov. 29, 1776—'On Tuesday last the remains of our late amiable and beloved fellow-citizen, the Hon. Peyton Randolph, Esquire, were conveyed in a hearse to the College Chapel, attended by the worshipful brotherhood of Freemasons, both Houses of Assembly . . . ' "

DANIEL ROBERDEAU

PENNSYLVANIA

Born January 5, 1727, on the Island of St. Christoper, British West Indies.

Died January 5, 1795, in Winchester, Virginia.

Buried in Rural Burying Ground of the Presbyterian Church, Winchester, Virginia. His body was removed in the early 1860's and reinterred in Mount Hebron Cemetery, Winchester, Virginia.

SIGNER OF THE ARTICLES OF CONFEDERATION

Daniel Roberdeau

BIOGRAPHICAL

Emigrated to America at an early age, settling in Philadelphia. Engaged in the lumber business.

Member, Continental Congress, 1777-79. Brigadier General of Pennsylvania Militia, July 4, 1776, to March, 1777 (the first of this rank). In Congress he was known as an advocate of strictest economy and the foe of inefficiency and dishonesty.

Member, State Assembly, 1756-1760. Manager of the Pennsylvania Hospital, 1756-58, and 1766-1776. Member of Pennsylvania Council of Safety.

Moved to Alexandria, Virginia, in 1785.

MASONIC

Member, First Lodge (St. John's) in Philadelphia, and on record as a visitor to Lodge No. 2, Philadelphia. See Vol. 1, p. 106, of *Old Masonic Lodges in Pennsylvania*, where he is shown as a visitor recorded in the old minute book of the Tun Tavern Lodge.

Subscribed £15 toward the erection of Masonic Hall, Philadelphia, March, 1752, and March, 1754.

See "Daniel Roberdeau", in *Genealogy of the Roberdeau Family*, Washington, 1876, by Roberdeau Buchanan, p. 43: "The earliest mention the writer has found of Daniel Roberdeau is in 1749, when, at the age of twenty-two, his name appears in a list of subscribers for an assembly to be given in Philadelphia . . . A few years after this, we find Daniel Roberdeau a member of the 'Mystic tie', the evidence being a paper now framed and hanging in a conspicuous place in the Masonic Hall in Philadelphia. The import is as follows, and constitutes the earliest documentary record of our ancestor in this country:

"Philadelphia, March 13, 1754,

'Whereas, at a meeting of the Grand First Lodges, on Thursday, the 12th day of March, 1752, a committee was then appointed and fully authorized to look out for a suitable lot, whereon to erect a building for the accommodation of said

Lodges, Philadelphia Assembly, and other uses. The undersigned subscribe the several sums, etc . . . ' Then follows the name of Daniel Roberdeau and subscription for fifteen pounds."

Additional information from the same reference is taken from Daniel Roberdeau's old receipt book:

"April 18, 1755, receipt for £11, 4, 8, 'in full for sundry jobs done at the lodge on account of the assembly', and again, June 11, 1755, £1, 14, 5½, 'in full, a balance due the Lodge', &c, probably his annual subscription."

This same reference, p. 100: "It is believed that no likeness of General Roberdeau now exists."

ARTHUR ST. CLAIR

PENNSYLVANIA

Born March 23, (O. S.), 1736, in Thurso Caithness, Scotland. (Lossing and BDAC give the year as 1734)

Died August 31, 1818, in Laurel Hill, in Western Pennsylvania.

Buried in Greensburg, Pennsylvania, Presbyterian Grove Cemetery.

**GENERAL OFFICER IN THE
CONTINENTAL ARMY**

BIOGRAPHICAL

Attended University of Edinburgh; studied medicine under Dr. John Hunter. Came to America in 1759 and served in Canada under Generals Amherst and Wolfe, 1759-1760.

Settled in Ligonier Valley, Pennsylvania, in 1764; Justice of the Court of Quarter Sessions and Common Pleas there.

Colonel, Pennsylvania Militia in 1775; Colonel, 2nd Pennsylvania Battalion, January 3, 1776; Brigadier General, Continental Army, August 9, 1776; Major General, February 19, 1777, and served to close of the war; Major General and Commander, United States Army, March 4, 1791; resigned, March 5, 1792. Member of the Court-martial that tried and convicted Major John André in 1780.

Member, Continental Congress from November 2, 1785, to November 28, 1787, and its President in 1787, when the Ordinance of 1787 was passed.

First Governor of Northwest Territory upon its formation in 1789, and served until November 22, 1802. Returned to Ligonier Valley and engaged in the iron business.

One of the original members of the Society of the Cincinnati, and President of the Pennsylvania Society, 1783.

MASONIC

Petitioner for charter of Nova Caesarea Lodge No. 10 at Cincinnati. The warrant for this lodge was issued by the Grand Lodge of New Jersey, September 8, 1791. (Case)

"His remains lie buried in Greensburg, Pennsylvania, where the Masons erected a monument to his memory over his grave." (Roth)

The History of Bro. Gen. LaFayette's Fraternal Connections with the Right Worshipful Grand Lodge, F. & A. M. of Pennsylvania, (Julius F. Sachse, 1916), states on page 5: "Lafayette reached Philadelphia, August 10, 1784—presented with address by Brothers A. St. Clair, William Irving, and General Anthony Wayne."

JONATHAN BAYARD SMITH

PENNSYLVANIA

(Grand Lodge of Pennsylvania)

Born February 21, 1742, in Philadelphia, Pennsylvania.

Died June 16, 1812, in Philadelphia, Pennsylvania.

Buried in the graveyard of the Second Presbyterian Church, Philadelphia, Pennsylvania.

SIGNER OF THE ARTICLES OF CONFEDERATION

BIOGRAPHICAL

Princeton graduate, 1760, and Trustee of the College from 1779 to 1808.

Member, Continental Congress, 1777 and 1778.

Secretary of the Philadelphia Committee of Safety, 1775-77. Lieutenant Colonel, Pennsylvania Associators, in 1777. Appointed Justice of the Court of Common Pleas in 1778.

"One of the founders in 1779 of the University of the State of Pennsylvania and a member of its board of trustees until its consolidation in 1791 with the College of

Philadelphia into the University of Pennsylvania, serving as a trustee of the latter institution until his death." (BDAC, p. 1831)

Member, Board of Aldermen of Philadelphia, 1792-94, and Auditor General of Pennsylvania, 1794.

MASONIC

His Masonic record is fully documented. Member of Military Lodge No. 3, Philadelphia. Committee approved him: he was ballotted for and received EA degree, February 18, 1783; FC degree, February 21, 1783; and MM degree, April 15, 1783. Treasurer of the Lodge, June 17, 1783; elected Junior Warden, December 26, 1783, and Senior Warden, June 15, 1784. Elected Worshipful Master, December 21, 1784. Recorded as visitor to Lodge No. 2, Philadelphia, April 11, 1785.

Elected Right Worshipful Grand Master of Masons in Pennsylvania, and served in this office on two different occasions, from 1789 to 1794, and again from 1798 to 1802.

JOHN STARK

NEW HAMPSHIRE

Born August 28, 1728, in Londonderry, New Hampshire.

Died May 8, 1822, probably at his home in Manchester, New Hampshire.

Buried with military honors in a cemetery on his own land, the site marked by a granite obelisk erected in 1829.

GENERAL OFFICER IN THE
CONTINENTAL ARMY

BIOGRAPHICAL

Members of Rogers' Company in the French & Indian War.

Colonel, 1st New Hampshire, April 23 to December, 1775; Colonel, 5th Continental Infantry, January 1 to December 31, 1776; Colonel, 1st New Hampshire, November 8, 1776; resigned March 23, 1777; Brigadier General, New Hampshire Militia, 1777; Brigadier General. Continental Army, October 4, 1777, and served to close of the war. Brevet Major General, September 30, 1783. Member of the court-martial which tried and convicted Major John André in 1780.

MASONIC

"Made a Mason in Masters Lodge, Albany, 1778." (Case)

The following extracts are from records of the Masters Lodge, as printed in the *Early History and Proceedings of the Grand Lodge of New York, 1781-1815*, page XXI, under the subject, "Early History of Masonry in New York":

"Albany, 9th January 1778.

The petition of Brigadier Gen. John Starke being presented to the body, he was balloted for, met with the unanimous consent of the members present, and was initiated accordingly. Brig. Gen. John Starke paid £5 for his initiation fee, 8s. to the Tyler, and 4s. for Extra Lodge."

BARON FRIEDRICH WILHELM AUGUST HEINRICH FERDINAND von STEUBEN

PRUSSIA

Independence National Historical Park Collections

Born September 17, 1730, in Magdeburg, Prussia.

Died November 28, 1794, in Steubenville, New York.

Buried on his land in Steubenville, Oneida County, New York.

GENERAL OFFICER IN THE CONTINENTAL ARMY

BIOGRAPHICAL

General Staff Officer in the army of Frederick the Great of Prussia, 1761. Volunteered to serve the American cause and sailed for America, September 26, 1777. His services were accepted by Congress and he was ordered to report to General Washington at once. Arrived at Valley Forge, February 23, 1778, and began his great work of creating the American Army.

As Drillmaster at Valley Forge, he welded the "rabble in arms" into the fighting army which went from there to ultimate victory for the American cause. His bluff and hearty manner endeared him to the troops. His method of drilling was to take the arms of the private soldier and show him by example how they should be used.

Volunteer Inspector General, March 28, 1778; Major General and Inspector General, Continental Army, May 5, 1778. Served under Major General Lafayette in the Virginia campaign of 1781, and commanded a division at Yorktown. By the Act of April 15, 1784, it was "Resolved, that the resignation of Baron Steuben . . . be accepted . . . that the thanks of the United States in Congress assembled, be given Baron Steuben . . . "

President of the New York Society of the Cincinnati, 1786.

MASONIC

"Baron Von Steuben was a member of Holland and Trinity Lodges, New York." (Roth, p. 81)

Grand Lodge of Iowa: "Made a member in Germany; became a member of Trinity Lodge No. 10 (now No. 12) of New York, later affiliating with Holland Lodge No. 8."

The Sesqui-Centennial Commemorative Volume of Holland Lodge No. 8. published by the Lodge in 1938, page 109, lists Steuben's name as a member in 5788.

"Visited Holland Lodge No. 8, October 17, 5788." "December 12, 5788-invited to dinner on St. John's Day next, and accepted."— "December 22, 5788—The Senior Warden at the last regular meeting informally proposed to the Lodge the admission of Brothers Steuben and Saderstrom as honorary members, which proposition was then agreed to by all the members who were present . . . "—"December 27, 5788—Steuben in attendance and spoke in French acknowledging the honor bestowed on him."— "February 6, 5789—Steuben present and listed as Past Master." (O R, Holland Lodge No. 8, New York)

RICHARD STOCKTON

NEW JERSEY

Independence National Historical Park Collections

Born October 1, 1730, at "Morven", near Princeton, New Jersey.

Died February 28, 1781, at "Morven", near Princeton, New Jersey.

Buried in Quaker Cemetery, Princeton, New Jersey.

SIGNER OF THE
DECLARATION OF INDEPENDENCE

BIOGRAPHICAL

Graduated in the first class from Princeton College in 1748; studied law; admitted to the bar in 1754, and commenced practice in Princeton, New Jersey.

Elected a member of the Second Continental Congress, June 22, 1776, and re-elected, November 30, 1776, but declined that office on December 2, 1776.

Colonel and Inspector of the Northern Army. Taken prisoner by the Tories at the home of his friend, Mr. Covenhoven, November 30, 1776, and held in provost jail in New York City until December 29, 1776.

Associate Justice of New Jersey Supreme Court, February 28, 1774, to June 17, 1776. Elected Chief Justice of that Court on August 31, 1776, but declined the Office. Unsuccessful candidate for Governor of New Jersey, August 31, 1776.

MASONIC

"Justice Stockton was the first signer of a petition for a Masonic Lodge in Princeton, known as St. John's Lodge, and became its first Master in 1765." (*The New Age*, April, 1946) This petition is recorded in the *Proceedings of the Grand Lodge of Massachusetts, 1733-1792*, p. 99:

"Prince Town, New Jersey Sept. 24th 1765. Right Worshipfull.

Whereas we the Subscribers being desirous of being formed into a regular and lawful Lodge do now make Application to you for a Warrant to Constitute the same, also to appoint the first Mast which I nominate Richard Stockton of the said Place . . . NB: let it be nominated St. Johns . . . "

Petition signed by Richard Stockton and six others, and addressed to Jeremiah Gridley, Esqr.

"Charter Master of St. John's Lodge, Princeton, September 24, 1765. May have been made in Scotland." (Case)

The Grand Secretary of the Grand Lodge of New Jersey has confirmed the fact that Richard Stockton is the only representative of New Jersey who signed the Declaration of Independence and who was a Mason.

JOHN SULLIVAN

NEW HAMPSHIRE

Born February 17, 1740, in Somersworth, New Hampshire.

Died January 23, 1795, in Durham, New Hampshire.

Buried in the Sullivan family cemetery in Durham, New Hampshire.

SIGNER OF THE ARTICLES OF ASSOCIATION AND A GENERAL OFFICER IN THE CONTINENTAL ARMY

Independence National Historical Park Collections

BIOGRAPHICAL

Studied law; admitted to the bar, and began practice in Durham in 1760. Received LL. D. degree from Harvard College in 1780.

Member, Continental Congress, 1774-75, and again, 1780-81.

Brigadier General, Continental Army, June 22, 1775; Major General, August 9, 1776; taken prisoner at Long Island, August 27, 1776; exchanged, December, 1776. Resigned on account of ill health, November 30, 1779, with the thanks of Congress.

Washington appointed him Judge of the United States District Court of New Hampshire in 1789, and he served in that office until his death.

Attorney General of New Hampshire, 1782-86; the first "President" or Governor of New Hampshire, 1786-89. New Hampshire was the first to establish a State government, effective January 5, 1776, due largely to Sullivan's influence.

MASONIC

The first Grand Master of Masons in New Hampshire, July 8, 1789.

Brother Harold O. Cady, P.G.M., Grand Secretary of the Grand Lodge, F. & A. M., New Hampshire, has supplied this information from the records in his office: Brother Sullivan was a member of St. John's Lodge No. 1, of Portsmouth, New Hampshire, and received the Entered Apprentice and Fellow Craft degrees on March 19, 1767. He was made a Master Mason on December 28, 1768. He was elected Grand Master of the Grand Lodge of New Hampshire on July 8, 1789, presided as Grand Master-elect on July 16, 1789, and installed in that office on April 8, 1790. His installation was delayed as he had never served as Master of a Lodge. He was elected Master of St. John's Lodge No. 1 Portsmouth, on December 3, 1789, which qualified him for the office of Grand Master. Impaired health forced him to resign the office after only five months of service (October 10, 1790).

JETHRO SUMNER

NORTH CAROLINA

Born in 1733, on farm called "Manor", Nansemond County, about one mile from Suffolk, Virginia.

Died March 18, 1785, in Warren County, North Carolina.

Buried in Warren County, North Carolina, near old Shocco Chapel and old Bute Court House. His tombstone is inscribed "To the memory of Jethro Sumner, one of the heroes of '76."

GENERAL OFFICER IN THE CONTINENTAL ARMY

Jethro Sumner

BIOGRAPHICAL

Colonel, 3rd North Carolina, April 15, 1776; Brigadier General, Continental Army, January 9, 1779, and served to close of the war.

President of the North Carolina Society of the Cincinnati in 1783.

Very little is known of the private life of this officer in the Continental Army.

MASONIC

" . . . In addition to those already mentioned there were such worthy veterans of the North Carolina Continental Line as . . . Brigadier General Jethro Sumner . . . all of Royal White Hart Lodge No. 2 in Halifax." (*GL Proc. North Carolina, 1912,* p. 76)

The North Carolina Lodge of Research Transactions, Vol. VI, 1936, contain an article, "How Blandford Bute Lodge was Formed", by Brother J. Edward Allen. The following quotations are taken from his account: (p. 163) " . . . A word should be said about some of the men whose names appear on the rolls and the Minutes . . . Jethro Sumner was the same General Jethro Sumner who fought valiantly in the Revolutionary War and who is buried on Guilford Battle Ground."

(p. 164) "At a lodge held at Buffalo at High Twelve the 29th of April, 5766, present: . . . Jethro Sumner as Stewart. Lodge 12th May 5766—Jethro Sumner is Tyler, and then appointed Treasurer of the Lodge."

(p. 165) "Lodge 24th June 5766, Jethro Sumner is Treasurer."

(p. 173) "Jethro Sumner appointed Deputy Master of the Lodge."

WILLIAM THOMPSON

PENNSYLVANIA

Born June 5, 1736, in the north of Ireland.

Died September 5, 1781, in Carlisle, Pennsylvania.

Buried in cemetery known as the "Old Graveyard", Carlisle, Pennsylvania.

GENERAL OFFICER IN THE
CONTINENTAL ARMY

Detail of General William Thompson from "Death of General Montgomery in the attack on Quebec", by John Trumbull, Yale University Art Gallery

BIOGRAPHICAL

Thompson's parents emigrated to Pennsylvania when he was a young man. He married Catherine Ross, a sister of George Ross, a signer of the Declaration of Independence.

Commissioned a Captain of light horse on May 4, 1758. His service in the French & Indian War entitled him to land in any part of the royal domain. Thompson, a surveyor by profession, was delegated by his brother officers to locate these lands, which were finally established in Kentucky. Later Thompson lost all of the land when he refused to sign a required oath of allegiance to the King. An early patriot favorable to the cause of independence. With others in Carlisle, he organized a "Committee of Safety" in May, 1775, to establish military districts in Cumberland County. Colonel Thompson was placed in Command of the Second District.

Colonel, Pennsylvania Rifle Regiment, June 25, 1775; Colonel, 1st Continental Infantry, January 1, 1776; Brigadier General, Continental Army, March 1, 1776; taken prisoner at Three Rivers, Canada, June 8, 1776; exchanged, October 25, 1780.

A detailed biography of General Thompson is available at The J. Herman Bosler Memorial Library, Carlisle, Pennsylvania. These few facts have been made available by Willa Weller, Library Assistant there. His commission as Colonel in the Continental Army, signed by John Hancock, is in their possession.

MASONIC

Member of Royal Arch Lodge No. 3, Philadelphia, as shown by these abstracts from Lodge records:

"December 23, 1778 - Lodge of Emergency . . . Transactions - General Thompson was ballotted for and approved etc. . . .

December 24, 1778 - Lodge of Emergency . . . Transactions - Bro. Coats reports that by a dispens'n from the G. M. this Lodge was called for the Benefit of Major General Thompson, (A Modern Mason) who is under the necessity (being Prisoner on Parole) of going speedily to New York, he was accordingly Initiated, Pass'd, and

Rais'd, and paid his Entrance Dues to Br. Doctor Coats, 10 Dollars."

January 7, 1779 - William Thompson was present at the regular meeting. He is also shown as having signed the by-laws of the lodge." (O R, Lodge No. 3)

JAMES MITCHELL VARNUM

RHODE ISLAND

Born December 17, 1748, in Dracut, Massachusetts.

Died January 10, 1789, in Marietta, Ohio.

Buried at Campus Martius, and later reinterred in Oak Grove Cemetery, Marietta, Ohio.

GENERAL OFFICER IN THE CONTINENTAL ARMY

BIOGRAPHICAL

Graduate, College of Rhode Island (later Brown University), 1769. Studied law at East Greenwich, Rhode Island; admitted to the bar in 1771 and commenced practice there.

Colonel, Rhode Island Regiment, May 3 to December, 1775; Colonel, 9th Continental Infantry, January 1 to December 31, 1776; Colonel, 1st Rhode Island, January 1, 1777; Brigadier General, Continental Army, February 21, 1777; resigned, March 5, 1779; was also Major General, Rhode Island Militia.

Member, Continental Congress, 1780-2, 1786, and 1787.

Judge of United States Court in the Northwest Territory in 1787, with office in Marietta, Ohio, and served in that post until his death.

President of the Rhode Island Society of the Cincinnati, 1786.

MASONIC

Orator of St. John's Day Festival in Providence, December 28, 1778. His funeral at Marietta, Ohio, in 1789, brought many Freemasons together. (Case)

Grand Lodge of Iowa: No record found of when or where he became a Mason. A frequent visitor at St. John's Lodge, Providence, Rhode Island, during the winter of 1778-79. Delivered the St. John's Day address in this Lodge in 1778 and 1782. The record of his burial is the first evidence of a Masonic gathering in what is now Ohio.

History of Freemasonry in Ohio, W. M. Cunningham, Vol. 1: " . . . Occurred the first Masonic incident of note. On January 10, 1789, the Brethren assembled to bury with Masonic honors an eminent and distinguished Brother and Revolutionary hero, Judge James Mitchell Varnum."

JOHN WALKER

VIRGINIA

Born February 13, 1744, at "Castle Hill", near Cobham, Albermarle County, Virginia.

Died December 2, 1809, near Madison Mills, Orange County (now Madison County), Virginia.

Buried in family cemetery on the Belvoir estate near Cismont, Albemarle County, Virginia.

No Likeness Available

LIEUTENANT COLONEL AND AIDE-DE-CAMP TO GENERAL WASHINGTON

BIOGRAPHICAL

Walker apparently never served as a regular Aide, nor was his appointment of Washington's selection; it was merely a form of camouflage. The *Journals of the Council of the State of Virginia*, Vol. 1, p. 315, for Thursday, January 16, 1777, show that "a Gentleman of discernment, discretion, Veracity, and inviolable Attachment to the American Cause, ought forwith to be appointed Agent of Correspondence for the purpose aforementioned . . . " Walker's appointment the next month followed. See *Writings of Washington*, (Fitzpatrick), Vol. VII, p. 200: "John Walker had been sent to the headquarters of the Continental Army by the Virginia Legislature to keep it informed of events, the idea being that the Commander in Chief could not find the time necessary to write fully. Washington accepted this dangerous precedent with calmness and full persuasion that no ulterior motive prompted the action. He appointed Walker an aide-de-camp." Lieutenant Colonel and Aide-de-Camp to General Washington, February 19, 1777, to December 22, 1777.

On February 24th, 1777, Washington wrote from Morristown, New Jersey, to Governor Patrick Henry of Virginia:

"Dear Sir:

Mr. Walker has, I doubt not, informed you of the situation in which I have placed him, in order that he may obtain the best information, and, at the same time, have his real design hid from the World; thereby avoiding the evils which might otherwise result from such Appointments, if adopted by other States.

"It will naturally occur to you, Sir, that there are some Secrets, on the keeping of which so, depends, oftentimes, the salvation of an Army; Secrets which cannot, at least ought not to, be intrusted to paper; nay, which none but the Commander in Chief at the time, should be acquainted with.

"If Mr. Walker's Commission, therefore, from the Commonwealth of Virginia, should be known, it would, I am persuaded, be followed by others of the like nature from other States, and be no better than so many marplots. To avoid the precedent, therefore, and from your Character of Mr. Walker and the high Opinion I myself entertain of his abilities, Honour, and prudence, I have taken him into my Family as an Extra Aide-de-Camp, and shall be happy, if in this Character, he can answer your expectations . . . "

It appears that Walker's period of service at Washington's headquarters as a special liaison officer from the State of Virginia was a very brief one. He was succeeded at an undisclosed date by Captain William Pierce, who himself resigned this assignment on December 22, 1777.

Privately educated, and a graduate of the College of William and Mary, Williamsburg, Virginia, in 1764. Studied law; admitted to the bar, and commenced the practice of law.

Appointed United States Senator to fill the vacancy caused by the death of William Grayson, and served from March 31 to November 9, 1790; not a candidate for re-election.

MASONIC

Member, St. John's Lodge No. 1, Wilmington, North Carolina. (ALR, Vol. VI, p. 254).

See also *Proceedings of the Grand Lodge of North Carolina*, 1912, p. 76: " . . . In addition to those already mentioned there were such worthy veterans of the North Carolina Continental Line as Major John Walker . . . " from report of Grand Historian, Brother Marshall DeLancey Haywood.

GEORGE WALTON

GEORGIA

Born July 1, 1741, near Farmville, Prince Edward County, Virginia. (*Biographical Directory of the American Congress, 1774-1949*, gives the year as 1750).

Died February 2, 1804, at "Meadow Garden", near Augusta, Georgia.

Buried in Rosney Cemetery and reinterred, July 4, 1848, beneath the monument erected in Augusta, Georgia, to the Georgia signers of the Declaration of Independence.

SIGNER OF THE
DECLARATION OF INDEPENDENCE

Geo Walton.

Independence National Historical Park Collections

BIOGRAPHICAL

Attended common schools; moved to Savannah in 1769; studied law; admitted to the bar in 1774, and practiced in Savannah.

Member, Second Continental Congress, 1776-1781.

2nd Lieutenant, 1st Georgia, January 7, 1776; 1st Lieutenant, July 5, 1776; Colonel, Georgia Militia in 1778; wounded and taken prisoner at Savannah, December 29, 1778; exchanged, September, 1779.

United States Senator, November 16, 1795, to February 20, 1796.

"Chairman of the Reception Committee, and delivered the address of welcome upon the occasion of President Washington's visit to Augusta in 1791." (BDAC, p. 1972)

Twice Governor of Georgia, 1779 and 1789. Justice of Georgia, 1783-86, and again in 1793. Appointed first Judge of the Superior Courts of the Eastern Judicial District in 1790. Appointed Judge of the Middle Circuit of Georgia and served from 1799 until his death.

A Commissioner to treat with the Indians at Easton, Pennsylvania, and to negotiate a treaty with the Cherokees in Tennessee in 1783. Represented Georgia in the settlement of the boundary line between South Carolina and Georgia in 1786.

Served as Trustee of Richmond Academy and of the University of Georgia.

MASONIC

"Claim of membership in Solomon's Lodge, Savannah, not disputed." (Case)

All authorities give his lodge as Solomon's Lodge in Savannah, and all agree that the date of his initiation is not known.

Brother William Bordley Clarke, Past Master of this Lodge, writes: "I find him mentioned in our minutes (Solomon's Lodge) immediately at the close of the Revolution in 1785 and several times thereafter. When Solomon's Lodge was reconstituted in 1785, Bro. Walton took his degrees over again, and was then made an 'Ancient'. There is a death record in these minutes which was maintained until the year 1775. This record contained a roster of the Lodge up to that time. The name of Walton does not appear, and from this we may assume that he was made a member of the Lodge about the time of the outbreak of the Revolution in Georgia in 1775 or shortly thereafter."

Brother F. F. Baker, Grand Secretary of the Grand Lodge of Georgia, in a letter of February 14, 1927, states: "George Walton appears to have been a member of Solomon's Lodge #1 of Savannah, and his name appears on their membership roll as reconstituted in 1785."

There are also two references from the *Proceedings of the Grand Lodge of Georgia:* "Leaves from Georgia Masonry", 1947, p. 233: "That immortal document (Declaration of Independence) was signed by Brother George Walton." p. 234: "After the capture of Savannah the British published a list of prominent patriots whose capture was desired and for whom rewards were offered. On this list appears the name of the following Masons . . . George Walton."

GEORGE WASHINGTON

VIRGINIA

Born February 22, 1732, at "Wakefield", Westmoreland County, Virginia.

Died December 14, 1799, at Mount Vernon, Virginia.

Buried at Mount Vernon, Virginia.

COMMANDER IN CHIEF OF THE CONTINENTAL ARMY; SIGNER OF THE ARTICLES OF ASSOCIATION AND THE CONSTITUTION OF THE UNITED STATES

BIOGRAPHICAL

Outstanding American patriot. Many biographers have recorded all facets of his life.

Attended "old field" school near Fredericksburg, Virginia. Later attended Mr. Williams' private school.

Adjutant General of a Military District in Virginia, with rank of Major, in 1751. Representative of Governor Dinwiddie of Virginia in November, 1753, on an important assignment to the French Army in the Ohio Valley. Lieutenant Colonel in the French & Indian War in 1754 and aide-de-camp to General Braddock in 1755.

Member, Virginia House of Burgesses, 1758-1774.

Delegate to the First Continental Congress in Philadelphia in 1774. This was the first concerted action of the Colonies to force Great Britain to change its colonial policy. As a member of this Congress, Washington was one of the fifty-three signers of the Articles of Association. Thus he was among the leaders who took a determined stand to obtain redress for the wrongs of the mother country.

When the time for military action came, he took to the field to secure this redress, and, following the successful conclusion of the war, he helped frame the Constitution of the newly organized Republic and signed this document as a deputy from Virginia. Thus, from the first organized action of the Colonies to the establishment of the new government, Washington the man, the patriot and leader, the Mason, played an important part.

Member of the Second Continental Congress in 1775. Resigned to take command of the Continental Army.

Unanimously chosen General and Commander in Chief of all the forces raised or to be raised, June 15, 1775. He commanded the army throughout the war for independence; resigned his commission, December 23, 1783.

Member, Federal Constitutional Convention of 1787, serving as President during the sessions, which were held in Philadelphia.

First President of the United States, by unanimous choice; inaugurated in New

York City, April 30, 1789. Unanimously re-elected for a second time, but refused a third term, and retired March 3, 1797.

Lieutenant General and Commander of the United States Army, July 3, 1798, and served until his death.

Member, Society of the Cincinnati and its first President-General.

MASONIC

Washington's Masonic career has been well documented. He received the three degrees of Masonry in the "Lodge of Fredericksburgh", Virginia (now Lodge No. 4, Fredericksburg).

November 4, 1752 - Entered Apprentice

March 3, 1753 - Fellowcraft

August 4, 1753 - Master Mason

On December 20, 1779, Washington was proposed as Grand Master of the United States by the Grand Lodge of Pennsylvania, and a second proposal was made on January 13, 1780. On December 27, 1779, the American Union Lodge, at Morristown, New Jersey, led in a convention to organize a National Grand Lodge, with George Washington as Grand Master.

The Proceedings of the Grand Lodge of Massachusetts, 1733-1792, p. 284, contain a letter from William Smith, Grand Secretary, Philadelphia, dated August 18, 1780, proposing a Grand Master General for the Thirteen United American States and reporting that they "had nominated His Excellency General George Washington . . . "

On page 289, Friday, January 12, 1781, there is the following minute: "Voted, that any determination upon the subject cannot with the Propriety and Justice due the Craft at large be made by this Grand Lodge Until a General Peace shall happily take place through the Continent."

On St. John's Day, December 27, 1782: "Bro. George Washington, Commander-in-Chief", is listed as a Visiting Brother in Solomon's Lodge No. 1, Poughkeepsie, New York.

Washington was named the first or Charter Master of Alexandria Lodge No. 39, on April 28, 1788, to serve to December 20, and was re-elected, serving in all twenty months. This Lodge No. 39 was then under the jurisdiction of the Grand Lodge of Pennsylvania; it is now Washington-Alexandria Lodge No. 22 under the jurisdiction of the Grand Lodge of Virginia. While he was Charter Master of this Lodge, a Deputy was appointed at the same time; there is no record of his having served as Master.

On March 6, 1789, Washington was made an honorary member of Holland Lodge (now Lodge No. 8) of New York. The original records of this Lodge read: "The Worshipful Master proposed his Excellency, George Washington, Esq., a Master Mason, for a member of this Lodge, which was properly seconded and the ballots being taken, he was unanimously elected." On March 7, Brother Washington was advised by letter of this action and was sent an Honorary Certificate. (*O R,* Holland Lodge No. 8)

On September 18, 1793, Washington laid the cornerstone of the National Capitol in Washington, in what has been said to be the greatest public Masonic occasion in American history. Washington, Master Mason, President of the United States, and America's first citizen, laid the cornerstone of the Capitol of the United States, with full Masonic ceremonies, in concert with the Grand Lodge of Maryland, several lodges under its jurisdiction, and Lodge No. 22, from Alexandria, Virginia.

GEORGE WEEDON

VIRGINIA

Born in 1734, in Westmoreland County, Virginia.

Died November, 1793, in Fredericksburg, Virginia.

Buried: There is no record of the place of burial. Traditionally, he was buried in the Masonic Cemetery, Fredericksburg, Virginia.

GENERAL OFFICER IN THE CONTINENTAL ARMY

National Archives

BIOGRAPHICAL

Lieutenant Colonel, 3rd Virginia, February 13, 1776; Colonel, August 13, 1776; Acting Adjutant General to General Washington, February 20, 1777; Brigadier General, Continental Army, February 27, 1777; resigned, June 11, 1783.

One of the original members of the Society of the Cincinnati, and President of the Virginia Society in 1783 and 1786.

MASONIC

Made a Mason in Port Royal Kilwinning Cross Lodge No. 2, Virginia, May 3, 1757, and later affiliated with Fredericksburg Lodge No. 4 (1767). (*GL Proc. Virginia, 1910,* p. 171 of the Appendix.) (Tatsch gives the date as May 3, 1756.)

See extract from minutes of Port Royal Kilwinning Cross Lodge No. 2, in the Library of the College of William & Mary, Williamsburg, Virginia: "Feb. 1767 - Bro. Geo. Weedon (afterward General) setting forth that he is an inhabitant of Fredericksburg, has become a member of that Lodge there and finding it inconvenient to attend this Lodge, desires to be excused attending here as a member the question being put the said petition was agreed to, and he is discharged his attendance as a member".

Weedon signed the by-laws of the Fredericksburg Lodge, giving his address as Fredericksburg. Dues paid to his account are recorded for 1767, 1768, 1769, 1772, and 1774.

Brother Edward H. Cann, Secretary of Fredericksburg Lodge No. 4, and Past Grand Master of Masons in Virginia, has advised that General Weedon was Worshipful Master of that Lodge in 1783.

WILLIAM WHIPPLE

NEW HAMPSHIRE

Born January 14, 1730, in Kittery, York County, Maine.

Died November 28, 1785, in Portsmouth, New Hampshire.

Buried in North Cemetery, Portsmouth, New Hampshire.

SIGNER OF THE
DECLARATION OF INDEPENDENCE

BIOGRAPHICAL

"Became a sailor and engaged in the slave trade; abandoned sailor life; liberated his slaves, and engaged in mercantile pursuits in Portsmouth, New Hampshire." BDAC, p. 1999)

Member of the Second Continental Congress, 1775-76 and 1778, but declined to be a candidate for renomination.

Brigadier General, New Hampshire Militia, 1777-78, and saw considerable active service.

Member, Provincial Congress at Exeter, 1775; member, State Assembly, 1780-84. Appointed Judge of State Supreme Court in 1782. Financial Receiver for New Hampshire, 1782-84.

MASONIC

"Made in old St. John's Lodge, Portsmouth, 1752". (Case)

"Secretary of Portsmouth Lodge reports he was raised January 2, 1752". (Roth)

See *Symbolic Freemasonry in New Hampshire, 1934,* by Harry Morrison Cheney, P. G. M., p. 220: "January 2, 1757 - the fact that Wm. Whipple . . . was a Mason rests upon this copy, taken verbatim from the record book of our Saint John's Lodge:

'At a lodge held at Mr. James Stoutley, this 2nd Jany 5752, being the first night of the Quarter, Mr. William Whipple Proposed & by Dispensation Balloted for & Unanimously Voted to be made a member of this Society.' "

Both Boyden and the *American Lodge of Research Transactions,* Vol. 6, No. 2, p. 256, give this same date.

OTHO HOLLAND WILLIAMS

MARYLAND

Born March 1, 1749, in Prince George County, Maryland.

Died July 5, 1794, in Millers' Town, Virginia.

Buried in Riverview Cemetery, Williamsport, Maryland. The Medairy Lodge of Masons erected a commemorative shaft over his grave.

**GENERAL OFFICER IN THE
CONTINENTAL ARMY**

BIOGRAPHICAL

First Lieutenant, Cresap's Company, Maryland Riflemen, June 21, 1775; Major of Stephenson's Maryland and Virginia Rifle Regiment, June 27, 1776; wounded and taken prisoner at Fort Washington, November 16, 1776; exchanged, January 16, 1778; Colonel, 6th Maryland, December 10, 1776; transferred to 1st Maryland, January 1, 1781; Brigadier General, Continental Army, May 9, 1782; retired, January 16, 1783.

At the close of the war, he was appointed Collector of Customs at Baltimore and held this office until his death.

President, Maryland Society of the Cincinnati, 1792.

MASONIC

"One of the first initiates in American Union Lodge at Roxbury, Massachusetts, February 26, 1776." (Case)

From photostat copies of Minutes of American Union Lodge, in the Library of the Grand Lodge of New York, his Masonic record is as follows: February 16, 1776 - proposed by Samuel Holden Parsons and a deposit of $4.00 made; February 26, 1776 - ballotted for, accepted, and Entered; March 11, 1776 - passed Fellowcraft, March 13, 1776 - raised to degree of Master Mason.

In 1780, with others, he petitioned the Grand Lodge of Pennsylvania for a charter for Military Lodge No. 27, Ancient York Masons, to be held in the Maryland Line Regiments. The records of the Grand Lodge of Maryland confirm his being Senior Warden of Maryland Lodge No. 27 in 1780.

WILLIAM WOODFORD

VIRGINIA

Born October 6, (O. S.), 1734, in Carolina County, Virginia.

Died November 13, 1780, in New York City, while a prisoner of war.

Buried in Old Trinity Churchyard, New York New York.

**GENERAL OFFICER IN THE
CONTINENTAL ARMY**

BIOGRAPHICAL

Served in the French & Indian War.

Colonel, 2nd Virginia, February 13, 1776; Brigadier General, Continental Army, February 21, 1777; wounded at Brandywine, September 11, 1777. Ordered to the relief of Charleston, he marched his troops 500 miles in 28 days. Taken prisoner at Charleston, May 12, 1780, and died in captivity, November 13, 1780.

Woodford was related to General Washington by marriage, and on intimate terms with him, as well as being one of the Commander in Chief's most trusted and confidential generals.

A full account of his life is given in an article in *The Daily Star,* Fredericksburg, Virginia, for April 11, 1922.

MASONIC

Member of Fredericksburg Lodge No. 4, Virginia. His signature on the by-laws is on record, and there is record of dues paid for 1770, 1771, and 1772.

DAVID WOOSTER

CONNECTICUT

Born March 2, 1711, in Stratford (now Huntington), Connecticut.

Died May 2, 1777, in Danbury, Connecticut, from wounds suffered while driving the British raiders back from Danbury.

Buried in Danbury, Connecticut, in what is now Wooster Cemetery. His grave was unmarked for 75 years, until this new cemetery was opened in 1854 and his body removed thereto.

GENERAL OFFICER IN THE CONTINENTAL ARMY

BIOGRAPHICAL

Yale graduate, 1738.

Served in the British Army on the expedition to Louisbourg in 1745. Returned to England; made a Captain in the regular service, under Sir William Pepperell, Colonel, and later, Brigadier General in the French & Indian War.

Major General, Connecticut troops, April, 1775; Colonel, 1st Connecticut, May 1, 1775; Brigadier General, Continental Army, June 22, 1775; died, May 2, 1777, of wounds received at Ridgefield, April 27, 1777. In June, 1777, Congress voted him a monument as a defender of American liberties, but it was never erected.

The present monument at Danbury was set up by the Grand Lodge of Connecticut, A. F. & A. M., the final stone being placed with Masonic honors on April 30, 1854. (Case)

MASONIC

He is presumed to have been made a Mason in a Military Lodge at Louisbourg, along with Lord Blayney, later Grand Master of England, as well as several of the charter members of the Lodge at New Haven, old Hiram No. 1 which he organized in 1750. Wooster was Charter Master of this, the first Masonic Lodge in Connecticut, in 1750. His remains rest under a beautiful memorial at Danbury, Connecticut. (Case)

"He was the first Master of Hiram Lodge No. 1, New Haven, in 1750." (Roth, p. 67)

"There also in 1750, he organized Hiram Lodge, one of the first Lodges of Free Masons in the colony, of which he was the first Master." (DAB, Vol. 20)

Freemasonry in the Thirteen Colonies, by J. Hugo Tatsch, declared (Wooster) "first introduced into Connecticut that Light which has warmed the widow's heart and illumined the orphan's pathway."

MASONIC MEMBERSHIP

of the

FOUNDING FATHERS

GROUP II

Membership in the Masonic Fraternity doubtful, supported only by tradition, contradictory evidence, or other unverified or undocumented information.

(26)

Extensive research thus far has failed to turn up conclusive proof that many of these early American patriots, the military and political leaders of the Revolutionary War period, were members of the Masonic Fraternity.

A thorough search of Grand Lodge records, standard reference books, manuscripts, and letters has produced in almost every instance only fragmentary evidence of membership. Some traditional references were found, some family histories claim membership for these individuals, but search thus far has not produced sufficient satisfactory evidence to accept them as members.

The lack of original records, the ever-present similarity of names, and the passing of time make it impossible to document fully many individuals to the satisfaction of the writer.

This does not necessarily mean that all, or some of the individuals whose names follow, were not Masons. Further research, still badly needed, may produce the necessary proofs later. But until then, we should not accord these men, staunch patriots though they were, the title of Freemason.

WILLIAM ALEXANDER (Earl of Stirling)

NEW JERSEY

Born in 1726 in New York, New York.

Died January 15, 1783, in Albany, New York.

Buried in Dutch Church Cemetery, Albany, New York, and later re-interred in Protestant Episcopal Cemetery there.

GENERAL OFFICER IN THE CONTINENTAL ARMY

BIOGRAPHICAL

British Army officer, and Aide-de-Camp to Governor Shirley. Went to England in 1755 in an effort to obtain title of Earl of Stirling, but could not obtain legal right to use the title. Returned to America in 1761; married the daughter of Philip Livingston.

Colonel, 1st New Jersey, November 7, 1775; Brigadier General, Continental Army, March 1, 1776; taken prisoner at Long Island, August 27, 1776; exchanged, September, 1776; Major General, Continental Army, February 19, 1777.

"It is a singular fact that at different periods during the war, Lord Stirling had under his command every brigade of the American Army except those of South Carolina and Georgia." (Lossing)

One of the founders of Kings College (now Columbia) and one of its first trustees.

MASONIC

"Quite generally believed to have been a Freemason, but there is no proof of his membership or activity. Card in Office of the Grand Secretary of the Grand Lodge of Massachusetts shows one of this name as member of St. John's Lodge, Boston." (Case)

In the *Transactions of the American Lodge of Research,* Vol. 2, No. 2, p. 445, Alexander is listed as a member of the American Philosophical Society as "one of 'thirty Additional Brothers' added to rolls from 1769 to 1789."

Vol. 5, No. 1, of above *Transactions,* p. 128: "Alexander (Stirling) passed F.C. in a lodge at Edinburgh, Scotland, 1753-61."

JOHN ALSOP

NEW YORK

Born in 1724, in New Windsor, Orange County, New York. (BDAC, p. 778)

Died November 22, 1794, in Newtown, Long Island, New York.

Buried in Trinity Church Cemetery, New York, New York.

SIGNER OF THE ARTICLES OF ASSOCIATION

BIOGRAPHICAL

Moved to New York City after completing his education; entered mercantile business, and later represented New York City in the colonial legislature.

Member, Continental Congress, September 14-October 26, 1774, and from May 10, 1775, to the latter part of that year.

"He was a prosperous merchant of unquestioned patriotism and integrity, and was a worthy member of the first American Congress in 1774-76." (Appleton)

One of the founders of New York Hospital, serving as its Governor, 1770-84. The eighth President of the New York Chamber of Commerce in 1784-85. Member of Trinity Church, New York City.

MASONIC

See *Old Masonic Lodges in Pennsylvania,* Sacshe, Vol. 1, p. 106. There is a John Alsop recorded as a visitor to Tun Tavern Lodge, Philadelphia. The same source, p. 82, records an Alsop as visitor at the meeting held June 28, 1749. No further identification or confirmation of these entries can be found.

BARON JOHANN DeKALB (commonly known as Baron DeKalb)
FRANCE

Born June 29, 1721, in Huettendorf, Bavaria.

Died August 19, 1780, near Camden, South Carolina.

Buried in Camden, South Carolina. Remains re-interred March 9, 1825, under monument in center of Camden, South Carolina, with Masonic ceremonies, with the Marquis de Lafayette the principal speaker.

GENERAL OFFICER IN THE CONTINENTAL ARMY

BIOGRAPHICAL

Served in the French Army from 1743 to 1764, and was sent on a confidential mission to America in 1768.

Returned to America in 1777 with the Marquis de Lafayette. Major General, Continental Army, September 15, 1777, to date from July 31, 1777. Died August 19, 1780, of eight wounds received at Camden, South Carolina, on August 16, 1780.

"Educated in the art of war in the French Army." (Lossing)

MASONIC

"DeKalb, it is supposed, was a member of a Military Lodge in the South." (Roth, p. 89)

"Traditionally buried with Masonic ceremony, but there is no record of his membership or activity in Freemasonry. This traditional connection with Freemasonry seems to have originated because his monument was laid with Masonic ceremony in the presence of Lafayette." (Case)

It is not known where he was made a Mason. It may have been in Army Lodge No. 29 in the Maryland Line. His biographer, Frederick Kapp, stated him to be a Freemason. See Kapp's *Life of John Kalb:* "Kalb was buried by his victorious adversaries, among whom there were many free masons, with military and masonic honors."

In the *Transactions of the American Lodge of Research,* Vol. 5, No. 2, p. 268, DeKalb is mentioned as member of Army Lodge No. 29.

Writing in *The New Age* for January, 1933, William L. Boyden, 33°, stated: "When and where he was made a Mason is not known. Schultz in his *History of Freemasonry in Maryland* says: 'There is reason to believe that he received them (the degrees) in the Army Lodge No. 29, chartered April 27, 1780, by the Grand Lodge of Pennsylvania, for the benefit of the Brethren of the Maryland Line of which General Mordecai Gist was Master, General Otho H. Williams, Senior Warden, and Major Archibald Anderson, Junior Warden—all of whom were Marylanders.' "

Masonic Journal, Portland, Maine, Vol. 16, November, 1903, p. 378: "Following the custom prevailing in the British Army, there were ten army lodges among the American troops during the Revolution. Prominent among these was the lodge attached to the Maryland line. General Mordecai Gist was its presiding Officer; with Colonel (afterwards General) Otho Holland Williams and Major Archibald Anderson as Wardens . . . the Baron DeKalb, who fell at Camden, was affiliated with this lodge; so also Count Kasimir Pulaski, who was killed at Charleston."

A Pilgrimage of Liberty, by Edgar Ewing Brandon, Athens, Ohio, 1944, gives a contemporary account of the Triumphal Tour of General Lafayette, 1825: " . . . The Master of the Lodge said in part: . . . General Lafayette had consented to lay the Corner Stone of a Monument to be erected at Camden, to the memory of Baron DeKalb, who was the friend of the rights of man . . . "

HORATIO GATES

VIRGINIA

Born in 1728, in Maldon, Essex, England.

Died April 10, 1806, in New York, New York.

Buried in Trinity Churchyard, New York City, but there is no tombstone to his memory, and the location of his grave is unknown. (Records of Trinity Parish, New York, New York).

GENERAL OFFICER IN THE CONTINENTAL ARMY

BIOGRAPHICAL

Had been a Major in the British Army. Brigadier General and Adjutant General, Continental Army, June 17, 1775; Major General, May 16, 1776. Served to the close of the war.

Elected to New York Legislature in 1800 and served one term.

President, Virginia Society of the Cincinnati in 1783.

MASONIC

"There is no record of his having been a Mason." (Roth)

"Gates was son-in-law of Erasmus James Phillips, Provincial Grand Master of Nova Scotia, but there is no proof of his (Gates') membership in any Masonic Lodge." (Case)

"At a meeting of Grand Lodge on December 18, 1778, 'Voted the Hon'ble General Gates and such of his Family who are Masons, be invited to dine at the feast' (St. John's Day)". (*GL Proc. Mass.*, Vol. 1, pp 268-9.)

"At a meeting of the Grand Lodge in Ample Form on Monday the 28th December 1778 to Celebrate the Festival of St. John the Evangelist in Free Mason Hall . . . Present Hon'ble General Gates and The family of Gen'l. Gates . . . " (*GL Proc. Mass.*, Vol. 1, p. 269)

The Proceedings of the Grand Lodge of Arkansas, 1919, p. 63, contain an address of Grand Orator Brother S. O. Whaley, November 18, 1919: " . . . The first Continental Congress was composed almost entirely of Master Masons . . . The Second Continental Congress appointed George Washington, a Master Mason, Commander in Chief of the Army. He surrounded himself with Masons. All of the Major Generals were Masons. General Gates . . . "

In *Masonic Soldiers of Fortune* by R. W. R. Stuart, District Deputy Grand Master, Grand Lodge F. & A. M., New York, page 32, there are minutes of a meeting of the Grand Lodge of Massachusetts in Ample Form, December 28, 1778, to celebrate the festival of St. John the Evangelist. Among those present was the Hon. General Gates. The author then goes on to say: "General Gates lived in Annapolis Royal, Nova Scotia, for some years and married a daughter of one of the officers of the garrison. (Erasmus James Phillips, Grand Master of Masons in Nova Scotia) There was a very active regimental lodge at Annapolis between 1738 and 1755. It was virtually a Military Lodge . . . and practically all the officers of the regiment were Masons, and I have no doubt that Gates, if he was not made a Mason previously in England . . . became a member of the Annapolis Royal Lodge . . . In view of the fact that he was present at a meeting of the Grand Lodge held in Ample Form, there can be no doubt concerning the Masonic status of General Horatio Gates." (Note: The Grand Lodge of Massachusetts advises that there are no records of the Annapolis Royal Lodge of Nova Scotia in its archives.)

ELBRIDGE GERRY

MASSACHUSETTS

Born July 17, 1744, in Marblehead, Massachusetts.
Died November 23, 1814, in Washington, D. C.
Buried in the Congressional Cemetery, Washington, D. C.

SIGNER OF THE DECLARATION OF INDEPENDENCE
AND THE ARTICLES OF CONFEDERATION

BIOGRAPHICAL

Harvard graduate, 1762.

Member, Continental Congress, 1776-1781, and again, 1782-85. General Chairman of the Committee of the Treasury. Member, United States Congress, March 4, 1789, to March 3, 1793.

Commissioner to France, 1797. Delegate to the Federal Constitutional Convention in 1787, but did not sign that document.

Fifth Vice President of the United States, March 4, 1813, until his death. His widow died in 1849, the last surviving widow of a signer of the Declaration of Independence.

Member, Massachusetts Provincial Congress, 1774-75. His efforts to redistrict Massachusetts to give the Republicans control gave us the term "gerrymander."

MASONIC

"Alleged membership in Philanthropic Lodge of Marblehead never substantiated." (Case)

Mrs. Muriel D. Taylor, Librarian of the Grand Lodge of Massachusetts, makes this information available from notes of William L. Boyden, from a letter of General Henry DeWitt Hamilton to Claude L. Allen, Grand Master of Massachusetts, under date of March 8, 1935 "I have known all the descendants of Elbridge Gerry . . . during the time since 1882. It is also true that it was traditional in the Gerry family that he was a Freemason." Mrs. Taylor further states that there is no card in the Grand Secretary's office on Gerry.

A letter written June 22, 1927, by Charles C. Hunt, Secretary, The Grand Chapter of the State of New York, Royal Arch Masons, states "Elbridge Gerry, Vice President of the United States in 1813, and a signer of the Declaration of Independence, was a member of Philanthropic Lodge of Marblehead, Mass. That Lodge is still in existence and probably you can get dates from Brother Frederick W. Hamilton, the Grand Secretary." Advice from the Librarian of the Grand Lodge of Massachusetts is that they have no Philanthropic Lodge records available for verifying this.

See also *Historical Sketch of Philanthropic Lodge.* by Stephen O. Hathaway, Jr., Secretary, 125th anniversary of Lodge March 25, 1885:

p. 14 - "The names of many members of those early days have been made familiar to us by tradition - Harris, Fettyplace, Lee, Orne, Gerry, Hooper." It was also noted that "many of its Brethren no doubt had joined the regiment of one thousand from this place, who had guided Washington and his army in their retreat from Long Island and over the cold water of the Delaware." (p. 12)

NATHANAEL GREENE

RHODE ISLAND

Born August 7, 1742, in Warwick, Rhode Island.

Died June 19, 1786, at Mulberry Grove, Georgia.

Buried in the Cemetery of Christ Episcopal Church, Savannah. In 1902 his remains were removed from the cemetery and re-interred beneath the Greene Monument in Johnson Square, Savannah.

GENERAL OFFICER IN THE CONTINENTAL ARMY

BIOGRAPHICAL

Brigadier General, Rhode Island troops, May 3, 1775; Brigadier General, Continental Army, June 22, 1775; Major General, August 9, 1776; Quartermaster General, March 2, 1778, to September 30, 1780. Served to November 3, 1783.

Returned to Rhode Island after the war; then went to his estate near Savannah, Georgia, in 1785.

A capable officer, who enjoyed the full confidence of Washington. It is said he was the one selected to command the American Army in case of Washington's death. He and Washington were the only two general officers who served throughout the war.

President, Rhode Island Society of the Cincinnati, 1783.

MASONIC

"Nathanael Greene was a Mason, having visited Lodges with Washington. The Grand Tyler of the Grand Lodge of Rhode Island states they have in their possession a Masonic medal once worn by General Greene." (Roth, p. 90)

"After the defeat at Camden (South Carolina) Washington placed Brother Nathanael Greene in charge of the Southern Army . . . " (Morse, p. 125)

On Monday, March 21, 1825, Lafayette, with the Grand Lodge of Georgia, laid the cornerstone of the monument to General Greene with Masonic ceremonies. A monument founded or dedicated with Masonic ceremony does not make the honored one a Mason. It would appear from correspondence beginning February 20, 1825, in Washington, from Lafayette to Col. E. F. Tattnall, the Masonic Fraternity was not invited as such, but as part of the general program of entertainment.

This cornerstone and monument were dedicated to the memory of General Nathanael Greene, "the saviour of the South."

The Grand Lodge of Rhode Island quotes from an article in *Freemasons Repository*, Vol. 27, pp. 629-632: " . . . He (Greene) was a Rhode Island Mason, identified with the Fraternity from early manhood, and never ceasing to hold it in high regard . . . "

PATRICK HENRY

VIRGINIA

Born May 29, 1736, at Studley, Hanover County, Virginia.
Died June 6, 1799, at "Red Hill" Plantation, Charlotte County, Virginia.
Buried at "Red Hill", Charlotte County, Virginia.

SIGNER OF THE ARTICLES OF ASSOCIATION

BIOGRAPHICAL

Studied law, and admitted to the bar in 1760. Member, Continental Congress, 1774-76. Henry was foremost in the movement to call a Continental Congress.

Colonel and Commander in Chief of the Virginia forces, September, 1775; resigned, February 28, 1776; appointed Colonel, 1st Virginia, February 13, 1776, which he declined. Member, House of Burgesses from Louisa County, May 20, 1765. Famous for his two speeches: Stamp Act speech of May 29, 1765, in the House of Burgesses at Williamsburg—"Caesar had his Brutus, etc." and the "Give me Liberty or give me Death" speech of March 20, 1775, in Richmond.

Declined appointment as United States Senator in 1794. President Washington offered him the position of Secretary of State, October 7, 1795, which he declined; three months later, Henry was asked by Washington to be Chief Justice of the United States, and Henry declined that position also. President John Adams also offered him the appointment of Minister of France, which was likewise declined.

The first republican Governor of Virginia, June 29, 1776, to 1779, and again, 1784-86; his fifth term expired November 30, 1786, and he made ready to settle in Prince Edward County, near Hampden-Sydney College. Elected to the State Senate in 1799, but did not take his seat.

MASONIC

"No satisfactory evidence of his membership. It is possible he was a member of the old Tappahannock Lodge of Virginia, whose records are lost." (Denslow)

The *New Age* for September, 1924, p. 564, lists the name Henry and others, with the undocumented information: " . . . were members."

The History of Lexington No. 1, Lexington, Kentucky, 125th Anniversary, p. 54, states that his Masonic apron is owned by Brother J. C. Cramer of Lexington Lodge. All efforts to verify this have thus far been unsuccessful.

The Proceedings of the Grand Lodge of Virginia for 1785 and 1797 show this name as a visitor, although a reprint of the 1785 *Proceedings,* page 15, shows only a "Henry". Similarly, reprints of the 1797 *Proceedings,* pp. 4 and 168, show only a "Henry."

ROBERT HOWE

NORTH CAROLINA

Born in 1732, in Bladen, New Brunswick County, North Carolina.

Died December 14, 1786, in Brunswick County, North Carolina.

Buried on Grange Farm, now a part of Columbus County, North Carolina.

GENERAL OFFICER IN THE CONTINENTAL ARMY

BIOGRAPHICAL

Colonel, 2nd North Carolina, September 1, 1775; Brigadier General, Continental Army, March 1, 1776; Major General, October 20, 1777, and served to the close of the war. Howe was the highest ranking officer from North Carolina in the Continental service.

Very little is known of his private life. See *The Historical & Scientific Society of Wilmington, N. C., - Sketch of Major General Robert Howe,* by John D. Bellamy, Jr., March 16, 1882, p. 22: Howe taken sick on way to Fayetteville and stopped at the residence of General Thomas Clark. A few days after December 14, 1786, he died and was buried on Grange Farm, then in Brunswick County (now, 1882, a part of Columbus

County). "Not even a stone marks his last resting place and nothing but a small hillock exists, to show that even a grave was ever there." (John D. Bellamy, "General Robert Howe", North Carolina Booklet, January, 1908, p. 192).

"In 1786, elected to the House of Commons, but taken ill in Bladen County on his way to the session, he died without taking his seat." (DAB)

Member, Society of the Cincinnati.

MASONIC

Howe is named as a member of Hanover Lodge, North Carolina, in the *Grand Lodge Proceedings* for that state for 1938, p. 22, but further details are lacking.

" . . . by such well known Masons as . . . Robert Howe in Brunswick." (*GL Proc. North Carolina*, 1912)

THOMAS JEFFERSON

VIRGINIA

Born April 13, 1743, at Shadwell, now Albemarle County, Virginia.

Died July 4, 1826, at "Monticello", near Charlottesville, Virginia.

Buried at "Monticello", near Charlottesville, Virginia.

SIGNER OF THE DECLARATION OF INDEPENDENCE

BIOGRAPHICAL

Graduate of the College of William & Mary, Williamsburg, Virginia, 1762. Studied law under George Wythe (who also signed the Declaration of Independence); admitted to the bar, and commenced practice in 1767. Prominent in pre-Revolutionary movements.

Member, Second Continental Congress, 1775-76, and 1783-85. While serving as a member of the Continental Congress, he was appointed chairman of a committee to prepare a draft of a Declaration of Independence from Great Britain; he made and presented the first draft that was submitted to the Congress, July 2, 1776.

Appointed a Minister Plenipotentiary to France, May 7, 1784, and then sole Minister to the King of France, March 10, 1785.

First Secretary of State under President Washington, September 26, 1789, to December 3, 1793; Vice President of the United States, March 4, 1797, to March 3, 1801; third President of the United States, March 4, 1801, to March 3, 1809, being elected by the House of Representatives after a tie vote with Aaron Burr.

Member, Colonial House of Burgesses, 1769-1774. Active in the founding of the University of Virginia; Governor of Virginia, 1779-1781.

MASONIC

Jefferson was said to have affiliated with the Door to Virtue Lodge No. 44, Albemarle County, Virginia, and also that he was made a Mason in France in the Famous Lodge of the Nine Sisters (La Loge Des Neuf Soeurs), but there is no supporting information for either claim.

"No positive evidence of where and when he was made a Mason." (Boyden)

". . . there is considerable contemporary evidence to indicate that Jefferson was himself a Mason." (Brown, p. 199)

"His presence at a cornerstone laying at the University of Virginia is no proof that he was a Freemason. No mention of the Fraternity appears in the millions of words he wrote and which are in print. Strict search has uncovered no evidence." (Case)

Moses Holbrook, Grand Commander of the Supreme Council, 33°, Southern Jurisdiction, United States of America, in a letter to Dr. J. M. Allen, Skaneateles, New York, dated at Charleston, S. C., August 2, 1826, says: "I have nothing new to write, except tomorrow we have a funeral procession for Thomas Jefferson, and all the societies are invited. I never knew that he was a Freemason."

From the Library of the Grand Lodge of Iowa, October 5, 1957: "No record. References to him as a Mason in contemporary writings."

JOHN LANGDON

NEW HAMPSHIRE

Born June 26, 1741, in Portsmouth, New Hampshire.
Died September 19, 1819, in Portsmouth, New Hampshire.
Buried in Langdon tomb in the Old North Cemetery, Portsmouth, New Hampshire.

SIGNER OF THE CONSTITUTION OF THE UNITED STATES

BIOGRAPHICAL

Attended Major Hale's school in Portsmouth, and was a merchant there before the war.

Member, Continental Congress, 1775-76, resigning to become Navy Agent to superintend the construction of several ships of war. Organized and financed General Stark's expedition against Burgoyne; participated in the battle of Bennington. Prominent in pre-Revolutionary affairs, and during the war, President of New Hampshire.

Member, Continental Congress in 1783. Delegate to the Federal Constitutional Convention in 1787.

United States Senator, March 4, 1789, to March 3, 1801; elected the first President pro-tempore of the United States Senate on April 6, 1789, in order that the Senate could organize and count the electoral votes for President and Vice President of the United States. Thus Langdon, officiating as the first President of the Senate, had the satisfaction of welcoming Washington to his new honors.

The office of Secretary of the Navy was offered him by President Jefferson, but he declined this appointment as well as the nomination for Vice President on the Republican ticket in 1812.

Governor of New Hampshire in 1788, 1805, and 1809-11.

MASONIC

"He is referred to as a Mason but his Masonic record has not been definitely traced. It would probably have been in St. John's Lodge No. 1 of Portsmouth, where his Brother Woodbury held membership." (Denslow)

RICHARD HENRY LEE

VIRGINIA

Born January 20, 1732, at "Stratford", Westmoreland County, Virginia.

Died June 19, 1794, at "Chantilly", Westmoreland County, Virginia.

Buried in old family burying ground at "Mount Pleasant", near Hague, Virginia.

SIGNER OF THE ARTICLES OF ASSOCIATION, THE DECLARATION OF INDEPENDENCE, AND THE ARTICLES OF CONFEDERATION

BIOGRAPHICAL

Educated at Wakefield Academy, England; returned to Virginia in 1751; studied law and history.

Member, Virginia House of Burgesses, 1758-1775; active in the organization of the Committees of Correspondence throughout the Colonies.

Member, First and Second Continental Congresses, 1774-1780, and 1784-87, and served as President of that body in 1784.

". . . brought forward the resolution, in accord with instructions given in the Virginia Convention of May 17, 1776, declaring 'that these united Colonies are, and of right ought to be, free and independent States', etc.; author of the first national Thanksgiving Day proclamation issued by Congress at York, October 31, 1777, after the capture of Burgoyne's army at Saratoga, N. Y." (BDAC, p. 1449)

Served as Colonel of the Westmoreland Militia in an engagement with the British at Stratford Landing on April 9, 1781.

United States Senator, March 4, 1789, until he resigned, October 8, 1792.

MASONIC

"Member, Hiram Lodge No. 59, Westmoreland, Va." (Hayden, p. 211). (Note: *Proceedings of the Grand Lodge of Virginia, 1777-1823*, p. 209, show Hiram Lodge chartered by that Grand Lodge on December 11, 1799, after Lee's death.)

"Alleged membership in Freemasonry never conclusively proven." (Case)

"In June, 1776, Richard Henry Lee, in the Continental Congress, moved that a committee be appointed to draft a Declaration of Independence. He was a Mason, and my heart thrills with fervor and praise when I recall that this first bold step was taken by a Freemason." (*GL Proc., Georgia*, 1911, p. 69, from the Grand Master's address.)

PHILIP LIVINGSTON

NEW YORK

Born January 15, 1716, in Albany, New York.

Died June 12, 1778, in York, Pennsylvania, while Congress was in session there.

Buried in Prospect Hill Cemetery, York, Pennsylvania.

SIGNER OF THE ARTICLES OF ASSOCIATION AND THE DECLARATION OF INDEPENDENCE

BIOGRAPHICAL

Yale graduate, 1737, and prominent New York City merchant. Delegate to Stamp Act Congress in October, 1765. Member, provincial house of representatives, 1763-69, and served as speaker in 1768; member, New York Committee of Correspondence. Prominent in commercial and education societies.

Member, First and Second Continental Congresses, 1774, until his death while attending the sixth session of the Congress in York, Pennsylvania.

MASONIC

"He was affiliated with Solomon's Lodge, New York". (Roth, p. 162). (Note: The Librarian of the Grand Lodge of New York advises there was no Solomon's Lodge in existence in New York at that time.)

"Alleged membership in Freemasonry never conclusively proven. Confused with others of the name." (Case)

"Brother Brown several times calls attention to the statement of Bro. Shirrefs (which seems to have escaped our notice) that so far as careful examination of Grand Lodge records can show the facts, only five of the signers of the Declaration of Independence in place of 'all but eight' are Freemasons: Benjamin Franklin, John Hancock, William Hooper, Philip Livingston, and Thomas Nelson, Jr." (*GL Proc. Pennsylvania,* 1909, p. 463 - Report on Correspondence)

THOMAS McKEAN

DELAWARE

Born March 19, 1734, in New London Township, Chester County, Pennsylvania.

Died June 24, 1817, in Philadelphia, Pennsylvania.

Buried in Laurel Hill Cemetery, Philadelphia, Pennsylvania.

SIGNER OF THE ARTICLES OF ASSOCIATION, THE DECLARATION OF INDEPENDENCE, AND THE ARTICLES OF CONFEDERATION

BIOGRAPHICAL

Educated privately by Rev. Francis Allison at New Castle, Delaware. Studied law, admitted to the bar in 1755 and commenced practice in New Castle, Delaware. Appointed Deputy Attorney-General for Sussex County in 1756; resigned in 1758 and went to England, resumed study of law at the Middle Temple in London.

Member, Continental Congress, 1774-1783, and its President in 1781; member, Stamp Act Congress in New York City, 1765.

Member, Delaware House of Assembly, 1762-1775, and served as Speaker in 1772; Collector of Port of New Castle in 1771. President of the State of Delaware, 1777.

Colonel, Pennsylvania Militia in 1776. Chief Justice of Pennsylvania, 1777-1799. Member of Pennsylvania Convention which ratified the Constitution of the United States, December 12, 1787. Governor of Pennsylvania, 1799-1808; then retired from public life.

McKean and John Dickinson were the only two members of Congress who took up arms in defense of the measures they had been advocating.

Vice President of the Pennsylvania Society of the Cincinnati.

MASONIC

"Alleged membership in Freemasonry and activity in Pennsylvania have not been conclusively proven." (Case)

See *History of Perseverance Lodge No. 21, F. & A. M., Harrisburg, Pa.*, by William Henry Egle and James M. Lamberton, Harrisburg, 1901, p. 281: "Governor McKean . . . were Visitors." An undated and unnamed newspaper clipping in the Library of The Historical Society of Montgomery County, Pennsylvania, (could possibly be *The Harrisburg Telegraph*): "In reference to the 118th anniversary of Lodge No. 21, Dr. William H. Egle, the State Librarian, delivered the historical address . . . 'Down through the corridors of a century, Lodge 21 has enshrined among its members many names . . . whose fame are part of the history of our state and nation . . . Governors McKean . . . were visitors."

A letter from Brother J. Douglas Royal, Secretary of Perseverance Lodge No. 21, dated March 16, 1957, says there is no information available in the records of the lodge which would verify this statement.

There is mention of a Brother Thomas McKean on page 56 of the Report of the Committee on History and Research in the *Proceedings of the Grand Lodge of Delaware* for 1937, but no further verification.

DANIEL MORGAN

VIRGINIA

Born in 1736, probably in Hunterdon County, New Jersey.
Died July 6, 1802, in Winchester, Virginia.
Buried in Mount Hebron Cemetery, Winchester, Virginia.

GENERAL OFFICER IN THE CONTINENTAL ARMY

BIOGRAPHICAL

Moved to Charles Town, Virginia (now West Virginia) in 1754, and in 1755 began his military career in General Braddock's army.

Captain, Company of Virginia Rifleman, July, 1775; taken prisoner at Quebec, December 31, 1775; Colonel, 11th Virginia, November 12, 1776; Regiment designated 7th Virginia, September 14, 1778; Brigadier General, Continental Army, October 13, 1780, and served to the close of the war.

Commanded Virginia Militia in 1794, to help put down the Whiskey Insurrection in Pennsylvania.

Member, Fifth United States Congress, March 4, 1797, to March 3, 1799; declined to be a candidate for re-election on account of ill health.

Member, Society of the Cincinnati.

MASONIC

"There is no record of his having been a Mason." (Roth, p. 94)

"Many other prominent Virginians, conspicuous among whom was Daniel Morgan, the famous leader of Morgan's riflemen, are numbered in the proud ranks of Virginia's Freemasons." (Morse, p. 128)

"There is no evidence of his Masonic membership or activity. His alleged apron in the Greensboro Masonic Museum is only connected with him by hearsay." (Case)

The Masonic Herald, Rome, Georgia, for March, 1903: "General Daniel Morgan, of Revolutionary fame, was a warm Freemason."

The Builder, May, 1926: "On December 3, 1780, following the fiasco of Gates at Camden, General Greene was appointed to the command of the Army of the South. Among his prominent officers were Colonel Henry Lee (Light Horse Harry), Daniel Morgan, Col. Wm. Washington, Col. Otho Williams—all Brother Masons."

ROBERT MORRIS

PENNSYLVANIA

Born January 20, 1734, in or near Liverpool, England.

Died May 8, 1806, in Philadelphia, Pennsylvania.

Buried in the family vault of William White and Robert Morris, behind Christ Church, Philadelphia, Pennsylvania.

SIGNER OF THE DECLARATION OF INDEPENDENCE, THE ARTICLES OF CONFEDERATION, AND THE CONSTITUTION OF THE UNITED STATES

BIOGRAPHICAL

Emigrated to America in 1747, and settled in Oxford, Maryland. Attended public schools; became a prominent merchant in Philadelphia.

Member, Continental Congress, 1776-78; member, Federal Constitutional Convention in 1787. United States Senator, March 4, 1789, to March 3, 1795, but declined to be a candidate for renomination.

Superintendent of Finances of the United States, 1781 to the close of the war. Established the Bank of North America.

Member, State Assembly, 1778-1780; member, State House of Representatives, 1785-87.

"Declined the position of Secretary of the Treasury in the cabinet of President Washington; became financially involved by unsuccessful land speculation, which caused him to be imprisoned for debt from February 16, 1798, to August 26, 1801." (BDAC, p. 1591)

MASONIC

"Alleged membership in Freemasonry and ownership of 'his' apron have never been conclusively proven." (Case)

Letter from Brother William J. Paterson, former Librarian and Curator of the Grand Lodge of Pennsylvania, dated March 21, 1957, states: "We have made several inquiries regarding Robert Morris and James Smith, signers, and the answer we received, that these two men were not members of the Masonic Fraternity."

Brother Paterson also writes, on another occasion: "Relative to Robert Morris, a signer, several historians speak of him as a Mason; but there is no positive proof that he was. A Masonic apron was presented to him by George Washington in 1774. This is a known fact."

"Morris has often been mentioned as being a Mason, but no definite proofs have been found." (Roth, p. 83)

THOMAS NELSON, JR.

VIRGINIA

Born December 26, 1738, in Yorktown, Virginia.

Died January 4, 1789, at "Mont Air", Hanover County, Virginia.

Buried in Grace Episcopal Churchyard Cemetery, Yorktown, Virginia.

SIGNER OF THE DECLARATION OF INDEPENDENCE

BIOGRAPHICAL

Attended private schools, and was graduated from Trinity College, Cambridge, England, in 1761.

Member, Second Continental Congress, 1775-77.

Captain, 1st Virginia, February 22, 1776; resigned, August 7, 1777; Commander of Virginia State forces, August, 1777, to 1782; resigned on account of ill health resulting from military service, and was publicly thanked by Washington and by Congress for his services. Participated in the siege of Yorktown, in 1781, commanding the Virginia Militia.

Member, Virginia House of Burgesses, 1774; member first Provincial Convention in Williamsburg in 1774. Governor of Virginia, 1781.

MASONIC

"His traditional membership and activity at Yorktown have never been conclusively documented." (Case)

"Member of Harmony Lodge No. 2, N. C." (Roth)

A letter of April 4, 1927, written by C. C. Callahan, of Virginia, states that Nelson was Worshipful Master of Lodge No. 9 at Yorktown.

Traditional story relates that Nelson was a visitor, with Washington and Lafayette, to Lodge No. 9, Yorktown, Virginia, after the siege of Yorktown, but is without foundation in fact.

See *Great American Masons,* Geo. W. Baird, Washington, 1924, p. 61: "When the cornerstone of the Washington Monument was laid in Richmond about the year 1830, the then Grand Master of Masons, Robert G. Scott, said:

'The campaign of this year is ever memorial for the capture of Cornwallis at Yorktown. In that village was Lodge No. 9, where after the siege was ended, Washington, Lafayette, Marshall, Nelson came together and by their union bore abiding testimony to the beautiful tenets of Masonry.'

There are no other records of the visit of Nelson to Lodge 9 on that occasion, but as Grand Master Scott and hosts of other Masons who enjoyed a personal and intimate acquaintance with Nelson were living at that time, there can be no question of the accuracy of the information."

JOHN PENN

NORTH CAROLINA

Born May 17, 1741, near Port Royal, Caroline County, Virginia.

Died September 14, 1788, near Williamsboro, in Granville County, South Carolina. (W. Eugene Rice, in *Masonic Membership of signers of the Declaration of Independence,* gives Caroline County, Virginia, as place of Penn's death).

Buried near Island Creek. Later reinterred at the Guilford Courthouse National Military Park, Greensboro, North Carolina. (Greensboro, N. C. *Daily News* for July 1, 1962)

SIGNER OF THE DECLARATION OF INDEPENDENCE
AND THE ARTICLES OF CONFEDERATION

BIOGRAPHICAL

Educated by private tutors; studied law; admitted to the bar in 1762, and commenced practice in Bowling Green, Caroline County, Virginia. Moved to North Carolina in 1774, and served in Provincial Congress there in 1775.

Member, Second Continental Congress, 1775-1780. Active in North Carolina affairs at the time of Cornwallis' invasion.

Member, Board of War in North Carolina, 1780; Receiver of Taxes for North Carolina in 1784.

MASONIC

"Alleged membership not conclusively shown." (Case)

In the *Grand Lodge of North Carolina Proceedings* for 1912, p. 75, it is stated that "Colonel William L. Taylor, of Granville County, a zealous Mason, as his father was before him, states that his father and Penn had attended lodges together in North Carolina."

Information from the Library of the Grand Lodge of Iowa on October 5, 1957, states Penn was known to have attended Masonic Lodges in North Carolina, but no further proof given.

CASIMIR PULASKI

POLAND

Born March 4, 1748, in Podolia, Poland.
Died October 11, 1779, on board U. S. brig "Wasp".
Buried probably on St. Helena's Island, 50 miles from Charleston. Other authorities say he was buried at sea, off the Georgia coast.

GENERAL OFFICER IN THE CONTINENTAL ARMY

BIOGRAPHICAL

Educated for the law, but military events influenced him to enter the army. An officer in the Polish Army, he came to America in March, 1777, after his estates in Europe had been confiscated.

Brigadier General, Continental Army, and Chief of Dragoons, September 15, 1777; designated as commander of an independent corps, known as the Pulaski Legion, March 28, 1778. Died on board the U. S. brig "Wasp" on October 11, 1779, of wounds received October 9, 1779, at the siege of Savannah, Georgia.

MASONIC

"Gould says: 'Pulaski was raised in a Military Lodge in Georgia.'" (Roth, p. 85)

"His monument laid with Masonic ceremonies, but there is no record of his Masonic membership or activity." (Case)

Pulaski's traditional connection with Freemasonry seems to have originated because his monument was laid with Masonic ceremony in the presence of Lafayette. The cornerstone of the monument was laid and the monument dedicated to Pulaski, "a departed friend of liberty."

BENJAMIN RUSH

PENNSYLVANIA

Born December 24, 1745, in Byberry Township (near Bristol), Pennsylvania.

Died April 19, 1813, in Philadelphia, Pennsylvania.

Buried in Christ Church Graveyard, Philadelphia, Pennsylvania.

SIGNER OF THE DECLARATION OF INDEPENDENCE

BIOGRAPHICAL

Educated by private tutors and at a private school in Nottingham, Maryland. Graduated from Princeton University in 1760; studied medicine in Philadelphia, Edinburgh, London, and Paris, and commenced practice in Philadelphia in August, 1769.

Member, Continental Congress, 1776-77.

One of the most outstanding physicians of the Revolutionary War period in the Colonies. Surgeon in May, 1775-76; entered the Revolutionary Army as Surgeon-General of Hospitals, Middle Department, April 11, 1777; Physician General of Hospitals, Middle Department, July 1, 1777; resigned, April 30, 1778, and resumed practice of medicine.

Professor of Medicine, Philadelphia Medical College, 1789. Member, American Philosophical Society; founder of Pennsylvania Hospital in Philadelphia; President of Philadelphia Medical Society, Vice President and one of the founders of Philadelphia Bible Society; one of the founders of Dickinson College, Carlisle, Pennsylvania. Treasurer of United States Mint, 1799, and served in that office until his death in 1813.

MASONIC

"There is no Masonic record, but it is often claimed that he was a member; from his close association with Washington the writer believes he was." (Roth, p. 156)

"Alleged membership and later withdrawal have not been documented." (Case)

Card in the Library of the Grand Lodge of Pennsylvania: "Following death of Bro. Capt. Wm. Leslie, British 17th Regt. ft. at Battle of Princeton, N. J., January, 1777, attended by Dr. Benj. Rush. Rush had monument erected over his grave. Reported a member, but doubtful."

PHILIP SCHUYLER

NEW YORK

Born November 22, 1733, in Albany, New York.

Died November 18, 1804, in Albany, New York.

Buried in Albany Rural Cemetery, Albany, New York.

GENERAL OFFICER IN THE CONTINENTAL ARMY

BIOGRAPHICAL

Attended public schools in Albany and was privately tutored.

Served in the French & Indian War in 1755; active in civil government of his state after the peace of 1763. Engaged in lumber business, and later built the first flax mill in America.

Major General, Continental Army, June 19, 1775; resigned, April 19, 1779.

Member, Continental Congress, 1775-77, and again, 1778-1781. Member, United States Senate, March 4, 1789, to March 3, 1791; unsuccessful candidate for re-election. Re-elected later and served from March 4, 1797 to January 3, 1798, when he resigned on account of ill health.

Commissioner to settle boundary between New York and Massachusetts in 1764. New York State Senator, 1780-84, and 1786-1790, and again, 1792-97.

Member, Society of the Cincinnati.

MASONIC

"No record of his membership or activity in Freemasonry." (Case)

Little Masonic Library, Vol. 3 of 1924 edition, p. 279: "The northern department (of the Army) in 1777 was in charge of General Philip Schuyler, who is believed to have been made a Mason in a military lodge during the French and Indian War."

"It is generally held that General Schuyler was a member of the Fraternity, but if so I cannot substantiate it." (*GL Proc. New York. 1900-01*, p. 309)

ROGER SHERMAN

CONNECTICUT

Born April 19, 1721, in Newton, Massachusetts.
Died July 23, 1793, in New Haven, Connecticut.
Buried in Grove Street Cemetery, New Haven, Connecticut.

SIGNER OF THE ARTICLES OF ASSOCIATION, THE DECLARATION OF INDEPENDENCE, THE ARTICLES OF CONFEDERATION, AND THE CONSTITUTION OF THE UNITED STATES

BIOGRAPHICAL

Signer of the Articles of Association, the Declaration of Independence, the Articles of Confederation, and the Constitution of the United States - the only member of the Continental Congress to sign all four of these great state papers. A member of the committee appointed to draft the Declaration of Independence.

Attended public schools. With only a limited education, he studied to improve his opportunities; read law and was admitted to the bar in 1754.

Prominent state legislator from 1745 to 1779; member, Connecticut Assembly, State Senate, Judge of Superior Court. Member, Council of Safety, 1777-79.

Member, First and Second Continental Congresses, 1774-1781, 1783, and 1784. A member of the Committee appointed to draft the Declaration of Independence. Delegate to the Federal Constitutional Convention in Philadelphia in 1787.

Member, First United States Congress, March 4, 1789, to March 3, 1791; United States Senator, June 13, 1791, and served until his death.

Mayor of New Haven, 1784, and served until his death. Treasurer of Yale College.

MASONIC

"He was a member of the Fraternity, probably Hiram No. 1, Connecticut." (Roth, p. 53)

"Lodge not known. The Masonic apron worn by him has been added to the historical collection of Yale University, of which he was one time Treasurer." (Boyden)

The Grand Secretary of the Grand Lodge of Connecticut advises there is a tradition that he was a Mason.

"Not a Freemason. Two of his sons were. 'His' apron, once in Yale memorabilia, cannot be traced to him. There is no evidence of any kind to support the opinion that Roger Sherman was himself a Freemason." (Case)

See *Masonic Papers*, September, 1938, of the Research Lodge No. 281, F. & A. M., Seattle, Washington, p. 91: "Delegates with uncertain Masonic records . . . 'Roger Sherman of Connecticut was an unusual man' . . . only man who signed the four principal epochmaking documents in American history that parallel the Magna Charta - But there is no information as to his Lodge membership."

WILLIAM SMALLWOOD

MARYLAND

Born in 1732, in Charles County, Maryland.

Died February 12, 1792, in Prince George County, Maryland.

Buried at his home "Smallwood's Retreat", in Charles County, Maryland.

GENERAL OFFICER IN THE CONTINENTAL ARMY

BIOGRAPHICAL

Sent to England to be educated; returned to America in 1754 and assisted in the management of his father's estate.

Colonel, Maryland Regiment, January 14, 1776; Brigadier General, Continental Army, October 23, 1776; wounded at White Plains, October 28, 1776; Major General, September 15, 1780, and served to the close of the war.

Governor of Maryland in 1785; returned to his plantation, "Smallwood's Retreat", at the expiration of his term as Governor, and died there.

The Maryland Sons of the American Revolution erected a granite monument over Smallwood's grave, immediately in front of the house, July 4, 1898. "Smallwood's

Retreat" is part of Mattawoman, located on Mattawoman Creek, near where it empties into the Potomac, and lies opposite Gunston Hall, home of George Mason, Smallwood was a member of the vestry of Durham Episcopal Church, located near his home, which is still in regular use. (Permission to use certain biographical information granted by Mr. George T. Ness, Jr.)

President, Maryland Society of the Cincinnati, 1783.

MASONIC

"General Smallwood has been cited as having been a member of an army lodge." (Roth, p. 57)

"No record, but claimed by Bloom. Traditionally a member of Military Lodge (27) A. Y. M." (Case)

"It is supposed that General Wm. Smallwood and Col. John Eager Howard were made Masons in this (Army Lodge No. 27) Lodge." *GL Proc. Maryland, 1910-11*, p. 110)

"Was member Alexandria Masonic Lodge, and, together with Washington and other neighbors belonging to the order, held Masonic meetings in one of the upper rooms in Smallwood's Retreat." It has not been possible to verify this statement. Brother Charles A. Cornnell, Secretary of Alexandria-Washington Lodge No. 22, A. F. & A. M., in Alexandria, Virginia, advises on December 7, 1963: "The records of Alexandria-Washington Lodge No. 22 do not contain the name of General William Smallwood."

JAMES SMITH

PENNSYLVANIA

Born July 1, 1719, in Northern Ireland. (BDAC gives year
of birth as 1713)
Died July 11, 1806, in York, Pennsylvania.
Buried in First Presbyterian Churchyard, York, Pennsylvania.

SIGNER OF THE DECLARATION OF INDEPENDENCE

BIOGRAPHICAL

Emigrated to America in 1727; attended Philadelphia Academy (now the University of Pennsylvania). Studied law and admitted to the bar in 1745; began practice in Shippensburg, Pennsylvania; later moved to York.

Member, Second Continental Congress, 1776-78.

An organizer and Colonel of Pennsylvania Militia, 1775-76. Member, General Assembly of Pennsylvania, 1780.

MASONIC

Brother William J. Paterson, former Librarian and Curator of the Grand Lodge of Pennsylvania, writes on March 21, 1957: "We have made several inquiries about Robert Morris and James Smith, signers, and the answer we received, that these two men were not members of the Masonic Fraternity."

A card in the Library of the Grand Lodge of Pennsylvania shows three James Smiths: one, Tun Tavern Lodge, Philadelphia, June 14, 1751; another, made a Mason in Lodge No. 2, Philadelphia, September 11, 1754; and the third, listed as member of Lodge No. 18, Dover, Delaware, May 9, 1786. On page 46 of the Dues Record of Lodge No. 2 is this information: "Sept. 11, 1754 - To making you a Mason, £3-0-0; Dec. 27, 1754 - To raising you the . . . 3 degrees, £1-2-6; January 7, 1755 - To making you a Member, £0-7-6." No further verification could be located.

ANTHONY WAYNE

PENNSYLVANIA

Born January 1, 1745, in Easttown, Pennsylvania.

Died December 15, 1796, in Presque Isle (now Erie), Pennsylvania.

Buried in Erie, Pennsylvania, but later re-interred in St. David's Episcopal Church Cemetery, Radnor, Pennsylvania.

GENERAL OFFICER IN THE CONTINENTAL ARMY

BIOGRAPHICAL

Attended Philadelphia Academy, became a land surveyor, and was employed for a time in Nova Scotia.

Member, State House of Representatives, in 1774 and 1775.

Colonel, 4th Pennsylvania Battalion, January 3, 1776; Brigadier General, Continental Army, February 21, 1777; wounded at Stony Point, July 16, 1779. Served to close of the war. Brevet Major General, September 30, 1783; Major General and Commander, United States Army, March 5, 1792. Governor Pennypacker of Pennsylvania has said that Wayne "fought farther North, farther South, and farther West than any General of the Revolution."

Member, Second United States Congress, March 4, 1791, to March 17, 1792, when the seat was declared vacant. He declined to be a candidate for re-election in 1792.

His successful negotiations with, and military victories over, the Indians after the Revolutionary War opened up the Northwest United States to settlers.

Member, Society of the Cincinnati.

MASONIC

History of Freemasonry in New York. McClenachan, New York, 1892, Vol. 3, p. 528: "From time to time the Grand Lodge Officers had been called upon to perform dedicatory services, and in many instances to perform fitting ceremonies at the monuments of eminent and distinguished brothers . . . In the beauty of summer, on July 16, 1857, at Stony Point . . . were the Masonic honors to the memory of the brave and fearless General Anthony Wayne rendered under the efficient charge of the Deputy Grand Master, Right Worshipful Robert Macoy."

" . . . and what a long roll of heroes of the Revolution, who were Masons; the fearless Israel Putnam, 'Light Horse' Harry Lee, 'Mad Anthony' Wayne, the Carolina 'Swamp Fox', Francis Marion, and the Fabian General, Nathaniel Greene." (*GL Proc. Georgia, 1911,* p. 70)

"There is no record of Gen. Anthony Wayne's Masonic career, but the fact of his being a member of the Fraternity is undoubted. In 1857 a monument over his grave was dedicated at Stony Point by the Grand Lodge (NY), R. W. Robert Macoy acting as Grand Master." (*GL Proc. New York, 1900,* p. 313) (Note: Wayne's grave is not at Stony Point.)

The History of Bro. Gen. LaFayette's Fraternal Connections with the Right Worshipful Grand Lodge, F. & A. M. of Pennsylvania, (Julius F. Sachse, 1916), in the Library of the Grand Lodge of Pennsylvania, makes this statement on page 5: "Lafayette reached Philadelphia, August 10, 1784—presented with address by Brothers A. St. Clair, William Irving, and General Anthony Wayne."

"Gen. Anthony Wayne was one of the few Revolutionary officers who was not a Freemason." (*OML,* Vol. II, p. 346)

SAMUEL BLATCHLEY WEBB

CONNECTICUT

Born December 15, 1753, in Wethersfield, Connecticut.
Died December 3, 1817, in Claverack, New York.
Buried in the Reformed Dutch Churchyard, Claverack, New York.

LIEUTENANT COLONEL AND AIDE-DE-CAMP TO GENERAL WASHINGTON

BIOGRAPHICAL

First Lieutenant, 2nd Connecticut, May 1, 1775; wounded at Bunker Hill, June 17, 1775; Major and Aide-de-Camp to General Israel Putnam, July 22, 1775; Lieutenant Colonel and Aide-de-Camp to General Washington, June 21, 1776, to January 1, 1775; wounded at White Plains, October 28, 1776, and at Trenton, January 2, 1777; Colonel of one of the Sixteen Additional Continental Regiments, January 11, 1777; taken prisoner on the expedition to Long Island, December 10, 1777, and was a prisoner of war on parole until exchanged, December, 1780. Transferred to 3d Connecticut, January 1, 1781, and served to June 3, 1783. Brevet Brigadier General, September 30 1783.

Served as Grand Marshal of the Day at Washington's first inauguration.

Member, Society of the Cincinnati.

MASONIC

The American Lodge of Research *Transactions,* Vol. VI, No. 2, mentions a Samuel Webb, member of Union Lodge No. 5, in Stamford, in 1794, but no other evidence is available.

JOHN WITHERSPOON

NEW JERSEY

Born February 5, 1723, in the Parish of Tester, near Edinburgh, in the Presbytery of Haddington, Scotland. (W. Eugene Rice, in *Masonic Membership of the Signers of the Declaration of Independence*, gives the date as February 5, 1722.)

Died November 15, 1794, on his farm, "Tusculum", near Princeton, New Jersey.

Buried in the President's Lot in the Witherspoon Street Graveyard, Princeton, New Jersey.

SIGNER OF THE DECLARATION OF INDEPENDENCE AND THE ARTICLES OF CONFEDERATION

BIOGRAPHICAL

Graduate of Edinburgh University, 1739. Studied theology at Edinburgh; licensed in 1743. Ordained Presbyterian minister of the Parish of Beith in 1745. Active writer and preacher in Scotland; declined calls to Rotterdam in 1759, Dundee in 1762, and Dublin in 1766. Emigrated to America in August, 1768. Active leader in pre-Revolutionary days.

Member, Provincial Congress of New Jersey, June 10-22, 1776. Member, Second Continental Congress, June 22, 1776, to December 1, 1779, and again, December 1, 1780, to December 1, 1781, and from May 20 to November 5, 1782.

Member of secret Committee of Congress on the conduct of the war. Drafted instructions in June, 1781, to the American peace commissioners. After the war, he continued his interest in public affairs; was prolific writer. Became blind in 1792. His works were collected and published after his death.

". . . declined the presidency of College of New Jersey (now Princeton University) in 1766, but accepted the second invitation of that institution, and was inaugurated as President, August 17, 1768; became a leader of Presbyterians in America." (BDAC, p. 2036)

MASONIC

"Admitted by many writers that he was a Mason, but there is no proof." (Roth, p. 158)

"Evidence of his Masonic activities in America seems to be fabricated. Possibility of his membership not doubted." (Case)

Brother Harvey C. Whildey, Grand Secretary of the Grand Lodge of New Jersey, writes on November 1, 1957, quoting from *History of Freemasonry in New Jersey*, by David McGregor, Grand Historian, commemorating the 150th anniversary of that Grand Lodge: "Dr. John Witherspoon, one of the signers, is said to have been a member of the Fraternity. but, as in the case of Aaron Burr, the claims are in conflict with his known activities. He is said to have conducted a Masonic church service in Ryegate, Vermont, on June 24, 1782, while in fact he was in close attendance at the meetings of Congress in Philadelphia at that time." The records of the Continental Congress show him to have been present in Philadelphia attending sessions of Congress on Friday, the 22nd of June, 1782, and on Monday, the 25th of June, 1782.

MASONIC MEMBERSHIP

of the

FOUNDING FATHERS

GROUP III

No evidence of Masonic membership or activity has as yet been found for these individuals.

(146)

There follow the names of the remainder of the group of 241 early American military and political leaders of the Revolutionary War period for whom no information has as yet been located which would indicate even possible membership in the Masonic Fraternity.

Some of the patriots in Group II may yet be fully documented; it is doubtful, however, if any of the several reviewed in Group III will be found to have been Masons, in view of the extensive search that has already been made by many writers and Masonic historians over the years.

ANDREW ADAMS (CONNECTICUT)

SIGNER OF THE ARTICLES OF CONFEDERATION. Born January 7, 1736, in Stratford, Connecticut. Died November 26, 1797, in Litchfield, Connecticut. Buried in East Cemetery, Litchfield, Connecticut.

BIOGRAPHICAL: Yale graduate, 1760. Studied law. Practiced in Stratford and Litchfield. Member, Continental Congress, 1777-1782; member, Council of Safety for two years. Major and then Colonel in militia; served in the Continental Army under General Wooster. Member, State House of Representatives, 1776-1781; Speaker in 1779 and 1780. Chief Justice of State Supreme Court in 1793, and served until his death.

MASONIC: An Andrew Adams was a member of Harmony Lodge No. 42, of Waterbury, Connecticut. James R. Case comments (July 16, 1960): "Andrew Adams, signer of the Articles of Confederation, was not a Mason. Harmony Lodge No. 42 was chartered in 1797 at Waterbury, not at Litchfield, where the Judge lived and died. The Andrew Adams conspicuous in Connecticut Freemasonry was a son or nephew, and was Worshipful Master of Lodge No. 42 in 1817."

JOHN ADAMS (MASSACHUSETTS)

SIGNER OF THE ARTICLES OF ASSOCIATION AND THE DECLARATION OF INDEPENDENCE. Born October 30, 1735, in Braintree (now Quincy), Massachusetts. Died July 4, 1826, in Quincy, Massachusetts. Buried beneath Old Congregational Church, Quincy, Massachusetts.

BIOGRAPHICAL: Harvard graduate, 1755; studied law, admitted to the bar in 1758, and began practice in Suffolk County. Member, First and Second Continental Congresses, 1774-78. Member of the Committee appointed to draft the Declaration of Independence. Adams proposed Washington for General of the American Army. United States Commissioner to France, 1778; Minister Plenipotentiary to Holland in 1782, and successfully negotiated a loan and treaty of commerce. First Minister to Great Britain, 1785 to 1788. First Vice President of the United States, serving with Washington, April 30, 1789, to March 3, 1797; second President of the United States, March 4, 1797, to March 3, 1801. His last official act in office was to appoint John Marshall Chief Justice of the Supreme Court of the United States. Served as a delegate to the Constitutional Convention of Massachusetts when eighty-five years of age.

MASONIC: "They (John and Samuel Adams) were not Masons but neither was there any reason for them to be anti-Masons." (Brown, p. 171) "Not a Freemason, as shown in his correspondence." (Case) *The Little Masonic Library*, Vol. 3, 1924 edition, p. 247: "On further investigation, it appears certain that neither of the Adamses was a Mason; and this is the conclusion of the authorities of the Grand Lodge of Massachusetts." See *History of Lodge 61, F. & A. M., Wilkes-Barre, 1794-1897*, by Oscar Jewell Harvey, Wilkes-Barre, 1897, p. 82: "I am not, never was, and never shall be a Free Mason"—quoted during the Anti-Masonic era.

SAMUEL ADAMS (MASSACHUSETTS)

SIGNER OF THE ARTICLES OF ASSOCIATION, THE DECLARATION OF INDEPENDENCE, AND THE ARTICLES OF CONFEDERATION. Born September 27, 1722, in Boston, Massachusetts. Died October 2, 1803, in Boston, Massachusetts. Buried in Old Granary Burial Grounds, Boston, Massachusetts.

BIOGRAPHICAL: Harvard graduate, 1740. Member, Continental Congress, 1774 to 1782, when he resigned. Member, State Constitutional Convention in 1788. Unsuccessful candidate for election in 1788 to the first United States Congress. Lieutenant Governor of Massachusetts, 1789-1794, and Governor from 1794-97.

MASONIC: "They (John and Samuel Adams) were not Masons, but neither was there any reason for them to be anti-Masons." (Brown, p. 171) *The Little Masonic Library,* Vol. 3, 1924 edition, p. 247: "On further investigation, it appears certain that neither of the Adamses was a Mason; and this is the conclusion of the authorities of the Grand Lodge of Massachusetts." "He never was a Mason, but was continually associated with members of the Fraternity." (Roth, p. 155) "Not positively identified with any of this name known to have been a member of the Fraternity." (Case)

In the September, 1924 *Master Mason,* Frederick W. Hamilton, Massachusetts Grand Secretary, showed that neither the great Samuel Adams, John Adams, nor John Quincy Adams could have been Freemasons.

The *name* Samuel Adams appears three times in Massachusetts Grand Lodge records. One was a member of Trinity Lodge, Lancaster, an undistinguished person. Another was acting Deputy Junior Grand Warden at the constitution of United Lodge at Topsham, Maine, then a part of Massachusetts. This was in 1805; *the* Samuel Adams died in 1803. Governor Samuel Adams was present when Grand Master Paul Revere laid the cornerstone of the State House at Boston in 1795; but nothing in the record indicates that the Governor was a Mason.

ARMAND CHARLES TUFFIN, Marquis de La Rouërie (FRANCE)
(commonly known as Colonel Armand)
GENERAL OFFICER IN THE CONTINENTAL ARMY. Born April 13, 1750, in parish of Saint Leonard, at Fougeres, France. Died January 30, 1793, at the Château de la Guyomarais, near Lamballe, (in Côtes-de-Nord) France. It is almost certain he was buried in the immediate vicinity.

BIOGRAPHICAL: Colonel, 3rd Cavalry, Pulaski Legion, May 10, 1777; succeeded Pulaski in command of the Legion, October 11, 1779; October 21, 1780, the name of command changed to "Armand's Partisan Corps", which he commanded until the close of the war. Brigadier General, Continental Army, March 26, 1783, to November 2, 1783. Served at Valley Forge and Yorktown. Some writers claim Armand was the first of the Frenchmen to arrive in America to help the colonists' cause. His outstanding service was recognized in an Act of Congress, February 27, 1784. Returned to France in 1783; active in revolutionary movements in his own country, and was a prisoner in the Bastille for a time in 1789. No evidence of Masonic membership or activity has been found.

JOHN ARMSTRONG (PENNSYLVANIA)
GENERAL OFFICER IN THE CONTINENTAL ARMY. Born October 13, 1717, in Brookborough Parish, County Fermanagh, Ireland. Died March 9, 1795, in Carlisle, Pennsylvania. Buried in Old Carlisle Cemetery, Carlisle, Pennsylvania.

BIOGRAPHICAL: Educated in Ireland; became a civil engineer. Emigrated to America; settled in Carlisle, Pennsylvania. Brigadier General, Continental Army, March 1, 1776; resigned, April 4, 1777. Brigadier General, Pennsylvania Militia, April 5, 1777; Major General, Pennsylvania Militia, January 9, 1778, to the close of the war. Member of Continental Congress in 1778-1780, and again in 1787-88.

Armstrong advocated plans for a convention to create a Constitution for the United States, and used his influence to have Pennsylvania adopt the Constitution in 1787. He endorsed Washington for first President. No information on Masonic membership or activity.

ABRAHAM BALDWIN (GEORGIA)

SIGNER OF THE CONSTITUTION OF THE UNITED STATES. Born November 22, 1754, in North Guilford, Connecticut. Died March 4, 1807, in Washington, D. C. Buried in the Congressional Cemetery, Washington, D. C.

BIOGRAPHICAL: Graduated from Yale College, 1772; licensed preacher, September 26, 1775. Chaplain, 2nd Connecticut Brigade, 1777-1783. Studied law during his service in the Army; admitted to the bar in 1783; practiced in Fairfield, Connecticut. Member, Continental Congress, 1785-88, and of the first and succeeding four United States Congresses, March 4, 1789, to March 3, 1799. Member, Federal Constitutional Convention in 1787. United States Senator, March 4, 1799; elected President pro tempore of the Senate, December 7, 1801, and April 17, 1802. R-elected to the Senate in 1805, and served until his death. Moved to Augusta, Georgia, in 1784, and continued law practice. Originator of plan for, and author of the charter of the University of Georgia, and served as President for several years.

MASONIC: "Not known to have been a Mason." (Case) See the American Lodge of Research *Transactions*, Vol. 6, No. 3, p. 359—"Addressed A U L with a 'very polite discourse' St. John's Day, December 27, 1779, at Morristown . . . Called 'Rev. Dr.' and not 'Bro'."

JOHN BANISTER (VIRGINIA)

SIGNER OF THE ARTICLES OF CONFEDERATION. Born December 26, 1734, at "Hatcher's Run", near Petersburg, in Dinwiddle County, Virginia. Died September 30, 1788, at "Hatcher's Run". Buried in family burying ground on his estate, "Hatcher's Run."

BIOGRAPHICAL: Attended private school in Wakefield, England; graduate in law from the Temple in London. Returned to Virginia and commenced practice of law in Petersburg. Member, Virginia Assembly in 1765, 1766-1774, and 1775; State House of Delegates in 1776, 1777, and 1781-83. Member, Continental Congress from March 16, 1778, to September 24, 1779. Major and Lieutenant Colonel in Virginia Militia, 1778-1781. No evidence of Masonic membership or activity.

JOSIAH BARTLETT (NEW HAMPSHIRE)

SIGNER OF THE DECLARATION OF INDEPENDENCE AND THE ARTICLES OF CONFEDERATION. Born November 21, 1729, in Amesbury, Massachusetts. Died May 19, 1795, in Kingston, New Hampshire. Buried in the rear of Universalist Church Cemetery, Kingston, New Hampshire.

BIOGRAPHICAL: The first to vote for the Declaration, and the second to sign, after John Hancock. Attended public schools; studied medicine, and commenced practice in Kingston, New Hampshire, in 1750; was medical agent to General Stark at Bennington. Colonel, New Hampshire Militia, 1777-79. Member, Continental Congress, 1775-76. Elected again in 1778 but resigned the same year; appointed

Chief Justice of the Court of Common Pleas in 1779. Justice of Superior Court in 1784 and Chief Justice in 1788. Elected to United States Senate in 1789, but declined, and at the same time resigned as Chief Justice. President of New Hampshire, 1790-94, becoming the first Governor under the new state Constitution, which changed the title from President to that of Governor.

MASONIC: "The signer was not a Mason. He was confused with another Dr. Josiah Bartlett (1759-1820), first candidate and sometime Secretary of Union Lodge (now No. 40), at Danbury, Conn. Later Charter Master of King Solomon's Lodge in Charlestown, which erected the first Bunker Hill Monument. Grand Master of Masons in Massachusetts, 1798." (Case) "There is no record of his having been a Mason." (Roth, p. 164) "Records would appear to disclose that he was a member of Union Masonic Lodge No. 40 at Danbury, Connecticut. He was spoken of as a Mason by known members of the Fraternity." (taken from a page in the *New Age*, not identified as to date) Conflicting and circumstantial evidence was found in printed material and correspondence, but no source was given for the information.

RICHARD BASSETT (DELAWARE)

SIGNER OF THE CONSTITUTION OF THE UNITED STATES. Born April 2, 1745, on his father's plantation, Kent County, Maryland. Died August 15, 1815, at "Bohemian Manor", Cecil County, Maryland. Buried in Wilmington and Brandywine Cemetery, Wilmington, Delaware.

BIOGRAPHICAL: Studied law; admitted to the bar; practiced in Delaware. Captain of troop of Dover Light Horse, Delaware, in the Colonial Army. Delegate to Annapolis Convention; state legislator. Delaware was the first state to ratify the Constitution, and Bassett was a leading member of its ratifying convention; served as Governor of Delaware, January 9, 1799, to March 3, 1801. Member, United States Senate, March 4, 1789, to March 3, 1793; he is credited with being the first man to cast his vote to locate the Capital of the United States on the Potomac River. Chief Justice of the Court of Common Pleas from September 6, 1793, to January 8, 1799. Appointed United States Circuit Judge by President Adams, March 3, 1801. No evidence of Masonic membership or activity has been found.

GEORGE BAYLOR (VIRGINIA)

LIEUTENANT COLONEL AND AIDE-DE-CAMP TO GENERAL WASHINGTON. Born January 12, 1752, in Newmarket, in the Shenandoah Valley, Virginia. Died November 19, 1784. Letter of May 11, 1932, in pension files in National Archives, Washington, D. C.: "Wounded in engagement in New Jersey and died as result of said wounds November 19, 1784, on Island of Bermuda, where he had gone for his health." Buried: Servant brought back his will, watch, etc., so apparently he was buried in Bermuda.

BIOGRAPHICAL: Served as Washington's Aide from August 15, 1775, to January 9, 1777. Colonel, 3d Continental Dragoons, January 9, 1777. Surprised, wounded and taken prisoner at Tappan, September 28, 1778; exchanged ———. His regiment consolidated with 1st Continental Dragoons, November 9, 1782; retained in command of same and served to the close of the war. Brevet Brigadier General, September 30, 1783. Member, Society of the Cincinnati. No evidence of Masonic membership or activity has been found.

RICHARD BLAND (VIRGINIA)

SIGNER OF THE ARTICLES OF ASSOCIATION. Born May 6, 1710, in Orange County, Virginia. Died October 26, 1776, in Williamsburg, Virginia. Buried in private cemetery on the Jordan Point Plantation on the James River.

BIOGRAPHICAL: Graduate of both the College of William and Mary in Williamsburg and the University of Edinburgh. An advocate of Colonial rights, but wished to avoid break with the Mother County. In 1765 he opposed Henry's resolutions against the Stamp Act. Member, Virginia House of Burgesses, 1745-1775. Member of the Virginia Committee of Correspondence in 1773. Member, Continental Congress, 1774 and 1775; again chosen, but declined to serve. Bland was known as "The Virginia Antiquary." No evidence has been located which would indicate membership in the Masonic Fraternity.

WILLIAM BLOUNT (NORTH CAROLINA)

SIGNER OF THE CONSTITUTION OF THE UNITED STATES. Born March 26, 1749, near Windsor, Bertie County, North Carolina. Died March 21, 1800, in Knoxville, Tennessee. Buried in First Presbyterian Church Cemetery, Knoxville, Tennessee.

BIOGRAPHICAL: Entered the service of revolutionary North Carolina in 1776; paymaster of various units of North Carolina troops during the Revolution. State Senator, 1788-1790. Member, Continental Congress in 1782, 1783, 1786, and 1787. Delegate to the Constitutional Convention in 1787. Appointed by President Washington first Governor of "the Territory South of the River Ohio" (Tennessee) in 1790. President of the Convention that framed the first Constitution of Tennessee in 1796, and served as United States Senator from Tennessee from August 2, 1796, until expelled, July 8, 1797. Impeachment proceedings were dismissd, but during the trial he was elected State Senator in Tennessee and chosen its president when session opened on December 3, 1797.

MASONIC: It is believed he was a Mason, but no record has been found of his membership. A note in the Biographical File of the Library of the Grand Lodge of New York contains this information: "Some Masonic writers claim he was a member of Unanimity Lodge No. 54, Edenton, North Carolina. Certainly an error, as there was no lodge at Edenton until 1809.—Blount died in 1800." See *The History of Freemasonry in Tennessee*, 1789-1943, by Charles Albert Snodgrass, 32°, KCCH, Nashville, 1944, p. 413: "William Blount, one of the Framers and Signers of the American Constitution in 1787; the first United States Senator from Tennessee . . . although intimately associated with distinguished Masons in North Carolina, was probably not a Mason, though often reported to be a member of the Fraternity." From the same reference: "A pamphlet published by the Grand Lodge of the District of Columbia in 1937 . . . contains a list compiled by the late Brother William L. Boyden . . . giving names of the Framers and Signers of the Constitution who were known to be Masons—among them Wm. Blount, member of Unanimity Lodge No. 54, Edenton, N. C. This is apparently an error as Unanimity Lodge No. 54 at Edenton was not organized until after 1807."

SIMON BOERUM (NEW YORK)

SIGNER OF THE ARTICLES OF ASSOCIATION. Born February 29, 1724, in New Lots (now Brooklyn), New York. Died July 11, 1775, in Brooklyn, New York. Buried in Glenwood Cemetery, Brooklyn, New York.

BIOGRAPHICAL: Attended the Dutch school at Flatbush, New York. After graduation, engaged in agriculture and milling. Appointed County Clerk of Kings County by Governor Clinton in 1750; also became Clerk of the Board of Supervisors, and held both positions until his death. Member of the Colonial Assembly, 1761-1775, and deputy to the provincial convention in April, 1775. Member of Continental Congress, 1775. Very little is known of the life of this early patriot. No evidence of Masonic membership or activity has been found.

CARTER BRAXTON (VIRGINIA)

SIGNER OF THE DECLARATION OF INDEPENDENCE. Born September 10, 1736, at "Newington", near King & Queen Court House, Virginia. Died October 10, 1797, in Richmond, Virginia. Buried at "Chericoke", King William County, Virginia.

BIOGRAPHICAL: Graduate College of William and Mary, 1755. Went to England after graduation, and returned to America in 1760. Member of Virginia House of Burgesses, 1761-1771, and in 1775; member, Virginia Council of State, 1786-1791, and from 1794 until his death. Member, Second Continental Congress, August 15, 1775, to August 11, 1776. There is no evidence that he was a Mason.

PIERCE BUTLER (SOUTH CAROLINA)

SIGNER OF THE CONSTITUTION OF THE UNITED STATES. Born July 11, 1744, in County Carlow, Ireland. Died February 15, 1822, in Philadelphia, Pennsylvania. Buried in Christ Churchyard, Philadelphia, Pennsylvania.

BIOGRAPHICAL: Came to America as an officer in the British Army; was stationed in Boston; resigned prior to the Revolutionary War and settled in Charleston, South Carolina. Major in South Carolina Militia, 1777-1781. Member, Continental Congress, 1787-88, and of the United States Senate from January 22, 1789, to October 25, 1796, when he resigned; elected again to the Senate to fill a vacancy caused by the death of John Ewing Colhoun, and served from November 4, 1802, until his resignation, November 21, 1804. Member of the Constitutional Convention of 1787. No evidence of Masonic membership or activity has been found.

CHARLES CARROLL (of Carrollton) (MARYLAND)

SIGNER OF THE DECLARATION OF INDEPENDENCE. Born September 19, 1737, in Annapolis, Maryland. (W. Eugene Rice, in *Masonic Membership of the Signers of the Declaration of Independence,* gives the date as September 20, 1737.) Died November 14, 1832, in Baltimore, Maryland. Buried in the Chapel of Doughoregan Manor, near Ellicott City, Maryland.

BIOGRAPHICAL: The last survivor of the fifty-six immortal patriots who signed the Declaration. Studied law in France and England. Member, Continental Congress, July 4, 1776, to November 15, 1776; and from February 15, 1777, to 1778, when he resigned. Again elected in 1780, but declined to serve. Served on the Committee that visited Valley Forge to investigate complaints against General Washington. Continental Commissioner to Canada in 1776; member, Board of War, 1776-77. Member, Maryland Senate, 1777 to 1800. United States Senator, March 4, 1789, to November 30, 1792. Retired to private life in 1801.

MASONIC: "He was not a Mason, being the only Roman Catholic among the signers." (Roth, p. 156) "Not a Freemason." (Case) Brother J. W. Smith, Curator of the Masonic Museum of the Grand Lodge of Maryland, writes on February 11,

1957: "The original Charles Carroll of Carrollton was not a Mason so far as I have been able to discover, although some have said that he was a Mason." Carroll was present, July 4, 1828, when the "first stone" of the B. & O. Railroad was laid with Masonic ceremony. He participated in the parade and exercises. Not a Mason himself, several of his Carroll cousins were.

SAMUEL CHASE (MARYLAND)
SIGNER OF THE ARTICLES OF ASSOCIATION AND THE DECLARATION OF INDEPENDENCE. Born April 17, 1741, in Princess Anne, Somerset County, Maryland. Died June 19, 1811, in Washington, D. C. Buried in Old St. Paul's Cemetery, Baltimore, Maryland.

BIOGRAPHICAL: Studied law; admitted to the bar in 1761 when only 20 years old. Began practice in Annapolis, Maryland. Member, General Assembly of Maryland, 1764-1784; Judge of Baltimore Criminal Court, 1788, and Judge of General Court of Maryland, 1791. Commissioner to Canada in 1774 to induce the Canadians to join in the revolution against Great Britain. Member, Continental Congress, 1774-78, and 1784 and 1785. Appointed by Washington as Associate Justice of the Supreme Court of the United States in 1796; served until his death in 1811, surviving impeachment proceedings filed against him in 1804 because of his arbitrary decisions in cases involving the Alien and Sedition Acts. Acquitted of all charges, March 5, 1805. There is no evidence that he was a Mason.

ABRAHAM CLARK (NEW JERSEY)
SIGNER OF THE DECLARATION OF INDEPENDENCE. Born February 15, 1726, near Elizabethtown (now Elizabeth), Essex County, New Jersey. Died September 15, 1794, in Rahway, New Jersey. Buried in Cemetery of Rahway Presbyterian Church, Rahway, New Jersey.

BIOGRAPHICAL: Attended private schools; studied law but never practiced. Active New Jersey state legislator before the Revolution. Member, Continental Congress, on three different occasions: June 22, 1776, to December 1, 1778; December 25, 1779, to November 5, 1783; November 2, 1787, to March 4, 1789. Member, United States Congress, March 4, 1791, and served until his death. There is no evidence that he was a Mason.

WILLIAM CLINGAN (PENNSYLVANIA)
SIGNER OF THE ARTICLES OF CONFEDERATION. Born, probably in Chester County, Pennsylvania. Died May 9, 1790, presumably in Chester County, Pennsylvania. Buried in Upper Octorara Burial Grounds, Chester County, Pennsylvania.

BIOGRAPHICAL: Member, Continental Congress in 1777-79, and one of the first signers of these Articles in 1778. See the *History of Upper Octorara Presbyterian Church,* published by J. Smith Futhey, Philadelphia, 1870: *p. 136:* Clingan is mentioned as one of many men "who occupied positions of influence in the state." Justice of the Peace from 1757 to 1786, and President of the County Courts, 1780-86. He left no descendants, and thus far no known portrait of him has been discovered. *p. 163:* Died May 9, 1790, at "advanced age" and buried in Upper Octorara Presbyterian Church Cemetery, together with his wife. Burial listed in ninth row, but no stone marks the grave at this time. Another of our early American patriots about whom very little is known. No evidence of Masonic membership or activity has been found.

GEORGE CLINTON (NEW YORK)

GENERAL OFFICER IN THE CONTINENTAL ARMY. Born July 26, 1739, in Little Britain, Ulster (now Orange) County, New York. Died April 20, 1812, in Washington, D. C. Buried in Congressional Cemetery, Washington, D. C.; reinterment in the First Dutch Reformed Church Cemetery, Kingston, New York, in May, 1908.

BIOGRAPHICAL: Studied law; admitted to the bar; practiced in Little Britain. Member, Continental Congress, May 15, 1775 to July 8, 1776, when he was ordered by Washington to take the field as Brigadier General of Militia. Elected first Governor of New York, April 20, 1777, serving to 1795. Re-elected, 1801-1804. Brigadier General, Continental Army, March 25, 1777, to November 3, 1783. Commanded forces in the actions at Forts Clinton and Montgomery, October 6, 1777. Brevet Major General, September 30, 1783. Vice President of the United States in 1805 during Jefferson's second term. Re-elected under President Madison and died in office. President, New York Society of the Cincinnati, 1794.

MASONIC: Not a Mason, although confused with his nephew, George, a member of Warren Lodge No. 17 of Little Britain, and representative to the Grand Lodge of New York, 1800.

GEORGE CLYMER (PENNSYLVANIA)

SIGNER OF THE DECLARATION OF INDEPENDENCE AND THE CONSTITUTION OF THE UNITED STATES. Born March 16, 1739, in Philadelphia, Pennsylvania. (W. Eugene Rice, in *Masonic Membership of the Signers of the Declaration of Independence*, gives the date as January 24, 1739.) Died January 23, 1813, at "Sommerseat", Morrisville, Pennsylvania. Buried in Friends Graveyard, Trenton, New Jersey.

BIOGRAPHICAL: Educated in the public schools of Philadelphia; entered into business there. Member, Continental Congress, 1776-78 and 1780-83. Consistent advocate of independence for the colonies, but was not a radical. Member, Federal Constitutional Convention in 1787. Member, First United States Congress, March 4, 1789, to March 3, 1791. Appointed one of the Commissioners to assist in negotiating treaty with the Cherokees and the Creeks in Georgia. This was his last public duty. Captain of Volunteer company at the outbreak of the war. Served in Pennsylvania House of Representatives, 1785-88, and was Collector of Excise Duties in 1791. Collection of these duties led to the "Whiskey Rebellion", 1794. "He never sought nor bought office, and was never heard to speak ill of any one." (DAB) There is no record of his having been a Mason.

DAVID COBB (MASSACHUSETTS)

AIDE-DE-CAMP TO GENERAL WASHINGTON. Born September 17, 1748, in Attleborough, Massachusetts. Died April 17, 1830, in Taunton, Massachusetts. Buried in Plain Burying Ground, Taunton, Massachusetts.

BIOGRAPHICAL: Harvard graduate, 1766; studied medicine in Boston and afterward practiced in Taunton, Massachusetts. Surgeon of Marshall's Massachusetts Regiment, May to December, 1775; Lieutenant Colonel of Jackson's Continental Regiment, January 12, 1777; regiment designated 16th Massachusetts, July 23, 1780; transferred to 9th Massachusetts, January 1, 1781; Aide-de-Camp to General Washington, June 15, 1781, to January 7, 1783; Lieutenant-Colonel Commandant, 5th Massachusetts, January 7, 1783; Brevet Brigadier General, September 30, 1783, and served to

November, 1783. Major General, Militia, 1786, and served with distinction during Shay's Rebellion. Member of Third United States Congress, March 4, 1793, to March 3, 1795. Moved to Maine in 1796, and served as State Senator in 1802, being President during this period; Lieutenant Governor in 1809. Chief Justice of the Hancock County Court of Common Pleas. Returned to Taunton in 1817, and died there. Member, Society of the Cincinnati. No evidence of Masonic membership or activity.

JOHN COLLINS (RHODE ISLAND)

SIGNER OF THE ARTICLES OF CONFEDERATION. Born June 8, 1717, in Newport, Rhode Island. Died March 4, 1795, in Newport, Rhode Island. Buried on his farm, "Brenton Neck", near Newport, Rhode Island.

BIOGRAPHICAL: Member, Continental Congress, 1778-1783; elected to the First United States Congress, but did not take his seat. Rhode Island fought vigorously, up to 1790, against calling a Convention to decide on entering the Federal Union, but on January 17 of that year it sanctioned such a call by a majority of one vote in the Senate. This vote was cast by Collins. Governor of Rhode Island, 1786-1790.

MASONIC: A petition to the General Assembly of his Majesty's Colony of Rhode Island, requesting permission to conduct a lottery to raise funds for the building of a Masons Hall in Newport, is signed by one John Collins of Newport, but no other evidence of Masonic membership has been found. *(GL Proc. Mass. 1733-1792*, p. 467 of the Appendix) The Grand Lodge of Massachusetts has no papers or records to prove that this John Collins is the one mentioned in these Proceedings.

THOMAS CONWAY (FRANCE)

GENERAL OFFICER IN THE CONTINENTAL ARMY. Born February 27, 1733, in County Kerry, Ireland. Died about 1800. No information found as to place of burial.

BIOGRAPHICAL: Brigadier General, Continental Army, May 13, 1777; Inspector General, with the rank of Major General, December 13, 1777; resigned, April 28, 1778. The story of the "Conway Cabal" adds further information about his role in American history. In 1793 he was back in France, where he espoused the Royalist cause, and was compelled to flee the country. He died in exile. There is no record of his having been a Mason.

STEPHEN CRANE (NEW JERSEY)

SIGNER OF THE ARTICLES OF ASSOCIATION. Born July, 1709, in Elizabethtown, New Jersey. Died July 1, 1780, in Elizabeth, New Jersey. Buried in First Presbyterian Church Cemetery, Elizabeth, New Jersey.

BIOGRAPHICAL: Served as Sheriff of Essex County under George the Second. Chosen by Elizabethtown Associates to go to England to lay a petition before the King in 1743. Judge of the Court of Common Pleas during the agitation over the Stamp Act. Member, State General Assembly, 1766-1773, and served as Speaker in 1771. Mayor of Elizabethtown, 1772-74; Member, Continental Congress, 1774-76; Member of State Council in 1776, 1777, and 1779. No evidence of membership or activity in the Masonic Fraternity in the Grand Lodge of New Jersey records.

THOMAS CUSHING (MASSACHUSETTS)
SIGNER OF THE ARTICLES OF ASSOCIATION. Born March 24, 1725, in Boston, Massachusetts. Died February 28, 1788, in Boston, Massachusetts. Buried in Granary Burial Ground, Boston, Massachusetts.

BIOGRAPHICAL: Attended Boston Latin School, and graduated from Harvard College in 1744; studied law, admitted to the bar, and commenced practice in Boston. Member, Provincial Assembly, 1761-1774, and served as Speaker. Commissary General of Massachusetts in 1775. Member, Continental Congress, 1774-76, but declined to be a candidate for re-election in 1779. Lieutenant Governor of Massachusetts, 1780-88, and Acting Governor in 1785. Delegate to the State Constitutional Convention which ratified the Federal Constitution in 1788. One of the founders of the American Academy of Arts and Sciences. No evidence of Masonic membership or activity.

FRANCIS DANA (MASSACHUSETTS)
SIGNERS OF THE ARTICLES OF CONFEDERATION. Born June 13, 1743, in Charlestown, Massachusetts. Died April 25, 1811, in Cambridge, Massachusetts. Buried in Old Cambridge Cemetery, Cambridge, Massachusetts.

BIOGRAPHICAL: Harvard graduate, 1762; studied law and began practice in Boston in 1767. Member of Sons of Liberty, and of the Continental Congress in 1776-78 and in 1784. Dana spent two years in England endeavoring to adjust the differences between Great Britain and the American Colonies; elected, September 28, 1779, secretary to accompany John Adams, who was appointed a Commissioner to negotiate a treaty of peace with Great Britain and a treaty of commerce with Holland. Commissioned, December 19, 1780, as duly accredited Minister to Russia, but was never received as such. Judge, Supreme Court of Massachusetts, 1785-1791, and Chief Justice, November 29, 1791, and served for fifteen years. Presidential elector in 1788, 1792, 1800, and 1808. A founder of the American Academy of Arts and Sciences. No evidence of Masonic membership or activity.

SILAS DEANE (CONNECTICUT)
SIGNER OF THE ARTICLES OF ASSOCIATION. Born December 24, 1737, in Groton, Connecticut. Died September 23, 1789, on board ship sailing from Gravesend, England, to Boston. Buried in Deal, on the Kentish coast, England.

BIOGRAPHICAL: Yale graduate, 1758; studied law, admitted to the bar in 1761, and began practice in Wethersfield, Connecticut. Member, Continental Congress, 1774-76. In March, 1776, Deane was selected to go to France, the first American to represent the united Colonies abroad. With Franklin and Arthur Lee, he successfully concluded two treaties with France, February 6, 1778, one of commerce and one providing for an offensive and defensive alliance. ". . . personally secured the services of Lafayette, DeKalb, and other foreign officers, for which he was accused of extravagance, and was recalled in 1777 and investigated by Congress; returned to France to procure transcripts of his transactions there, and found that the publication of some of his confidential dispatches had embittered that Government against him, and he was compelled to go to Holland, and thence to Great Britain, greatly impoverished; died on board ship . . . in 1842 Congress vindicated his memory by deciding that a considerable sum of money was due him, which was paid to his heirs." (BDAC, p. 1069) No evidence of Masonic membership or activity has been found.

PHILIPPE HUBERT DE PREUDHOMME DE BORRE (FRANCE)

GENERAL OFFICER IN THE CONTINENTAL ARMY. Born September 18, 1717, in the Parish of Saint-Servais, in Liege. Died—the date and place of his death have not been found. Buried—place not known.

BIOGRAPHICAL: An officer in the French Army, with thirty-five years of European service. Brigadier General, Continental Army, December 1, 1776; resigned, September 14, 1777, when a Congressional investigation was proposed into his conduct at the Brandywine. Left Charleston, South Carolina, for France, January 20, 1778, and served in the French Army until, April, 1780. "He was unpopular in the army, and totally unfit to command American troops." (Appleton) No information on Masonic membership or activity has been found.

JOHN PHILIP DeHAAS (PENNSYLVANIA)

GENERAL OFFICER IN THE CONTINENTAL ARMY. Born about 1735 in Holland. Died June 3, 1786, in Philadelphia, Pennsylvania. Buried, presumably in Philadelphia. (See *Pennsylvania Magazine of History and Biography*, Vol. 27, p. 50—excerpts from Day Book of David Evans: "June 4, 1786—Estate Gen. J. Philip DeHaas, making a mahogany coffin and case for deceased, £11.")

BIOGRAPHICAL: Emigrated to America in 1750, and settled in Lancaster County, Pennsylvania. Major of Pennsylvania Provincials in 1775; Colonel, 1st Pennsylvania Battalion, January 22, 1776; Colonel, 2nd Pennsylvania, October 25, 1776, to rank from January 22, 1776; Brigadier General, Continental Army, February 21, 1777, to November 3, 1783; went to Philadelphia in 1779 and rendered no subsequent service. No information of Masonic membership or activity has been found.

JOHN DeHART (NEW JERSEY)

SIGNER OF THE ARTICLES OF ASSOCIATION. Born in 1728, in Elizabethtown (now Elizabeth), New Jersey. Died June 1, 1795, in Elizabeth, New Jersey. Buried in St. John's Churchyard, Elizabeth, New Jersey.

BIOGRAPHICAL: Studied law; admitted to the bar, and practiced his profession. Member, Continental Congress, July 3, 1774, until his resignation on November 22, 1775. Re-elected February 14, 1776, but resigned June 13, 1776. Elected Chief Justice of the Supreme Court of New Jersey, September 4, 1776, and his declination of that office was accepted February 5, 1777. Mayor of Elizabethtown under the revised charter and served from November, 1789, until his death.

MASONIC: The Grand Lodge of New Jersey has no record of his membership or activity in the Masonic fraternity. See *Freemasonry in Pennsylvania*, Barrett and Sachse, Vol. 1, p. 142, where one of this name is mentioned: "Tues. Jan. 12, 1781—Extra Lodge—Lodge 2 A Y M under Provincial Grand Lodge.—Masters Lodge open'd when the following Brethren VIZ: ... DeHart ... has now taken the Sublime Degree as Master Masons & accordingly returned & Gave Thanks". There appears to be no information prior to this date. The index, however, identifies this DeHart as Jacob, with record of his application, approval, and receiving the three degrees.

FRIEDRICH WILHELM DE WOEDTKE (PRUSSIA)

GENERAL OFFICER IN THE CONTINENTAL ARMY. Born in 1740, in Prussia. Died July 28, 1776, of illness while in the service, at Lake George, New York. "Buried with military honors due his rank." (Lossing) Buried probably in the Ticonderoga-Lake George area of New York State.

BIOGRAPHICAL: Served many years in the army of Frederick the Great, attaining the rank of Major. Came to America on the recommendation of Benjamin Franklin. Brigadier General, Continental Army, March 16, 1776; ordered to join the Northern Army under General Schuyler. DeWoedtke was apparently with the American Army when it retreated from Canada to Crown Point in June, 1776. General Gates arrived at Crown Point on July 5 to take command. DeWoedtke attended a Council of War at which it was agreed the army should retire to Fort Ticonderoga, sending all sick to Fort George. It is possible that DeWoedtke went to Lake George because he himself was already ill. General Gates' report to Washington, dated from "Tyconderoga, August 6, 1776 . . . Brigadier General, Baron de Woodtke, died at Lake George, the Beginning of last week. He was buried with the Honours due to his Rank . . ." (note: August 6, 1776, fell on Tuesday. "The beginning of last week" would be Sunday, July 28). No evidence of Masonic membership or activity.

WILLIAM HENRY DRAYTON (SOUTH CAROLINA)
SIGNER OF THE ARTICLES OF CONFEDERATION. Born in September, 1742, at Drayton Hall, near Charleston, South Carolina. Died September 3, 1779, in Philadelphia, Pennsylvania. Buried in Christ Church Cemetery, Philadelphia, Pennsylvania.

BIOGRAPHICAL: Attended Westminster School and Balliol College, Oxford, England, returning to South Carolina in 1764. Studied law; admitted to the bar. President of the Council of Safety in 1775; Chief Justice in 1776. Member, Continental Congress, 1778, and served until his death. Brigadier General James Hogun was a pallbearer at his funeral. Unusual record of service during the Revolution. A member of all the important Revolutionary bodies in the province, and chairman of several. Pursued the American course with zeal and energy. Except for Gouverneur Morris he was a member of more committees during this period than any other individual. ". . . visited England in 1770 and was appointed by King George III privy councilor for the Province of South Carolina; while on his way home from England he was appointed assistant judge, but took such an active part in the pre-Revolutionary movement that he was deprived of both positions." (BDAC, p. 1102). No evidence of Masonic activity or membership.

JAMES DUANE (NEW YORK)
SIGNER OF THE ARTICLES OF ASSOCIATION AND THE ARTICLES OF CONFEDERATION. Born February 6, 1733, in New York, New York. Died February 1, 1797, in Duanesburg, Schenectady County, New York. Buried beneath Christ Church in Duanesburg, New York.

BIOGRAPHICAL: Studied law; admitted to the bar, August 3, 1754. Clerk of the Chancery Court, 1765; Attorney General of New York State, 1767. Member, Continental Congress, 1774-1784. Chosen a member of the Annapolis Commercial Convention in 1786, but did not attend. President Washington appointed him the first Federal Judge for the District of New York in September, 1789; held this office until retirement on account of ill health in March, 1794. Mayor of New York City, February 4, 1784, to September, 1789; State Senator, 1782-85, and 1788-1790. No evidence of Masonic activity or membership.

PHILIPPE CHARLES JEAN BAPTISTE TRONSON DU COUDRAY (FRANCE)

GENERAL OFFICER IN THE CONTINENTAL ARMY. Born September 8, 1738, in Reims, France. Drowned in Schuylkill River, Philadelphia, Pennsylvania, September 16, 1777. Buried: "Yesterday was buried Monsieur du Coudray, a French officer of Artillery, who was lately made an Inspector-General of Artillery and Military Manufactures, with the rank of Major-General. . . . He was reputed the most learned and promising officer in France. He was carried into the Romish Chapel (St. Mary's Roman Catholic Church) and buried in the yard of that church." (Diary of John Adams for September 18, 1777). Congress in a body attended the Funeral Mass.

BIOGRAPHICAL: Major General and Inspector General of Ordnance and Military Manufactories, Continental Army, August 11, 1777. No information concerning Masonic membership or activity.

WILLIAM DUER (NEW YORK)

SIGNER OF THE ARTICLES OF CONFEDERATION. Born March 18, 1747, in Devonshire, England. Died April 18, 1799, in New York, New York. Buried in the family vault under the old church of St. Thomas; reinterment in Jamaica, Long Island, New York.

BIOGRAPHICAL: Attended Eton College, England. Served as Aide-de-Camp to Lord Clive, Governor General of India, in 1765. Emigrated to America in 1768; settled in Fort Miller, Washington County, New York. Built the first saw and grist mills there; erected the first cotton mill in what is now Paterson, New Jersey, and also built a cotton mill in Westchester County, New York. Member, Continental Congress, 1777-78. Assisted Alexander Hamilton in organizing the United States Treasury Department in 1789 and 1790. Appointed Justice of the Peace, by royal authority, on July 1, 1773; member, Provincial Congress, 1776 and 1777; appointed Judge of Court of Common Pleas in 1777 and re-appointed in 1778; served as first Judge of Charlotte (now Washington) County, New York. Member, State Assembly, 1786. No evidence of Masonic membership or activity.

LOUIS LE BEGUE DE PRESLE DUPORTAIL (FRANCE)

GENERAL OFFICER IN THE CONTINENTAL ARMY. Born November 14, 1743, in the parish of Saint-Salomon, at Pithiviers, Loiret, France. Died at sea in 1802, having embarked from Philadelphia for France.

BIOGRAPHICAL: Colonel, Engineers, July 8, 1777; Chief of Engineers, July 22, 1777; Brigadier General, Engineers, November 17, 1777; the Engineer in charge of laying out the encampment and fortifications at Valley Forge; appointed Commandant of Corps of Engineers and Sappers and Miners, May 11, 1779; taken prisoner at Charleston, May 12, 1780, and on parole to November, 1780; Major General, Chief Engineer, November 16, 1781; retired, October 10, 1783. Returned to France in the fall of 1781, and was Marechal-de-Camp (Major General), March 9, 1788, and Secretary of State for War from November 16, 1790 to December 2, 1791. Promoted to Lieutenant General January 13, 1792. Being of the nobility, he was suspected of disloyalty to the revolutionary regime, and went into hiding. Later escaped to America and purchased a farm in Bridgeport, Pennsylvania. Embarked for France in 1802 when Napoleon appealed to all former officers of the Royal Army to return to the colors. It is said he died during the passage and was buried at sea. No information on Masonic membership or activity.

ELIPHALET DYER (CONNECTICUT)

SIGNER OF THE ARTICLES OF ASSOCIATION. Born September 14, 1721, in Windham, Connecticut. Died May 13, 1807, in Windham, Connecticut. Buried in Windham Cemetery, Windham, Connecticut.

BIOGRAPHICAL: Yale graduate, 1740; Town Clerk; Captain of Militia in 1745; studied law, admitted to the bar in 1746, and began practice in Windham. Delegate to the Stamp Act Congress of 1765. Member, Continental Congress, 1774-79, and 1780-83. Colonel, Connecticut Militia, 1775 and 1776, and Brigadier General, Connecticut Militia, December 1776, to May, 1777; Lieutenant Colonel, Connecticut troops in French and Indian War, and commanded a regiment in the Canadian expedition of 1758. Declined appointment as Brigadier General in the Continental Army in 1776, considering he could serve the cause better in Congress. Member, Connecticut General Assembly, 1747, 1749, 1752, and 1753, and again from 1756 to 1784. A prominent state legislator; Judge of the Superior Court of Connecticut, 1766-1793, serving as Chief Judge from 1789 to 1793. There is no record of his being a Freemason.

MATTHIAS ALEXIS DE LA ROCHEFERMOY (commonly known as General Fermoy) (FRANCE)

GENERAL OFFICER IN THE CONTINENTAL ARMY. Born in 1737 in the West Indies. Died—date and place of death not known. Buried—d'Auberteuil says: "He died after retiring from service", but gives no date or place. (It was probably prior to 1782).

BIOGRAPHICAL: Brigadier General, Continental Army, November 5, 1776. In December, 1777, he applied for promotion to rank of Major General, which Congress refused. Displeased, he asked for permission to resign, and request was granted January 31, 1778. Later left this country. It is said he was a native of the West Indies, and it is thought he returned there. Tradition states he crossed the Delaware River in the same boat as Washington on December 25, 1776. No information on Masonic membership or activity.

WILLIAM FEW (GEORGIA)

SIGNER OF THE CONSTITUTION OF THE UNITED STATES. Born June 8, 1748, near Baltimore, Maryland. Died July 16, 1828, at Fishkill-on-the-Hudson, at the home of his son-in-law, Major Albert Chrystie. Buried in Reformed Dutch Church Cemetery, Fishkill Landing, Dutchess County, New York.

BIOGRAPHICAL: Moved to Orange County, North Carolina, in 1758. Studied law, admitted to the bar, and began practice in Augusta, Georgia, 1776. Member, Continental Congress, 1780-82, and 1785-88. United States Senator, March 4, 1789, to March 3, 1793; unsuccessful candidate for re-election in 1795. Member of the Federal Constitutional Convention in 1787. Member, General Assembly of Georgia, 1777, 1779, 1783, and 1793, and of the Executive Council in 1777 and 1778. An original Trustee for establishing the University of Georgia, 1785. Judge of the Circuit Court of Georgia, 1794-97. Moved to New York City in 1799, and served in State Assembly there from 1802 to 1805. United States Commissioner of Loans, 1804. Director of the Manhattan Bank, 1804-14, and President in 1814.

MASONIC: A card in the Library of the House of the Temple, in Washington, D. C., states he was apparently a member of Solomon's Lodge No. 1, Savannah, Georgia, and makes reference to *Early and Historic Freemasonry of Georgia,* by W. B. Clarke, p. 99, in which Few is mentioned but not claimed to be a Mason.

PEREGRINE FITZHUGH (VIRGINIA)

LIEUTENANT COLONEL AND AIDE-DE-CAMP TO GENERAL WASHINGTON. Born May 10, 1759, at "Rousby Hall," Calvert County, Maryland. Died November 28, 1811, in Sodus Point, New York. Buried in Sodus Point; later his body and gravestone were removed to the Old Burial Grounds, on the banks of Lake Ontario, Sodus, New York.

BIOGRAPHICAL: Cornet, 3rd Continental Dragoons, June 16, 1778; Lieutenant, ——1778; taken prisoner at Tappan, September 28, 1778; exchanged, October 25, 1780; was also Captain, 3d Continental Dragoons in 1781. Aide to General Washington, July 2, 1781, to December 23, 1781. Moved to Geneva, New York, in 1799, and to Sodus Point in 1803. Very little is known of this patriot's life. He was an intimate friend of Washington. Member, Society of the Cincinnati. No evidence of Masonic membership or activity.

THOMAS FITZSIMONS (PENNSYLVANIA)

SIGNER OF THE CONSTITUTION OF THE UNITED STATES. Born in 1741, in County Tubber, Wicklow, Ireland. Died August 26, 1811, in Philadelphia, Pennsylvania. Buried (traditional) in St. Mary's Roman Catholic Churchyard, Philadelphia, Pennsylvania.

BIOGRAPHICAL: Merchant in Philadelphia; served in Pennsylvania Assembly for many years. Commanded a company of volunteer home guards during the Revolutionary War. Signer of the Constitution of the United States. Pennsylvania's only Catholic signer of the Constitution. Member, Continental Congress, 1782 and 1783. Member, First, Second, and Third United States Congresses, March 4, 1789, to March 3, 1795; unsuccessful candidate for re-election in 1794 to the Fourth Congress. Delegate to the Federal Constitutional Convention in 1787. Member of the Hibernian Society, and contributed largely to the erection of St. Augustine's Church in Philadelphia; Trustee of the University of Pennsylvania. No evidence of Masonic membership or activity.

WILLIAM FLOYD (NEW YORK)

SIGNER OF THE ARTICLES OF ASSOCIATION AND THE DECLARATION OF INDEPENDENCE. Born December 17, 1734, in Setauket, Long Island, New York. Died August 4, 1821, in Westernville, Oneida County, New York. Buried in Presbyterian Church Cemetery, Westernville, New York.

BIOGRAPHICAL: Colonel and Major General, New York Militia. Prominent in ante-Revolutionary movements; and prominent in New York politics after the war, New York State Senator, 1777-78; and 1784-88, and again in 1808. Member, Continental Congress, 1774-77, and 1778-1783. Member, First United States Congress, March 4, 1789, to March 3, 1791; unsuccessful candidate for re-election in 1790. Presidential elector in 1792, 1800, 1804, and 1820. There is no record of his having been a Mason.

NATHANIEL FOLSOM (NEW HAMPSHIRE)

SIGNER OF THE ARTICLES OF ASSOCIATION. Born September 18, 1726, in Exeter, New Hampshire. Died May 26, 1790, in Exeter, New Hampshire. Buried in Winter Street Cemetery, Exeter, New Hampshire.

BIOGRAPHICAL: Active in military affairs; captain of a regiment in the French and Indian war; commanded the Fourth Regiment of troops at the outbreak of the Revolutionary War. Brigadier General of New Hampshire troops sent to Massachusetts, and served during the siege of Boston; Major General, New Hampshire Militia, May to August, 1775. Member, Continental Congress, 1774-75, and 1777-1780. Chief Justice, Court of Common Pleas.

MASONIC: There is no record of his membership in the Masonic fraternity in the Grand Lodge of Massachusetts. One of this same name appears in the *Proceedings of the Grand Lodge of New Hampshire*, Vol. 1, p. 1, covering the origin and proceedings of the Grand Lodge of New Hampshire: "At a meeting of the Deputies from the several Lodges in the State of New Hampshire, assembled at Portsmouth the eighth day of July, in the year of Masonry, 5789, Present . . . Nathaniel Folsom, Deputy from St. John's Lodge, Portsmouth, and elected Grand Treasurer." This same man still appears in Grand Lodge records, January 26, 1803, well after the death of the Folsom covered by this short sketch.

CHRISTOPHER GADSDEN (SOUTH CAROLINA)
GENERAL OFFICER IN THE CONTINENTAL ARMY AND SIGNER OF THE ARTICLES OF ASSOCIATION. Born February 16, 1724, in Charleston, South Carolina. Died August 28, 1805, in Charleston, South Carolina. Buried in St. Philip's Churchyard, Charleston, South Carolina.

BIOGRAPHICAL: Educated in England. Returned to America in 1740 and entered business in Philadelphia. One of the earliest opponents of Great Britain in South Carolina and a firm supporter of the Revolution. Delegate to the Stamp Act Congress, 1765. Member First Continental Congress, 1774-76. Colonel, 1st South Carolina, June 17, 1775; Brigadier General, Continental Army, September 16, 1776; resigned, October 2, 1777; taken prisoner at Charleston, May 12, 1780; exchanged in June, 1781. Lieutenant Governor, South Carolina, 1778-1780. Elected Governor in 1781, but declined. No information on Masonic membership or activity.

JOSEPH GALLOWAY (PENNSYLVANIA)
SIGNER OF THE ARTICLES OF ASSOCIATION. Born about 1729, in West River, Anne Arundel County, Maryland. Died August 29, 1803, in Watford, Hertfordshire, England. Buried in Churchyard of Watford, Hertfordshire, England.

BIOGRAPHICAL: Studied law, admitted to the bar, and practiced in Philadelphia; intimate with Benjamin Franklin. Member, Colonial House of Representatives, 1757-1775, serving as Speaker, 1766-1774. "One of the most popular of the leaders in Pennsylvania when the war of the Revolution broke out . . . in 1776 he abandoned the Whigs, and became the most virulent and proscriptive Loyalist of the time." (Lossing) Member, Continental Congress, 1774-75. Galloway signed the Articles of Association or Non-Importation Agreement, but opposed independence, remaining loyal to the King. He joined the British Army in New York under General Howe in December, 1776; moved to England in 1778, the same year the General Assembly of Pennsylvania convicted him of high treason and confiscated his estates, valued at about £40,000. Died in England after twenty-five years of exile. Member of American Philosophical Society, and Vice President, 1767-1775.

MASONIC: A Joseph Galloway was admitted as Master Mason in Washington Lodge No. 59, Pennsylvania, on June 14, 1796. This is no doubt another Galloway.

A review of the dates above shows that Galloway, the subject of this short sketch, was in England at that time.

NATHANIEL GORHAM (MASSACHUSETTS)

SIGNER OF THE CONSTITUTION OF THE UNITED STATES. Born May 27, 1738, in Charlestown, Massachusetts. Died June 11, 1796, in Charlestown, Massachusetts. Buried in Phipps Street Cemetery, Charlestown, Massachusetts.

BIOGRAPHICAL: Attended public schols and engaged in mercantile pursuits. State legislator, and took an active part in public affairs from the beginning of the Revolutionary War period. Member, Provincial Congress in 1774 and 1775; member, Board of War, 1778-1781. Member, Continental Congress, 1782, 1783, 1785-87, and served as President from June 6, 1786, to February 2, 1787. Delegate to the Federal Constitutional Convention of 1787, and also delegate to State Constitutional Convention which ratified the Federal Constitution in 1788. Judge, Common Pleas Court, July 1, 1785, until his resignation, May 31, 1796. No evidence of Masonic membership or activity has been found.

WILLIAM GRAYSON (VIRGINIA)

ASSISTANT SECRETARY AND AIDE-DE-CAMP TO GENERAL WASHINGTON. Born in 1740, in Prince William County, Virginia. (*Encyclopedia of Virginia Biography* gives the date as 1736.) Died March 12, 1790, in Dumfries, Virginia, while on his way to Congress. Buried on the old family estate at Belle Air, near Dumfries, Virginia.

BIOGRAPHICAL: Educated at University of Oxford, in England, and graduated from there; studied law at the Temple in London. Attended College of Philadelphia (now the University of Pennsylvania) and practiced law in Dumfries. Assistant Secretary to General Washington, June 21, 1776, to August 24, 1776. Lieutenant Colonel and Aide-de-Camp, August 24, 1776, to January 11, 1777. Colonel of one of the Sixteen Additional Continental Regiments, January 11, 1777; distinguished himself at the Battle of Monmouth; retired, April 22, 1779. Appointed a Commissioner to treat with Sir William Howe respecting prisoners while the Continental Army was at Valley Forge. Commissioner of the Board of War, December 7, 1779; resigned, September 10, 1781. Member, Continental Congress, 1784. Delegate to the Virginia Convention of 1788 for the adoption of the Federal Constitution, which he opposed. United States Senator, March 4, 1789, until his death. Member, Society of the Cincinnati. No evidence of Masonic membership or activity.

BUTTON GWINNETT (GEORGIA)

SIGNER OF THE DECLARATION OF INDEPENDENCE. Born April 1, 1732, in Down Hatherly, Gloucestershire, England. Died May 19, 1777, as a result of a duel with Brigadier General Lachlan McIntosh. Buried (probably) in Old Colonial Cemetery (later named Colonial Park), Savannah, Georgia.

BIOGRAPHICAL: A merchant in Bristol, England; emigrated to the colonies; settled in Charleston, South Carolina, engaging in commercial pursuits; moved to Savannah in 1765 and continued in business; in 1770, moved to St. Catherines Island, Georgia, and engaged in planting. Member, Second Continental Congress, 1776-77. "Acting President and Commander in Chief of Georgia from February to March, 1777; unsuccessful candidate for Governor of Georgia; engaged in a duel, May 16, 1777, with (Brigadier) General Lachlan McIntosh, which resulted in his death, near Savannah, Ga., May 19, 1777." (BDAC, p. 1246)

MASONIC: "There is no record of his having been a Mason." (Roth, p. 62) "No information." (Case) See *Leaves from Georgia Masonry*, published by the Education & Historical Commission of the Grand Lodge of Georgia, F. & A. M., second printing, 1947, p. 31, which states: "That immortal document (Declaration of Independence) was signed by Brother George Walton and Messrs. Hall and Gwinnett."

LYMAN HALL (GEORGIA)
SIGNER OF THE DECLARATION OF INDEPENDENCE. Born April 12, 1724, Wallingford, Connecticut. Died October 19, 1790, in Burke County, Georgia. Buried on his plantation near Shell Bluff, Burke County, Georgia; reinterment in 1848 beneath the monument in front of the Court House in Augusta, honoring Georgia signers of the Declaration of Independence.

BIOGRAPHICAL: Member, Second Continental Congress, 1775-1780. Yale graduate in 1747; ordained a Congregationalist preacher and served in Stratfield, Connecticut. Practiced medicine; moved to South Carolina in 1752, and later to Sunbury, Georgia. Moved back north in 1778 after the fall of Savannah and the confiscation of his property; returned to Savannah in 1782 and again practiced medicine. Served as Governor of Georgia, 1783.

MASONIC: Indications seem to show that he was a member of Solomon's Lodge No. 2, although it cannot be authenticated. "Alleged membership in Solomon's Lodge, Savannah, cannot be proven. His background renders it highly unlikely." (Case) *American Lodge of Research Transactions*, Vol. 2, No. 1 and 2, p. 97: "Dr. Lyman Hall appears to have been a Mason." William L. Boyden, in his *Masonic Presidents, Vice Presidents and Signers,* states: "Bro. Wm. B. Clarke, Savannah, Ga., the authority for early Freemasonry in that State says Hall appears to be a Mason. Records indicate, he says, that Masons living in Hall's neighborhood were members of Solomon's Lodge of Savannah. Minutes of this Lodge from 1734 to 1784 were destroyed by the British during their occupancy of Savannah in the Revolution, except for portions from 1756 to 1757." *Leaves from Georgia Masonry*, published by the Education & Historical Commission of the Grand Lodge of Georgia, F. & A. M., second printing, 1947, p. 31, states: "That immortal document (Declaration of Independence) was signed by Brother George Walton and Messrs. Hall and Gwinnett."

ALEXANDER HAMILTON (NEW YORK)
LIEUTENANT COLONEL AND PRINCIPAL AIDE-DE-CAMP TO GENERAL WASHINGTON, AND SIGNER OF THE CONSTITUTION OF THE UNITED STATES. Born January 11, 1757, on British colony of Nevis, one of the Leeward Islands. Died July 12, 1804, in New York, New York. Buried in Trinity Churchyard, New York, New York.

BIOGRAPHICAL: Emigrated to America in 1772; educated at Elizabethtown, New Jersey, and King's College (now Columbia University), New York. Studied law, admitted to the bar, and practiced in New York. Captain, Provincial Company, New York Artillery, March 14, 1776; principal Aide-de-Camp to General Washington, March 1, 1777, to February 16, 1781, but continued to serve until the end of April; Lieutenant Colonel, July 31, 1781, to command battalion of Light Infantry; served at Yorktown, commanding the American detachments which stormed and captured Redoubt No. 10 on the night of October 14/15; Brevet Colonel, September 30, 1783; Major General and Inspector General, United States Army, July 19, 1798; honorably discharged, June 15, 1800. Member, Continental Congress, 1782, 1783, 1787, and 1788. Member, Annapolis Convention in 1786; served in New York State Assembly, 1787, and member of Federal Constitutional Convention of 1787. Member, Washington's first Cabinet, as Secretary of the Treasury, 1789-1795; returned to New York City and resumed the practice of law. Member, Society of the Cincinnati, succeeding Washington as President-General. Mortally wounded in a duel with Aaron Burr at Weehawken, New Jersey, July 11, and died on July 12, 1804.

MASONIC: All research thus far has turned up no evidence of his activity in or connection with the Masonic Fraternity.

ALEXANDER CONTEE HANSON (MARYLAND)
ASSISTANT SECRETARY TO GENERAL WASHINGTON. Born October 22, 1749, in Annapolis, Maryland. Died January 16, 1806, in Annapolis, Maryland. Buried, possibly in St. Margaret's Churchyard, Anne Arundel County, Maryland.

BIOGRAPHICAL: Assistant Secretary to General Washington, June 21, 1776; toward the close of that year, he resigned on account of ill health. Educated at the College of Philadelphia (now the University of Pennsylvania). He was the son of the President of the Congress of the United States under the Articles of Confederation in 1781-82. No evidence of Masonic membership or activity.

JOHN HANSON (MARYLAND)
SIGNER OF THE ARTICLES OF CONFEDERATION. Born April 3, 1715, at "Mulberry Grove", near Port Tobacco, Charles County, Maryland. Died November 15, 1783, at "Oxon Hill", Prince Georges County, Maryland. Buried at "Oxon Hill", the residence of his nephew.

BIOGRAPHICAL: Member, State House of Delegates for nine terms, from 1757 to 1773. Member of the Stamp Act Congress in New York in 1765. Member, Continental Congress, 1780-83. On November 5, 1781, he was elected the first President of the Continental Congress of the Confederation, and in that capacity tendered General Washington on November 28, 1781, the thanks of Congress for the victory at Yorktown. An active leader and participant all during the Revolutionary War. The resolution authorizing the Maryland delegates to ratify the Articles of Confederation was read in Congress by Hanson on February 12, 1781. The final ratification and signing took place on March 1, 1781. The Federal Union was now an accomplished fact. The colonies were now a nation. While serving as President during the Confederation, Hanson arranged for the appointment of John Adams, Benjamin Franklin, John Jay, and Henry Laurens as Peace Commissioners, and also organized a Cabinet, a Foreign Department, Post Office, appointed a Secretary of State, and arranged for a seal of the United States, first used on September 16, 1782. No evidence of Masonic membership or activity.

BENJAMIN HARRISON (VIRGINIA)
SIGNER OF THE ARTICLES OF ASSOCIATION AND THE DECLARATION OF INDEPENDENCE. Born April 5, 1726, at "Berkeley", Charles City County, Virginia. Died April 24, 1791, in City Point, Prince George County, Virginia. Buried, presumably in Old Westover Church Cemetery. (BDAC, p. 1274). W. Eugene Rice, in *Masonic Membership of the Signers of the Declaration of Independence*, says "probably" buried at "Berkeley", Charles City County, Virginia.

BIOGRAPHICAL: Studied at the College of William and Mary. Member, First and Second Continental Congresses, 1774-78. ". . . as Chairman of the Committee of the Whole House he reported the resolution on June 10, 1776, offered three days before by Richard Henry Lee, declaring the independence of the American Colonies, and reported the Declaration of Independence, of which he was one of the signers, on July 4, 1776, . . ." (BDAC, p. 1274) Governor of Virginia, 1782-84, and prominent in state government affairs both before and after the Revolution, serving in the House of Burgesses, 1749-1775, and in the Virginia revolutionary convention of 1775; member, State House of Delegates, 1776-1782, and 1787-1791, serving as Speaker in 1778-1782, 1785, and 1786; delegate to the state convention for ratification of the Federal Constitution in 1788.

MASONIC: "There is no record of his having been a Mason." (Roth, p. 161) "Not positively identified with another of the name who visited Fredericksburg Lodge, October 10, 1770." (Case)

ROBERT HANSON HARRISON (MARYLAND)

LIEUTENANT COLONEL AND AIDE-DE-CAMP TO GENERAL WASHINGTON. Born in 1745, near Port Tobacco, Charles County, Maryland. Died April 2, 1790, "at his home on the Potomac, some twenty miles from Port Tobacco, Charles County, Maryland." Buried: "There has been much speculation as to the place of his burial, but it seems probable that it is Walnut Landing, near his mother's grave on his father's estate or in the churchyard of Durham Parish where his brother was rector. Some believe that it is in the old Episcopal church cemetery of Port Tobacco. Long ago this burying ground was covered with silt as Port Tobacco Creek filled up so that no grave or stone is now visible."

BIOGRAPHICAL: Educated for the law; established residence in Alexandria, Virginia by 1769. Lieutenant, 3d Virginia, September, 1775; nominated in November, 1777, to Board of War and Ordnance, but declined to serve. Lieutenant Colonel and Aide-de-Camp to General Washington, November 5, 1775, to May 16, 1776; Military Secretary to General Washington, May 16, 1776. Resigned in March, 1781. Appointed a member of the original Supreme Court of the United States by President Washington in 1789, but declined to serve on account of ill health. Appointed Chief Justice of the Supreme Court of Maryland, March 10, 1781, and a member of the Governor's Council. Chancellor for the State of Maryland, October 1, 1789, but declined that office. ". . . it is said that 'no person possessed the confidence of Washington more entirely than Col. Harrison and to few was he indebted for more valuable services.' . . ." Mr. George T. Ness, Jr., has kindly given permission to use much of the information in his copyrighted article, "A Lost Man of Maryland", which appeared in *The Maryland Historical Magazine*, Vol. 35, pp. 315-336. "A man of distinguished talents." (Case) No evidence of Masonic membership or activity.

JOHN HART (NEW JERSEY)

SIGNER OF THE DECLARATION OF INDEPENDENCE. Born July 1, 1707, in Stonington, Connecticut. Died May 11, 1779, on his estate near Hopewell, New Jersey. Buried in the First Baptist Church Cemetery, Hopewell, New Jersey.

BIOGRAPHICAL: Attended private schools; prominent State legislator, serving as Judge of Hunterdon County Courts, 1768-1775; member, New Jersey Provincial

Congress from May 23, 1775, to June 22, 1776; member, Committee of Safety from August 17 to October 4, 1775, and again from October 28, 1775, to January 31, 1776. "When the British invaded New Jersey his estate was devastated, and he was forced to flee to the forests to save his life; returned to his home after the capture of the Hessians by General Washington." (*BDAC*, p. 1277) Member, Continental Congress, June 22 to August 30, 1776. Member, first State General Assembly under the State Constitution in August, 1776, and re-elected in 1777 and 1778.

MASONIC: Brother Harvey C. Whildey, Grand Secretary of the Grand Lodge of New Jersey, advises on November 1, 1957: "Can find no reference whatever to John Hart." "He was a member of American Union Lodge." (from Gould, Vol. 6, p. 411) (Roth, p. 157). (Note: This is no doubt another John Hart, 1760-1800). "No information. His background (Congregationalist, farmer, not convivial) renders it highly unlikely." (Case)

JOHN HARVIE (VIRGINIA)
SIGNER OF THE ARTICLES OF CONFEDERATION. Born in 1742, in Albemarle County, Virginia. Died February 6, 1807, at "Belvidere", near Richmond, Virginia. Buried in Hollywood Cemetery, Richmond, Virginia.

BIOGRAPHICAL: Probably educated in Scotland. Studied law, admitted to the bar, and practiced. Served in the Continental Congress, 1777-79, and prominent as Virginia legislator; Purchasing Agent, Register of Land Office in 1780-1791, and Secretary of the Commonwealth of Virginia, May 19, 1788. "In Congress he was very apt to be found with the minority." (DAB) During the latter years of his life he engaged in building operations in Richmond, and was killed by falling from ladder, February 6, 1807, while inspecting the building of the Gamble House erected by him there. Harvie served as Mayor of Richmond, and Registrar of Land Offices of Virginia when Kentucky, Ohio, and the Great Northwest Territory were within its limits. No evidence of Masonic membership or activity.

WILLIAM HEATH (MASSACHUSETTS)
GENERAL OFFICER IN THE CONTINENTAL ARMY. Born March 2, 1737, in Roxbury, Massachusetts. Died January 24, 1814, in Roxbury, Massachusetts. Buried in Forest Hills Cemetery, Jamaica Plain (suburb of Boston), Massachusetts.

BIOGRAPHICAL: Colonel of a Massachusetts Regiment at Lexington and Concord, April to June 1775; appointed Major General, Massachusetts Militia, June 20, 1775; Brigadier General, Continental Army, June 22, 1775; Major General, Continental Army, August 9, 1776, and served to the close of the war. Member, Society of the Cincinnati.

MASONIC: "No evidence of his Masonic membership or activity." (Case) The Centennial Anniversary program of Washington Lodge, Roxbury, Massachusetts, 1896, p. 171, mentions Roxbury as the home of *Brother* and General William Heath. Card in the office of Grand Secretary of Grand Lodge of Massachusetts does not show where or when he got degrees.

THOMAS HEYWARD, JR. (SOUTH CAROLINA)

SIGNER OF THE DECLARATION OF INDEPENDENCE AND THE ARTICLES OF CONFEDERATION. Born July 28, 1746, on his father's plantation in St. Luke's Parish, South Carolina. Died March 6, 1809, on his plantation, "White Hall", in St. Luke's Parish, South Carolina. Buried in the old family burial grounds on his father's plantation, "Old House", in St. Luke's Parish, South Carolina.

BIOGRAPHICAL: Studied law in the Middle Temple at London, returned to South Carolina in 1771, admitted to the bar, and practiced there. Member, Second Continental Congress, 1776-78. Captain, South Carolina Artillery Company in 1776; wounded at Beaufort, February 9, 1779. Taken prisoner at Charleston, May 12, 1780; released in April, 1781. Member, Commons House of Assembly in 1772; member, Committee of Safety in 1775 and 1776; member, General Assembly, 1776-78; member, State House of Representatives, 1778-1784. Judge of State Courts, 1779-1789. Co-founder and first President of the Agricultural Society of South Carolina in 1785. "There is no record of his having been a Mason." (Roth, p. 162)

SAMUEL HOLTEN (MASSACHUSETTS)

SIGNER OF THE ARTICLES OF CONFEDERATION. Born June 9, 1738, in Danvers, Massachusetts. Died January 2, 1816, in Danvers, Massachusetts. Buried in the Holten Cemetery, Danvers, Massachusetts.

BIOGRAPHICAL: Studied medicine and practiced in Gloucester, Massachusetts, for a short time, and then in Danvers. Member, Continental Congress, 1778-1780, and 1782-1787; elected President pro-tempore, August 17, 1785. Member, Committee of Safety in 1775; member, State House of Representatives, 1787; State Senate, 1780-82, 1784, 1786, 1789, and 1790. Member, Third United States Congress, March 4, 1793, to March 3, 1795. Appointed Judge of the Probate Court for Essex County in 1796 and served until his resignation in 1815. No evidence of Masonic membership or activity.

STEPHEN HOPKINS (RHODE ISLAND)

SIGNER OF THE ARTICLES OF ASSOCIATION AND THE DECLARATION OF INDEPENDENCE. Born March 7, 1707, in Providence, Rhode Island. Died July 13, 1785, in Providence, Rhode Island. Buried in North Burial Ground, Providence, Rhode Island.

BIOGRAPHICAL: Attended public schools. Member, General Assembly, 1732-1752, and 1770-75, serving as Speaker, 1738-1744, and 1749. Member, First and Second Continental Congresses, 1774-1780. A prominent State legislator, and held three important offices at the same time: member of the State Assembly, member of Continental Congress, and Chief Justice of Rhode Island. Colonial Governor of Rhode Island, 1755-1768, except for a four year interval. A founder of Brown College and its first Chancellor.

MASONIC: "He was a member of Master's Lodge, October 25, 1748, Providence, R. I." (Roth, p. 160) "Alleged membership not conclusively proven. Doubtful because of Quaker connections." (Case) Brother Fred W. Johnstone, Acting Grand Secretary of the Grand Lodge of Rhode Island, writes on November 25, 1957: "Regarding Stephen Hopkins, no record could be found of his belonging to the Masonic Fraternity."

FRANCIS HOPKINSON (NEW JERSEY)

SIGNER OF THE DECLARATION OF INDEPENDENCE. Born September 21, 1737, in Philadelphia, Pennsylvania. Died May 9, 1791, in Philadelphia, Pennsylvania. Buried in Christ Church Cemetery, Philadelphia, Pennsylvania.

BIOGRAPHICAL: Awarded the first diploma granted by the University of Pennsylvania in 1757. Studied law, admitted to the bar in 1761, and began practice in Philadelphia. Moved to New Jersey in 1774 and resumed the practice of law in Bordentown. Member, Second Continental Congress, June 22 to November 30, 1776. Treasurer of Continental Loan Office in 1778; United States District Judge for the Eastern District of Pennsylvania, 1789-1791. Elected Associate Justice of the Supreme Court of New Jersey in 1776, but declined the office; Judge of the Admiralty Court of Pennsylvania, 1779, and reappointed in 1780 and 1787.

MASONIC: "There is no record of his having been a Mason." (Roth, p. 161) "Alleged membership not conclusively proven." (Case) From a memo prepared by Brother M. E. Vandever, Philadelphia: "The signer's father and grandfather were members. Thomas, the father, a member of St. John's Lodge No. 1, Philadelphia, and Francis, the grandfather, member of that same lodge."

TITUS HOSMER (CONNECTICUT)

SIGNER OF THE ARTICLES OF CONFEDERATION. Born in 1736, in what is now West Hartford, Hartford County, Connecticut. Died August 4, 1780, in Middletown, Connecticut. Buried in Mortimer Cemetery, West Hartford, Connecticut.

BIOGRAPHICAL: Yale graduate, 1757; studied law, and practiced in Middletown, Connecticut. Member, Continental Congress, 1775-76, and 1777-79. Prominent State legislator. Member, State House of Representatives, 1773-78, serving as Speaker in 1776 and 1778; member, State Senate from May, 1778, until his death. Judge of the Maritime Court of Appeals for the United States in 1780. No evidence of Masonic membership or activity.

ISAAC HUGER (SOUTH CAROLINA)

GENERAL OFFICER IN THE CONTINENTAL ARMY. Born March 19, 1742/3, on Limerick Plantation, Cooper River, South Carolina. Died October 17, 1797, in Charleston, South Carolina. Buried, presumably, in Charleston, South Carolina, as he had returned to his estate at the close of the war.

BIOGRAPHICAL: Received his education in Europe. Lieutenant Colonel, 1st South Carolina, June 17, 1775; Colonel, 5th South Carolina, September 16, 1776; Brigadier General, Continental Army, January 9, 1779; wounded at Stono Ferry, June 20, 1779, and at Guilford, March 15, 1781; served to the close of the war. Member, Society of the Cincinnati. No information on Masonic membership.

JEDEDIAH HUNTINGTON (CONNECTICUT)

GENERAL OFFICER IN THE CONTINENTAL ARMY. Born August 4, 1743, in Norwich, Connecticut. Died September 25, 1818, in New London, Connecticut. Buried in the family tomb in Old Cemetery in Norwichtown, Connecticut.

BIOGRAPHICAL: Harvard graduate, 1763. Active member of the Sons of Liberty. Colonel in the Lexington Alarm, April, 1775; Colonel, 8th Connecticut, July 6 to

December 10, 1775; Colonel, 17th Continental Infantry, January 1 to December 31, 1776; Colonel, 1st Connecticut, January 1, 1777; Brigadier General, Continental Army, May 12, 1777, and served to the close of the war. Brevet Major General, September 30, 1783. Delegate to the Federal Constitutional Convention of 1787. Appointed Collector of Customs at New London, Connecticut, by President Washington, a position he held for 26 years. A religious man, he served on the first Board of Foreign Missions set up in the United States. Treasurer of the State of Connecticut. President, Connecticut Society of the Cincinnati, 1783. "Not a Freemason." (Case)

SAMUEL HUNTINGTON (CONNECTICUT)
SIGNER OF THE DECLARATION OF INDEPENDENCE AND THE ARTICLES OF CONFEDERATION. Born July 3, 1731, in Windham, Connecticut. Died January 5, 1796, in Norwich, Connecticut. Buried in Norwichtown Old Cemetery, Norwich, Connecticut.

BIOGRAPHICAL: Attended the common schools; studied law, admitted to the bar in 1758, and practiced in Norwich, Connecticut. Member, Continental Congress, 1776-1784; served as President from September 28, 1779, to July 6, 1781, when he retired, receiving the thanks of Congress. Later served a short period in 1783. King's Attorney in 1765, and Associate Justice of the Superior Court of Connecticut from 1774 to 1784, serving as Chief Justice in 1784. Lieutenant Governor of Connecticut, 1785, and Governor from 1786 until his death.

MASONIC: "There is no record of his having been a Mason." (Roth) "Not a Freemason; confused with his nephew namesake and heir (1765-1817), Grand Master of Ohio, 1808." (Case)

RICHARD HUTSON (SOUTH CAROLINA)
SIGNER OF THE ARTICLES OF CONFEDERATION. Born July 9, 1748, in Prince William Parish, South Carolina. Died April 12, 1795, in Charleston, South Carolina. Buried in the Perrineau family vault in the Independent Congregational Church Cemetery.

BIOGRAPHICAL: Princeton graduate, 1765. Studied law; admitted to the bar and practiced in Charleston. Hutson remained a bachelor all his life. Member, Continental Congress, 1778-79. Captured at the fall of Charleston and was confined as a prisoner at St. Augustine, Florida, in 1780 and 1781 by Lord Cornwallis. Member, State House of Representatives, 1776-79, 1781, 1782, 1785, and 1788; member, Legislative Council of South Carolina, 1780-82. Served as Lieutenant Governor, 1782-83. Chancellor of the Court of Chancery of South Carolina, 1784-1791, and Senior Judge of this Court, 1791-95. No evidence of Masonic membership or activity.

JARED INGERSOLL (PENNSYLVANIA)
SIGNER OF THE CONSTITUTION OF THE UNITED STATES. Born October 27, 1749, in New Haven, Connecticut. Died October 31, 1822, in Philadelphia, Pennsylvania. Buried in First Presbyterian Church Cemetery, 4th & Pine Streets, Philadelphia, Pennsylvania.

BIOGRAPHICAL: Yale graduate, 1766; studied law, admitted to the bar in 1773. Finished his legal education at the Middle Temple, London, in 1774. Went to Paris in 1776; returned to Philadelphia in 1778, and commenced the practice of law. Member, Continental Congress, 1780-81. Member, Federal Constitutional Convention of 1787. United States District Attorney for the Eastern District of Pennsylvania; declined the appointment of Judge of the Federal Court in 1801. Unsuccessful Federalist candidate for the office of Vice President of the United States in 1812. The first Attorney General of Pennsylvania, 1790-99, and served again from 1811 to 1817. Presiding Judge of the District Court of Philadelphia County, in Philadelphia, until his death. No evidence of Masonic membership or activity.

WILLIAM IRVINE (PENNSYLVANIA)
GENERAL OFFICER IN THE CONTINENTAL ARMY. Born November 3, 1741, near Enniskillen, Fermanagh County, Ulster Province, Ireland. Died July 29, 1804, in Philadelphia, Pennsylvania. Buried in First Presbyterian Churchyard, Philadelphia; subsequently removed to Ronaldson Burying-Ground, South 9th Street, in Philadelphia. In 1950 his body re-interred in the burial ground of Gloria Dei (Old Swedes') Church, Philadelphia, now a National Shrine.

BIOGRAPHICAL: Dublin University graduate; studied medicine and was admitted to practice. Served as surgeon on a British man-of-war. Emigrated to America in 1763 and settled in Carlisle, Pennsylvania. Colonel, 6th Pennsylvania Battalion, January 9, 1776; taken prisoner at Three Rivers, June 8, 1776; paroled, August 3, 1776; exchanged, May 6, 1778; Colonel, 7th Pennsylvania, January, 1777, to rank from January 9, 1776; Brigadier General, Continental Army, May 12, 1779, and served to the close of the war. Superintendent of Military Stores, March 13, 1800. Member, Continental Congress, 1786-88. Member, Third United States Congress, March 4, 1793, to March 3, 1795. Commanded the State troops during the Whiskey Rebellion in 1794. Member of the Pennsylvania State Society of the Cincinnati; its President from 1801 to 1804.

MASONIC: "Not acknowledged as a Freemason by the Grand Lodge of Pennsylvania." (Case) Card in the Library of the Grand Lodge of Pennsylvania: "Irvine was the Commandant of troops at Fort Pitt in April, 1782, when Masonic brethren requested permission to absent themselves from camp to hold meetings, and the petition was complied with. The petition is in the archives of The Historical Society of Pennsylvania, Philadelphia, in the *Irvine Papers*, Vol. 5, page 79, dated April 15, 1782, and endorsed on back 'Free Masons Petition'." *The Washington-Irvine Correspondence from 1781 to 1783*, edited by C. W. Butterfield, Madison, Wisconsin, 1882, page 172, footnote 1, declares: ". . . As a matter of interest to the Masonic Fraternity in the West, and to show that Irvine was disposed to treat kindly the soldiers who behaved well, it may be mentioned that on the 15th of the previous month (May?) the following officers of his command sent to Gen. Irvine a petition, which was granted, asking the privilege of secretly meeting together as a most ancient society, the first and third Monday evenings in every month, except on occasions of emergency: J. H. Lee, Sergeant Major, Pa. detachment; Thomas Wood, Sergeant Major, 7th Va. Regt.; Simon Fletcher, Quartermaster's Sergeant, Pa. Detachment; William Semple, Sergeant; John Harris, Corporal; Matthew Fout, Sergeant; Michael Hanley; Matthew McAfee, Corporal; John Hutchison; Martin Sheridan; John Kean; J. Williams, Sergeant, 7th Va. Regt."

JOHN JAY (NEW YORK)
SIGNER OF THE ARTICLES OF ASSOCIATION. Born December 12, 1745, in New York, New York. Died May 17, 1829, in Bedford, near New York, New York. Buried in the family burying ground at Rye, New York.

BIOGRAPHICAL: Graduate of Kings College, now Columbia University, in 1764; studied law, and admitted to the bar in 1768. Colonel of New York Militia, 1775. Chief Justice of the State of New York, May, 1777, but resigned in December, 1778, to become President of the Continental Congress. Member, Continental Congress, 1774-77, and 1778 and 1779, and served as President from December 10, 1778, to September 28, 1779. American Minister Plenipotentiary to Spain, September 27, 1779; appointed one of the ministers to negotiate peace with England, June 14, 1781, and signed the Treaty of Paris. Appointed one of the ministers to negotiate treaties with the European powers, May 1, 1783. Returned to New York in 1784 and was appointed Secretary of Foreign Affairs, July, 1784, and held this position until the establishment of the Federal Government in 1789. Appointed the first Chief Justice of the Supreme Court of the United States by President Washington, September 26, 1789, and served to June 29, 1795, when he resigned. Appointed Envoy Extraordinary and Minister Plenipotentiary to Great Britain, April 19, 1794, and served until April 8, 1795, still retaining his position as Chief Justice. Governor of New York, 1795-1801; declined re-election, and also a re-appointment as Chief Justice of the United States.

MASONIC: Although he wrote a Masonically significant letter to George Washington on April 21, 1779, "There is no proof that he was a Freemason." (Denslow) This note appears in the Biographical File in the Library of the Grand Lodge of New York: "There is no record of his having been a Mason." An article in the *New Age* for November, 1934: "This distinguished patriot, like other outstanding leaders of the American Revolution, was a member of the Masonic Fraternity." Another *New Age* reference for February, 1938, p. 77, "gives ample proof he was a Mason", by quoting several items of the "long ago", but without any documentation: *American Masonic Record and Albany Literary Journal*, Vol. 4, of October 23, 1830; *Boston Daily Mirror*, Vol. 3, September 3, 1831; and *Kentucky Freemason*, Vol. 1, September, 1868.

DANIEL OF ST. THOMAS JENIFER (MARYLAND)
SIGNER OF THE CONSTITUTION OF THE UNITED STATES. Born in 1723, in Charles County, Maryland. Died November 16, 1790, in Annapolis, Maryland. Buried: "Believed to be buried near Annapolis, where he died." (*The Baltimore Sun*, September 9, 1937.)

BIOGRAPHICAL: A bachelor, active in pre-Revolutionary movement, and member of Continental Congress from 1778 to 1782. Hospital Surgeon's Mate, August 27, 1776, to October 6, 1780; Hospital Physician and Surgeon, September 20, 1781, and served to October, 1782. Member of Federal Constitutional Convention of 1787. Member of the Governor's Council in 1773; member and President of Committee of Safety for Maryland, 1775-77; President of the State Senate, 1777-1780; nominated for Governor in 1782 and 1785, but not elected. No evidence of Masonic membership or activity.

THOMAS JOHNSON, JR. (MARYLAND)
SIGNER OF THE ARTICLES OF ASSOCIATION. Born November 4, 1732, in Calvert County, Maryland. Died October 26, 1819, at "Rose Hill", Frederick, Maryland. Buried in All Saints Episcopal Churchyard; reinterred in Mount Olive Cemetery, Frederick, Maryland.

BIOGRAPHICAL: Studied law, admitted to the bar, and practiced law. Member, Continental Congress, 1774-77. It was Johnson who nominated George Washington as Commander in Chief of the American forces, June 15, 1775. Member, Federal Constitutional Convention of 1787. Appointed first United States Judge for the District of Maryland, September, 1789, but declined the office. Associate Justice of the Supreme Court of the United States, August 5, 1791, and served until February, 1793, resigning on account of ill health. Declined a Cabinet appointment of Secretary of State offered by Washington August 24, 1795. Appointed Chief Judge of the Territory of Columbia, by President John Adams, on February 28, 1801. A member of the Board of Commissioners of the Federal City, he assisted in laying out streets and designating sites for public buildings, and named the capital city "Washington." Senior Brigadier General of Maryland Militia, January 6, 1776. First Governor of the State of Maryland, 1777-79; member, Maryland House of Delegates in 1780, 1786, and 1787; Chief Judge of the General Court of Maryland in 1790 and 1791. No evidence of Masonic membership or activity.

WILLIAM SAMUEL JOHNSON (CONNECTICUT)
SIGNER OF THE CONSTITUTION OF THE UNITED STATES. Born October 7, 1727, in Stratford, Connecticut. Died November 14, 1819, in Stratford, Connecticut. Buried in Episcopal Cemetery, Stratford, Connecticut.

BIOGRAPHICAL: Yale graduate, 1744, and Harvard graduate, 1747; studied law; admitted to the bar, and practiced in Stratford. Connecticut Agent Extraordinary to the Court of England, 1767-1771, to determine the State title to Indian lands. Judge of Connecticut Supreme Court, 1772-74. Elected a member of the Continental Congress in 1774 but declined to serve. Member, Continental Congress, 1784-87. Delegate to the Stamp Act Congress in New York City in 1765. Delegate to the Federal Constitutional Convention in 1787. Member, United States Senate from March 4, 1789, to March 3, 1791, when he resigned. "The crowning event in Johnson's career was his work in the Federal Convention, of which he was one of the most generally respected members. . . .His diary shows that he did not miss a single day of the Convention from his first attendance (June 2) until the adjournment." (DAB) First President of Columbia College, 1787-1790.

MASONIC: Claimed to be a Mason by Dr. Charles E. Snyder in *Iowa Grand Lodge Bulletin* of May, 1938, p. 560, affiliation unknown, but there is no supporting information given. "Someone no doubt confused William Samuel Johnson with Samuel William Johnson, his son, made a Mason in St. John's Lodge (6) in Stratford, Connecticut, in 1793." (Case) (Note: Records of the Grand Lodge of New Jersey give the date of March 12, 1792).

GEORGE JOHNSTON (VIRGINIA)
LIEUTENANT COLONEL AND AIDE-DE-CAMP TO GENERAL WASHINGTON. Born, probably on his father's plantation, "Belvale", on Dogue Run, near Mount Vernon, Virginia. Died—date and place not known, but prior to February 21, 1786, per Land

Office Military Certificate signed by George Mason: "This will be delivered you by my neighbour, Mr. Archibald Johnston, eldest Brother of Colo. George Johnston, decd., and one of the Devisees in his Will. . . ." Buried—place not known; very likely at "Belvale".

BIOGRAPHICAL: Lieutenant Colonel and Aide-de-Camp to General Washington, January 20, 1777, to August 15, 1777, when he resigned. Captain, 2nd Virginia, September 21, 1775; Major, 5th Virginia, August 13, 1776. Very little is known of this earlyAmerican patriot, other than the brief military record given above. No evidence of Masonic membership or activity.

JAMES KINSEY (NEW JERSEY)
SIGNER OF THE ARTICLES OF ASSOCIATION. Born March 22, 1731, in Philadelphia, Pennsylvania. Died January 4, 1803, in Burlington, New Jersey. Buried in St. Mary's Churchyard, Burlington, New Jersey.

BIOGRAPHICAL: Attended the common schools; studied law; admitted to the bar in New Jersey in 1753, and practiced in the courts of Pennsylvania and New Jersey, while residing in Burlington, New Jersey. Member, Continental Congress, July 23, 1774, until his resignation on November 22, 1775. Member, State General Assembly, 1772-75, and member of Committee on Correspondence for Burlington County in 1774 and 1775. Chief Justice of the Supreme Court of New Jersey, November 20, 1789, and served until his death. No record or information of his membership in the Masonic fraternity.

EDWARD LANGWORTHY (GEORGIA)
SIGNER OF THE ARTICLES OF CONFEDERATION. Born in 1738, in or near Savannah, Georgia. Died November 2, 1802, in Baltimore, Maryland. Buried: Thomas W. Griffith's *Annal of Baltimore*, p. 176, states: "Died, also in this city, on the 2d November, aged 63 years, Edward Langworthy, Esq., . . ." No place of burial is given.

BIOGRAPHICAL: Attended a school kept in connection with the Bethesda Orphan House, founded by the Reverend George Whitefield, where he was an inmate; later he was an instructor there. Member, Continental Congress, 1777-79. "Opposed the rebel movement and signed a protest against certain patriotic resolutions adopted by Savannah citizens. Changed his views shortly and was a prominent 'Liberty Boy'." (*National Cyclopedia of American History*) Assisted in organizing the Georgia Council of Safety and became its Secretary, December 11, 1775. Moved to Baltimore in 1785, and engaged in newspaper work there until 1787; teacher of the classics in Baltimore Academy, 1787-1791. Clerk of Customs in Baltimore, 1795, until his death. No evidence of Masonic membership or activity.

JOHN LAURENS (SOUTH CAROLINA)
VOLUNTEER AIDE-DE-CAMP AND LIEUTENANT COLONEL AND AIDE-DE-CAMP TO GENERAL WASHINGTON. Born October 28, 1754, in Charleston, South Carolina. Died August 27, 1782, near Combahee Ferry, South Carolina. Buried on Plantation of a Mrs. Stock, with whose family he spent the evening before his death. Lossing notes: "A small enclosure, without a stone, marks his grave."

BIOGRAPHICAL: Volunteer Aide-de-Camp to General Washington, September 6, 1777, to August 27, 1782; Lieutenant Colonel and Aide-de-Camp, March 29, 1779. Wounded at Germantown, October 4, 1777, and at Monmouth, June 28, 1778; taken prisoner at Charleston, May 12, 1780. One of the two named to negotiate surrender terms with Cornwallis at Yorktown—"a pleasant duty inasmuch as Cornwallis was Constable of the Tower of London where the elder Laurens lay confined." (DAB) Sent on a mission to France early in 1782 to secure money and arms. His successful accomplishment earned him the thanks of Congress. One of the last casualties of the War. Mortally wounded, August 27, 1782, in action near Combahee Ferry, South Carolina. No evidence of Masonic membership or activity.

EBENEZER LEARNED (MASSACHUSETTS)
GENERAL OFFICER IN THE CONTINENTAL ARMY. Born April 18, 1728, in Oxford, Massachusetts. Died April 1, 1801, in Oxford, Massachusetts. Buried near his father's grave in Old Burying Ground, Oxford, Massachusetts.

BIOGRAPHICAL: Colonel of a Massachusetts Regiment, April 19, to December, 1775; Colonel, 3rd Continental Infantry, January 1, 1776; Brigadier General, Continental Army, April 2, 1777; resigned, March 24, 1778. An early and earnest advocate of the cause of the colonies. Member, Provincial Congress of Massachusetts, September 29, 1774. After his resignation from the Army, was active as member of the State Legislature, and in local political affairs. No record of Masonic membership or activity.

CHARLES LEE (VIRGINIA)
GENERAL OFFICER IN THE CONTINENTAL ARMY. Born in 1731, in Dernhall, Cheshire, England. Died October 2, 1782, in Philadelphia, Pennsylvania. Buried in Christ Churchyard, Philadelphia, Pennsylvania, "with military honors." (Lossing)

BIOGRAPHICAL: Lieutenant Colonel in the British Army; came to America in 1756, and saw service in the French & Indian War, returning to England at the close of the campaign. Returned to America in 1773. Resigned his commission in the British Army to serve in the Continental Army. Major General, Continental Army, June 17, 1775; taken prisoner at Baskenridge, December 13, 1776; exchanged, May 6, 1778; was informed that his services were no longer required, January 10, 1780. "Probably not a Freemason." (Case)

FRANCIS LIGHTFOOT LEE (VIRGINIA)
SIGNER OF THE DECLARATION OF INDEPENDENCE AND THE ARTICLES OF CONFEDERATION. Born October 14, 1734, at "Stratford", Westmoreland County, Virginia. Died January 11, 1797, at "Menoken", Richmond County, Virginia. (Heitman gives date of death as April 3, 1797) Buried in family burial ground, "Mount Airy", near Warsaw, Virginia.

BIOGRAPHICAL: Educated at private schools in Westmoreland County and by private tutors. Member, Second Continental Congress, 1775-1780; member of the Committee which formulated the Articles of Confederation. Member of the Virginia House of Burgesses, 1758-1775. Signed the Westmoreland Declaration against the Stamp Act. Virginia State Senator, 1778-1782.

MASONIC: "He has been claimed as a Mason but no record is available." (Roth, p. 158) "No information. Confused with a nephew of the same name who was a member of Alexandria-Washington Lodge." (Case) Letter dated November 1, 1957, from Colonel Cooper D. Winn, Jr., Superintendent of Robert E. Lee Memorial Foundation, Stratford Hall, Virginia, says this of Francis Lightfoot Lee: "I regret that we have no records at Stratford Hall to indicate such membership and my inquiries in the neighborhood have not developed any records from which the information you want may be obtained."

ANDREW LEWIS (VIRGINIA)

GENERAL OFFICER IN THE CONTINENTAL ARMY. Born May 30, 1720, in Donegal County, Ireland. Died September 26, 1781, in Bedford County, Virginia, while on the way to his home in Roanoke. Buried at Dropmore Farm, near Salem, Virginia.

BIOGRAPHICAL: Emigrated to America and settled in Virginia. Served in the French & Indian War, a Major in Washington's Virginia Regiment. Member, Virginia House of Burgesses for several years. Brigadier General, Continental Army, March 1, 1776; resigned, April 15, 1777. (Lossing says he was recommended by Washington for rank of Major General, but he was overlooked.) No evidence of Masonic membership or activity.

FRANCIS LEWIS (NEW YORK)

SIGNER OF THE DECLARATION OF INDEPENDENCE AND THE ARTICLES OF CONFEDERATION. Born March 21, 1713, at Llandaff, in Glamorganshire, Wales. Died December 30, 1803, in New York, New York. Buried in Trinity Churchyard, New York, New York.

BIOGRAPHICAL: Educated at Westminster School, London; emigrated to New York in 1735, and established businesses in New York and Philadelphia. Participated in the French & Indian War as Aide to General Hugh Mercer; captured in Oswego, New York, and taken as a prisoner to France. On his return, the Colonial Government recognized his services with a gift of 5000 acres of land. Member, Continental Congress, 1774-79. Delegate to Stamp Act Congress in New York City in 1765. Member, Committee of One Hundred in 1775, and Provincial Congress, 1776-77. Commissioner of the Board of Admiralty in 1779.

MASONIC: "There is no record of his having been a Mason." (Roth, p. 158) See *New York Grand Chapter Proceedings, 1897-99*, p. 291, remarks by M. W. William A. Sutherland: "It is told of Rev. Francis Lewis, one of the signers of the Declaration of Independence, that being taken a prisoner in the French and Indian War by the Tuscarora Indians, he a Welshman and a Freemason, was saved from this torture and the stake by the Masonic sign of distress, with the words accompanying the same spoken in the Welsh language." "No information. The signer was not a Reverend as far as I can learn." (Case) See also *Masonic Outlook* for July, 1926, p. 332, re Francis Lewis: "The Grand Secretary notes that his name does not appear in the Grand Lodge Register of New York. The fact that Lewis' name was not on the Grand Lodge Register does not necessarily mean that he was not a Mason and in good standing in this State, but it adds to the presumption that he was not."

WILLIAM LIVINGSTON (NEW JERSEY)

SIGNER OF THE ARTICLES OF ASSOCIATION AND THE CONSTITUTION OF THE UNITED STATES. Born November 30, 1723, in Albany, New York. Died July 25, 1790, in Elizabeth, New Jersey. Buried in Elizabeth, New Jersey; body removed to family vault in Trinity Churchyard, New York, New York, the following winter.

BIOGRAPHICAL: Yale graduate, 1741, at the head of his class. Studied law; admitted to the bar in 1748, and practiced in New York City. Member, Continental Congress, July 23, 1774, to June 22, 1776. Served as a Commissioner in 1754 to adjust boundaries between New York and Massachusetts, and in 1764 in similar capacity for New York and New Jersey. Brigadier General, New Jersey Militia, October 28, 1775, to August 31, 1776. Governor of New Jersey, August 31, 1776, until his death. Appointed one of the Commissioners to superintend the construction of Federal building in 1785, but declined, as he did the appointment to be Minister to The Hague tendered him June 23, 1785. Delegate to the Federal Constitutional Convention of 1787. No evidence of membership or activity in the Masonic fraternity.

JAMES LOVELL (MASSACHUSETTS)

SIGNER OF THE ARTICLES OF CONFEDERATION. Born October 31, 1737, in Boston, Massachusetts. Died July 14, 1814, in Windham, Maine. Death occurred while visiting relatives in Windham, Maine, but town records there give no further information.

BIOGRAPHICAL: Attended public schools; graduated from Boston Latin School in 1752; from Harvard College in 1756, and completed a post-graduate course there in 1759. Taught in the Boston Latin School, 1757-75. Member, Continental Congress, 1776-1782. Imprisoned by General Howe during the Revolutionary War, and taken to Halifax in 1775. Receiver of Continental taxes, 1784-88; Collector of Customs, Boston, 1788 and 1789; appointed Naval Officer of the Port of Boston and Charlestown and served from August 3, 1789, until his death. Member, Society of the Cincinnati. No evidence of Masonic membership or activity.

ISAAC LOW (NEW YORK)

SIGNER OF THE ARTICLES OF ASSOCIATION. Born April 13, 1735, at Raritan Landing, near New Brunswick, New Jersey. Died July 25, 1791, at Cowes, Isle of Wight, England. Buried, presumably at Cowes, Isle of Wight, England.

BIOGRAPHICAL: Member, Continental Congress, 1774-75. Active in pre-Revolutionary affairs. Delegate to Stamp Act Congress in 1765. He favored resistance to taxation without representation, but was opposed to the demand for independence and of armed conflict with Great Britain. Spoke against King and Parliament, "yet while his colleagues in Congress embraced the republican cause, he sought safety by adhering to the Crown." (Appleton) After the Declaration of Independence, he abandoned the patriot cause; accused of treason and arrested in 1776; named in an act of attainder of the state of New York, October 22, 1779, and his property, including a tract of land in Tryon County, was confiscated. Moved to England in 1783 and died there. One of the founders, and President of the New York Chamber of Commerce, 1775-1783. No record of any connection with or activity in the Masonic fraternity.

THOMAS LYNCH, SR. (SOUTH CAROLINA)

SIGNER OF THE ARTICLES OF ASSOCIATION. Born in 1727, in St. James' Parish, Berkeley County, South Carolina. Died December, 1776, in Annapolis, Anne Arundel County, Maryland, while en route to his home. Buried in St. Anne's Churchyard, Annapolis, Maryland.

BIOGRAPHICAL: Father of Thomas Lynch, Jr., a signer of the Declaration of Independence. Attended the common schools; engaged in planting. Delegate to the Stamp Act Congress of 1765. Member, Continental Congress, 1774-76; re-elected in 1776, but was unable to sign the Declaration of Independence on account of illness. "Early advocate of Colonial resistance to the encroachment of Crown and Parliament." (Appleton) Prominent state legislator, serving almost continuously from 1751 to 1772 in the State House of Assembly; delegate to the First and Second Provincial Congresses in 1775 and 1776; member of the first State General Assembly in 1776. No record of membership or activity in the Masonic fraternity.

THOMAS LYNCH, JR. (SOUTH CAROLINA)

SIGNER OF THE DECLARATION OF INDEPENDENCE. Born August 5, 1749, in Prince George's Parish, Winyah, South Carolina. Died October, 1779, at sea, en route to France; vessel lost at sea. W. Eugene Rice, in *Masonic Membership of the Signers of the Declaration of Independence,* gives the date as July 1, 1779.

BIOGRAPHICAL: Educated at Eton and Cambridge, England, and studied law at the Middle Temple in London. Returned to America in 1772; became a planter. Member, Continental Congress, 1776-77, but did not seek re-election on account of ill health. He was appointed to succeed his father as delegate to the Congress, and one of his last public acts was to sign the Declaration of Independence. Captain, 1st South Carolina, June 17, 1775, and subsequently of the Continental Line in the Revolutionary War in 1776. Member, first and second Provincial Congresses in South Carolina, 1774-76; member, State General Assembly in 1776. "There is no record of his having been a Mason." (Roth, p. 161)

ALEXANDER McDOUGALL (NEW YORK)

GENERAL OFFICER IN THE CONTINENTAL ARMY. Born July/August, 1732, at Inner Hebrides, Parish of Kildalton, Islay, Scotland. Died June 9, 1786, in New York, New York. Buried in the family vault, First Presbyterian Church, New York, New York.

BIOGRAPHICAL: Came to the Colonies in 1740, and settled near Fort Edward, New York. Colonel, 1st New York, June 30 to November, 1775; Brigadier General, Continental Army, August 9, 1776; Major General, October 20, 1777, and served to the close of the war. Member, Continental Congress, 1781, 1782, 1784, and 1785. Declined to accept appointment of Minister of Marine in 1782. An ardent patriot, imprisoned for authorizing some Revolutionary pamphlets. Member, New York Senate from 1783 until his death. First President, New York Society of the Cincinnati, 1783; first President, Bank of New York.

MASONIC: "No record of membership in the New York Grand Lodge records." (Case) William Moseley Brown, in his *George Washington—Freemason,* Richmond, 1952, cites as non-Masonic correspondence, letters from George Washington to Alexander McDougall between 1777 and 1781.

LACHLAN McINTOSH (GEORGIA)

GENERAL OFFICER IN THE CONTINENTAL ARMY. Born March 17, 1725, near Raite, in Badenoch, Scotland. Died February 20, 1806, in Savannah, Georgia. Buried in Colonial Cemetery, Savannah, Georgia.

BIOGRAPHICAL: Emigrated to America with his parents in 1736, and settled in Georgia; as a young man, went to Charleston, South Carolina, and was a clerk in the counting-room of Henry Laurens. Returned to Georgia, married, and was a land surveyor. Colonel, 1st Georgia, January 7, 1776; Brigadier General, Continental Army, September 16, 1776; wounded in a duel with Governor Button Gwinnett of Georgia, May 16, 1777; taken prisoner at Charleston, May 12, 1780; exchanged, December, 1780, and served to the close of the war; Brevet Major General, September 30, 1783. Delegate to Georgia's Provincial Congress in 1775, held in Savannah; member of a Commission appointed to settle the boundary dispute between South Carolina and Georgia. President, Georgia Society of the Cincinnati, 1783.

MASONIC: "No information on Masonic membership." (Case) *Early and Historic Freemasonry of Georgia*, by William Bordley Clarke, Savannah, 1924, p. 101: (paragraph regarding General Washington's visit to Savannah in 1791) states: "When the President landed he was received by Colonel James Gunn and General James Jackson, both members of the Lodge. The welcoming committee selected by the citizens was composed of Brothers N. W. Jones, John Houstoun and Joseph Habersham, members of the Lodge, together with General Lachlan McIntosh and Joseph Clay."

JAMES MADISON (VIRGINIA)

SIGNER OF THE CONSTITUTION OF THE UNITED STATES. Born March 16, 1751, in Port Conway, King George County, Virginia. Died June 28, 1836, at "Montpelier," Orange County, Virginia. Buried in private cemetery at "Montpelier."

BIOGRAPHICAL: Graduate of the College of New Jersey (now Princeton University), 1771; studied law but never practiced. He seems to have regarded law solely as preparation for a political career. Member, Continental Congress, 1780-83, and 1786-88. Prominent delegate to the Federal Constitutional Convention in Philadelphia in 1787. Member, United States Congress, March 4, 1789, to March 3, 1797. Declined the mission to France tendered by President Washington in 1794, and also the position of Secretary of State tendered the same year. Co-author with Alexander Hamilton and John Jay of the series of papers, "The Federalist", which explained and advocated adoption of the new Constitution. Secretary of State in Jefferson's cabinet, May 2, 1801, to March 3, 1809. Fourth President of the United States, March 4, 1809, to March 3, 1817. Prominent in Virginia government, 1775-79, as legislator and member of Committee of Safety and Council of State. Delegate to the Virginia Constitutional Convention of 1829; Rector at the University of Virginia, Charlottesville, and Visitor to the College of William and Mary, Williamsburg.

MASONIC: "His (Madison's) Masonic membership has never been proved and has been a matter of debate for many years. Many researchers . . . think Madison was a member of Hiram Lodge No. 59, Westmoreland Court House, Virginia. This lodge was granted a temporary dispensation, September 20, 1799, and a permanent charter, December 11, 1799, becoming dormant about 1814." (Denslow) A letter in the Madison papers in the Library of Congress, dated February 11, 1795, from

John Francis Mercer, Governor of Maryland, reads in part: ". . . I have had no opportunity of congratulating you before on your becoming a free Mason—a very ancient and honorable fraternity . . ." This would indicate that if Madison were a Mason, he had joined the fraternity before 1795, which would rule out membership in Hiram Lodge No. 59. It is altogether possible Madison was initiated in some unfamiliar lodge and later affiliated with Hiram Lodge as a charter member. Denslow continues: "The best evidence of his membership, however, is in the attacks made on him during the anti-Masonic period when he was taunted for being a Freemason."

The latest and most conclusive evidence has been furnished by Dr. Donald O. Dewey, Associate Editor of *The Papers of James Madison*, sponsored by the University of Chicago and the University of Virginia. Dr. Dewey writes on November 20, 1961: ". . . I think that I now have pretty conclusive proof that Madison was not a Mason. In a letter of 24 January 1831 (LC: Madison Papers), which Madison wrote to Stephen Bates, he explained that he delayed so long in responding to a pamphlet sent by Bates, because of his lack of information concerning Masonry. He says: 'ignorant as I was of the true Character of Masonry and little informed as I was of the grounds on which its extermination was contended for; and incapable as I was and am, in my situation of investigating the controversy. I never was a Mason, and no one perhaps could be more a Stranger to the principles, rites and fruits of the institution. I had never regarded it as dangerous or noxious; nor on the other hand as deriving importance from any thing publicly Known of it. From the number and character of those who now Support the Charges against Masonry, I cannot doubt that it is at least Susceptable of abuse outweighing any advantages promised by its patrons'." Dr. Dewey further comments on the letter of February 11, 1795, from Governor Mercer, in these words: "I again checked the Mercer letter of 11 February 1795 in which Mercer welcomes Madison to Masonry. This is apparently some sort of joke, for actually what Mercer is doing is congratulating Madison on his recent marriage. I don't get the joke, myself, but if you read between the lines you'll see that it is an initiation into marriage rather than into Masonry to which Mercer refers."

The authenticity of this letter of January 24, 1831, has been questioned recently. It is claimed that the letter is unsigned, was not written by Madison himself, and was folded, sealed and posted to Madison at Montpelier. "It appears to have been written by Bates and like his previous letter, was postmarked from Washington. The Library of Congress has classified this letter among the letters to Madison and not among those written by Madison. There is no question but what the purported Madison letter is spurious." (page 88, *Masonic Stamp Unit Newsletter,* Vol. 2, No. 11, for June, 1962.) Dr. Dewey has graciously given permission to reproduce his comments on the article: "Although the letter is not in James Madison's hand, it is in the hand of his step-son, John Payne Todd, who frequently served as Madison's amanuensis. This letter was written at a time when Madison seldom wrote his own letters because he was extremely ill. As with Madison himself, so with his amanuenses, it was customary to write drafts or file copies of his letters on the back of envelopes. Since this was written on the back of a cover addressed to Madison, the writer for the *News-letter* has assumed that the letter referring to the Masonic connection was sent *to,* rather than *by,* Madison. Before we can accept this interpretation, however, we would have to ask how the letter of 24 January could have come in an envelope postmarked 5 January! I doubt very much that the Library of Congress classified the letter among the letters *to* Madison, as is alleged, but even if this was done, it was done in error. A comparison with Bates' handwriting immediately disproves the allegation that Bates wrote this letter. And, to sum up, my conclusion is just the opposite of that in the *Newsletter:* there is no reason whatever to believe that Madison did not dictate this letter. Unfortunately the recipient's copy has not been found. If it ever is found, I suspect that it will turn out to be in the hand of Todd, or Dolley Madison, or of her brother John C. Payne, and that Madison himself has laboriously scrawled his signature at the bottom." Dr. Dewey continues: ". . . Unless you are sick to the death of James Madison, there is one other muddle which you might want to correct. Although the letter which we have been quoting is dated January 24, 1831, it should be dated January 24, 1832. In the letter Madison makes it clear that he is answering Bates' letter of October 31, 1831. Todd made the quite common error of dating a January letter with the date of the previous year. Moving the matter up a year also seems to bring it more into the center of the Anti-Masonic crusade."

HENRY MARCHANT (RHODE ISLAND)
SIGNER OF THE ARTICLES OF CONFEDERATION. Born April 9, 1741, at Martha's Vineyard, Massachusetts. Died August 30, 1796, in Newport, Rhode Island. Buried in the Common Burial Ground, Newport, Rhode Island.

BIOGRAPHICAL: Attended school in Newport, Rhode Island, and graduated from Philadelphia College (now the University of Pennsylvania) in 1762. Studied law; admitted to the bar about 1767, and practiced in Newport, Rhode Island. Member, Continental Congress, 1777-1780, 1783, and 1784. Attorney General of Rhode Island, 1771-77; prominent in ante-Revolutionary affairs. United States District Judge for the District of Rhode Island, 1790-96. No evidence of Masonic membership or activity.

JOHN MATHEWS (SOUTH CAROLINA)
SIGNER OF THE ARTICLES OF CONFEDERATION. Born in 1744, in Charleston, South Carolina. Died November 17, 1802, in Charleston, South Carolina. Buried, presumably, in Charleston, South Carolina.

BIOGRAPHICAL: Passed the Middle Temple at London as barrister in 1764; returned to South Carolina in 1772. Member, Continental Congress, 1778-1782. An active leader of the Revolutionary party in South Carolina. Captain in Colleton County regiment during the Revolutionary War. Member, "General Committee of Ninety-Nine" in 1774; member, first and second Provincial Congresses of South Carolina, 1775-76. Associate Judge of the Circuit Court, 1776. Member, State House of Representatives, 1776-1780, and again in November, 1784. Served as Speaker of that body in 1777 and 1778. Governor of South Carolina in 1782 and 1783. Elected by legislature one of three judges of the Court of Chancery in March, 1784; one of the three judges of the Court of Equity at the time of reorganisation of the judiciary system of South Carolina, February, 1791; resigned in November, 1797. No evidence of Masonic membership or activity.

RICHARD KIDDER MEADE (VIRGINIA)
LIEUTENANT COLONEL AND AIDE-DE-CAMP TO GENERAL WASHINGTON. Born July 14, 1746, in Nansemond County, Virginia. Died February 9, 1805, "at the seat of Matthew Page, Esq., in Frederick County" of gout aggravated by the hardships of military life. Buried—place has not been located.

BIOGRAPHICAL: Lieutenant Colonel and Aide-de-Camp to General Washington, March 12, 1777, to the middle of October, 1780. Captain, 2nd Virginia, October 24, 1775. He superintended the execution of Major André. In the spring of 1781, he became a volunteer Aide-de-Camp to Major General von Steuben, and served as such throughout the Virginia campaign and at Yorktown. Returned to private life in November, 1781. Member, Society of the Cincinnati. No evidence of Masonic membership or activity.

ARTHUR MIDDLETON (SOUTH CAROLINA)

SIGNER OF THE DECLARATION OF INDEPENDENCE. Born June 26, 1742, at "Middleton Place" on the Ashley River, near Charleston, South Carolina. Died January 1, 1787, at "The Oaks", near Charleston, South Carolina. Buried in vault on his estate, "Middleton Place", St. Andrews' Parish, near Charleston, South Carolina.

BIOGRAPHICAL: Educated privately and in Charleston schools; attended school at Hackney, Westminster School, and St. John's College, Cambridge University, in England. Studied law at the Middle Temple, London, but did not practice. Returned to South Carolina in 1763. Member, Second Continental Congress, 1776-78, and 1781-83. Served in the Revolutionary War; taken prisoner at Charleston, May 12, 1780; exchanged in June, 1781. Prominent in state government, 1765-1776. Elected Governor of South Carolina in 1778, but declined. Member, State House of Representatives, 1778-1780; 1785-1786; also served in State Senate in 1781 and 1782. Member, Board of Trustees of Charleston College. "There is no record of his having been a Mason." (Roth, p. 160)

HENRY MIDDLETON (SOUTH CAROLINA)

SIGNER OF THE ARTICLES OF ASSOCIATION. Born in 1717, probably on his father's plantation, "The Oaks", near Charleston, South Carolina. Died June 13, 1784, in Charleston, South Carolina. Buried behind the chancel of the Church of St. James Parish, Berkeley County, South Carolina.

BIOGRAPHICAL: Educated privately and in England. Member, Continental Congress, 1774-76. The second President of the Continental Congress, succeeding Peyton Randolph, and served from October 22, 1774, to May 10, 1775, in that capacity. Prominent state legislator, serving from 1742 to 1774, and from 1775 to 1780 in several state offices: Council of Safety, 1775 and 1776; Provincial Congress of South Carolina in 1775 and 1776; State Senate, 1778-1780. As delegate to the Continental Congress, received the thanks of the South Carolina Provincial Congress for his services in the cause of liberty. No information has been located which would show him to be a member of the Masonic fraternity.

THOMAS MIFFLIN (PENNSYLVANIA)

GENERAL OFFICER OF THE CONTINENTAL ARMY, MAJOR AND AIDE-DE-CAMP TO GENERAL WASHINGTON, AND A SIGNER OF THE ARTICLES OF ASSOCIATION AND THE CONSTITUTION OF THE UNITED STATES. Born January 10, 1744, in Philadelphia, Pennsylvania. Died January 20, 1800, in Lancaster, Pennsylvania, while attending sessions of the State Legislature. Buried in Trinity Lutheran Churchyard, Lancaster, Pennsylvania.

BIOGRAPHICAL: Graduate, University of Pennsylvania, 1760. Major and Aide-de-Camp to General Washington, July 4, 1775 (Washington's second appointment); Major and Quartermaster General, Continental Army, August 14, 1775; with rank of Colonel, December 22, 1775; with rank of Brigadier General, May 16, 1776;

and with rank of Major General, February 19, 1777; resigned as Quartermaster General, November 7, 1777, but continued in the performance of that duty to December 8, 1777; Member, Board of War, November 7, 1777; resigned as Major General, February 5, 1779. Member of the First (1774-76) and Second (1782-84) Continental Congresses, and served as President in 1783. Delegate to the Federal Constitutional Convention in 1787. President of the Supreme Executive Council of Pennsylvania, October, 1788, to October, 1790, and again a member of the State House of Representatives in 1799 and 1800; Speaker, 1785-88. Governor of Pennsylvania, 1790-99. Member, American Philosophical Society, 1765-1799; Trustee of the University of Pennsylvania, 1778-1791. President, Pennsylvania Society of the Cincinnati, 1789. "There is no record of his having been a Mason." (Roth, p. 80)

JAMES MOORE (NORTH CAROLINA)
GENERAL OFFICER IN THE CONTINENTAL ARMY. Born in 1737 in New Hanover County, North Carolina. Died April 9, 1777, in Wilmington, North Carolina, his health undermined by exposures during the military campaigns. Buried in Wilmington, North Carolina, but place of burial is not known.

BIOGRAPHICAL: Captain in the French & Indian War; Colonel of Artillery, 1768. Colonel, 1st North Carolina, September 1, 1775, the first regiment raised for the defense of the State. Brigadier General, Continental Army, March 1, 1776. In command of the Army of the Department of the South, September, 1776. Member of Committee to prepare an address to all the people of the Colony to protest closing of the port of Boston; member Committee of Safety for New Hanover County. Member, State Legislature in 1764, and later, representing New Hanover County in 1769 and 1770; member, Third Provincial Congress, 1775. No information on Masonic membership or activity.

GOUVERNEUR MORRIS (NEW YORK-PENNSYLVANIA)
SIGNER OF THE ARTICLES OF CONFEDERATION AND THE CONSTITUTION OF THE UNITED STATES. Born January 31, 1752, in Morrisiana, now a part of New York City. Died November 6, 1816, in Morrisiana. Buried in St. Anne's Episcopal Churchyard, Bronx, New York, New York.

BIOGRAPHICAL: Signer of the Articles of Confederation, representing New York, and of the Constitution of the United States, representing Pennsylvania. Educated by private tutors; graduated from Kings College (now Columbia University), 1768; studied law, admitted to the bar in 1771, and practiced in New York City. Member, Continental Congress, 1777-78. Commissioner to England in 1789; Minister Plenipotentiary to France, January 12, 1792, to August 15, 1794. Member, United States Senate, April 3, 1800, to March 3, 1803. Member of the Federal Constitutional Convention of 1787. Member, New York Provincial Congress, 1775-77; Lieutenant Colonel, State Militia, in 1776. Member, first State Council of Safety in May, 1777; member, first State Assembly, 1777-78; Assistant Minister of Finance in 1781, and served four years. Chairman of the Erie Canal Commission, 1810-13.

MASONIC: The subject of Morris' membership or activity in the Masonic Fraternity has been a favorite topic of Masonic writers for some time. There is a card in the Library of the Grand Lodge of New York with this notation: "No Masonic record found in a search of the following references: Biographical folder in the

Library; Prominent Masons file; *Outlook* Index; *Freemasonry in the Thirteen Colonies,* J. Hugo Tatsch; *Transactions of the American Lodge of Research; Washington and his Masonic Compeers,* Sidney Hayden; *Masonry in the Formation of our Government,* Philip A. Roth; McClenachan's *History of Freemasonry in New York; Beginnings of Freemasonry in America,* Melvin M. Johnson."

LEWIS MORRIS (NEW YORK)
SIGNER OF THE DECLARATION OF INDEPENDENCE. Born April 8, 1726, in Morrisania (now a part of New York City), Westchester County, New York. Died January 22, 1798, in Morrisania, Westchester County, New York. Buried in St. Anne's Episcopal Churchyard, Bronx, New York.

BIOGRAPHICAL: Instructed by private tutors, and was graduated from Yale College in 1746. Member, Continental Congress, 1775-77. Member, Federal Constitutional Convention in 1787. Served in New York State Legislature and New York Provincial Congress. Served in State Senate, 1777-1781 and 1784-88. Appointed by the Crown a Judge of the Court of Admiralty in 1760, and resigned in 1774. Brigadier General and Major General, New York Militia. Member of first Board of Regents of the University of New York and served from 1784 until his death. "There is no record of his having been a Mason." (Roth, p. 155)

JOHN MORTON (PENNSYLVANIA)
SIGNER OF THE ARTICLES OF ASSOCIATION AND THE DECLARATION OF INDEPENDENCE. Born July 1, 1724, in Ridley Township, Delaware County, Pennsylvania. Died April 15, 1777, in Ridley Park, Delaware County, Pennsylvania. Buried in St. Paul's Churchyard, Chester, Pennsylvania.

BIOGRAPHICAL: The first of the fifty-six signers of the Declaration of Independence to die. Member of the Stamp Act Congress in New York in 1765. Member, Continental Congress, 1774-77. Prominent in Pennsylvania political affairs from 1757 on. Associate Justice, Supreme Court of Appeals of Pennsylvania, 1774. Morton cast the deciding vote of the Pennsylvania delegation on the adoption of the Declaration of Independence. "There is no record of his having been a Mason." (Roth, p. 159)

WILLIAM MOULTRIE (SOUTH CAROLINA)
GENERAL OFFICER IN THE CONTINENTAL ARMY. Born December 4, 1730, in Charleston, South Carolina. Died September 27, 1805, in Charleston, South Carolina. Buried, presumably, in Charleston, South Carolina.

BIOGRAPHICAL: Colonel, 2nd South Carolina, June 17, 1775; Brigadier General, Continental Army, September 16, 1776; taken prisoner at Charleston, May 12, 1780, and was on parole to November, 1781; Major General, Continental Army, October 15, 1782, and served to close of the war. Governor of South Carolina for several terms. President, South Carolina Society of the Cincinnati in 1783. "It is said that he was a member of the Craft, but proofs are lacking." (Roth, p. 56)

STEPHEN MOYLAN (PENNSYLVANIA)

AIDE-DE-CAMP TO GENERAL WASHINGTON. Born ———, 1737, in Cork, Ireland. Died April 11, 1811, in Philadelphia, Pennsylvania. Buried in St. Mary's Graveyard, Philadelphia, Pennsylvania, but the location of the grave is not now known.

BIOGRAPHICAL: Aide-de-Camp to General Washington, March 6, 1776, to June 5, 1776. Mustermaster General, Continental Army, August 11, 1775; Colonel Quartermaster General, June 5, 1776; resigned as Quartermaster General, September 28, 1776, but remained on the staff of General Washington until appointed Colonel, 4th Continental Dragoons, January 5, 1777, and served to November 3, 1783; Brevet Brigadier General, November 3, 1783. After the war, Moylan was active in Chester County political affairs, and later appointed by Washington to the post of Commissioner of Loans in Pennsylvania, and served from December 9, 1793, until his death. A prominent Philadelphia merchant before and after the Revolutionary War. The first and last President of the Friendly Sons of St. Patrick of Philadelphia. President, Pennsylvania Society of the Cincinnati. No information has been found which would connect him with the Masonic Fraternity.

FRANCIS NASH (NORTH CAROLINA)

GENERAL OFFICER IN THE CONTINENTAL ARMY. Born in 1742, at "Templeton Manor," Amelia County (later Prince Edward County), Virginia. Died October 7, 1777, of wounds received at the battle of Germantown, Pennsylvania. Buried in the Churchyard of Towamencin Mennonite Church, Kulpsville, Pennsylvania.

BIOGRAPHICAL: Lieutenant Colonel, 1st North Carolina, September 1, 1775; Colonel, April 10, 1776; Brigadier General, Continental Army, February 5, 1777; died, October 7, 1777, or wounds received at the battle of Germantown, October 4, 1777. The highest ranking American officer killed in the battle of Germantown. No Masonic record.

WILLIAM PACA (MARYLAND)

SIGNER OF THE ARTICLES OF ASSOCIATION AND THE DECLARATION OF INDEPENDENCE. Born October 31, 1740, at "Wye Hall", near Abingdon, Queen Anne County, Maryland. Died October 23, 1799, at "Wye Hall", Queen Anne County, on Wye Island, Maryland. Buried in family burial ground at "Wye Hall", Queen Anne County, Maryland.

BIOGRAPHICAL: Graduate, Philadelphia College, 1759; studied law in Annapolis, Maryland, and the Middle Temple in London; admitted to the bar in 1764, and began practice in Annapolis the same year. Member, Continental Congress, 1774-79. Appointed by President Washington as Judge of the United States District Court for Maryland, 1789, and served until his death. State Senator, 1777-79; Chief Judge of the Superior Court of Maryland, 1778-1780; Chief Justice of the Court of Appeals in Prize and Admiralty cases, 1780-82. Governor of Maryland, 1782-86, at the time Washington resigned his Commission as Commander in Chief of the Continental Army, December 23, 1783. Honorary member of the Society of the Cincinnati.

MASONIC: "There is no record of his having been a Mason." (Roth, p. 157) "No information." (Case) From the Grand Lodge of Maryland, February 11, 1957: "There seems to be no Masonic record in Maryland of William Paca. This, however does not mean that he was not a Maryland Mason, because our early records are incomplete."

EDMUND PENDLETON (VIRGINIA)

SIGNER OF THE ARTICLES OF ASSOCIATION. Born September 9, 1721, in Carolina County, Virginia. Died October 23, 1803, in Richmond, Virginia. Buried at Edmundsbury, near Bowling Green, Virginia. Reinterment in north aisle of Bruton Parish Church in Williamsburg, Virginia, in 1907.

BIOGRAPHICAL: Studied law; admitted to the bar in 1741, and practiced law. Member, Continental Congress, 1774 and 1775. Member, Virginia House of Burgesses, 1752-1774, and member of Committee of Correspondence in 1773. Member of the Colonial Convention in 1774, and President of the Committee of Safety in 1775. Governor of Virginia, 1774-76. Member, State House of Delegates in 1776 and 1777. Judge of General Court and the Court of Chancery, 1777, and presiding Judge of the Court of Appeals in 1779.

MASONIC: "Member, Fairfax Lodge No. 43, Culpeper, Virginia, he is listed in the proceedings of the Grand Lodge of Virginia in 1800-01-02, and in 1803 death list. His name is on the lodge record as *Edward*, but most Masonic historians agree that this was an error and should have been *Edmund*." (Denslow) Brother Archer B. Gay, Past Grand Master of Masons in Virginia, in a letter written January 27, 1961, states that Edmund Pendleton "was not, so far as we know, a Mason." He suggests "Edmund" has been confused with "Edward" Pendleton, whose name does appear in the roster of Fairfax Lodge No. 43.

CHARLES PINCKNEY (SOUTH CAROLINA)

SIGNER OF THE CONSTITUTION OF THE UNITED STATES. Born October 26, 1757, in Charleston, South Carolina. Died October 29, 1824, in Charleston, South Carolina. Buried at Snee Farm, near Episcopal Church of Christ Church Parish, about five miles from Mt. Pleasant, South Carolina. There is a monument in Christ Church Graveyard to his memory, but it does not cover his body.

BIOGRAPHICAL: Studied law at the Middle Temple, London; admitted to the bar, and commenced practice in 1779. Member, Continental Congress, 1784-87. Member of the Federal Constitutional Convention in 1787. Received President Washington on his visit to Charleston in 1791. Served in the United States Senate from December 6, 1798, to 1801, when he resigned. Minister to Spain, June 8, 1801, to November 22, 1804. Member, United States Congress, March 4, 1819, to March 3, 1821. Member, State House of Representatives, 1779-1784, 1786-89, 1792-96, 1805, 1806, and 1810-14. Governor of South Carolina, 1789-1792, and 1796-98, and again from 1806 to 1808.

MASONIC: Charles Pinckney has sometimes been confused with a Freemason of the same name who is mentioned as a Provincial Grand Steward in the *South Carolina Gazette* for December 5, 1754, *three years before this signer was born.*

CHARLES COTESWORTH PINCKNEY (SOUTH CAROLINA)

SIGNER OF THE CONSTITUTION OF THE UNITED STATES. Born February 25, 1746, in Charleston, South Carolina. Died August 16, 1825, in Charleston, South Carolina. Buried in St. Michael's Churchyard, Charleston, South Carolina.

BIOGRAPHICAL: Went to England at an early age and received education and training in the law there. Returned to Charleston in 1769; began practice in 1770. Not a member of any Continental or United States Congress, but as a delegate to the Federal Constitutional Convention he signed the Constitution of the United States.

Captain, 1st South Carolina, June 17, 1775; Lieutenant Colonel, ———; Colonel, September 16, 1775; taken prisoner at Charleston, May 12, 1780; exchanged February, 1782; served to November 3, 1783; Brevet Brigadier General, November 3, 1783; Major General, United States Army, July 19, 1798; honorably discharged, June 15, 1800. President Washington offered him a seat on the Supreme Court of the United States, as well as cabinet portfolio of Secretary of State or War, but he declined. Served as Minister to France in 1796. While in France on this mission, in the midst of personal danger, said: "Millions for defense but not one cent for tribute." Member, Society of the Cincinnati. After a long record of public service, he lived in retirement for about twenty five years, before his death occurred. "There is no record of his being a Mason." (New York Grand Lodge Library)

ENOCH POOR (NEW HAMPSHIRE)
GENERAL OFFICER IN THE CONTINENTAL ARMY. Born June 21, 1736, in Andover, Massachusetts. Died September 8, 1780, in Paramus, New Jersey. Buried in the Churchyard at Hackensack, New Jersey. (Lossing)

BIOGRAPHICAL: Colonel, 2nd New Hampshire, May 23 to December, 1775; Colonel, 8th Continental Infantry, January 1, 1776; Colonel, 2d New Hampshire, November 8, 1776; Brigadier General, Continental Army, February 21, 1777. His funeral was attended by Washington, Lafayette, and many other officers.

MASONIC: "Probably not a Freemason. No evidence of his membership or activity in New Hampshire or the army, or when buried." (Case) An article in the *Masonic Monthly Magazine* of New Haven lists Poor with officers of a Military Lodge. Some say No. 19; others, American Union. From the fact that he commanded a brigade in Sullivan's army against the Iroquois, which army was accompanied by Lodge No. 19, Pennsylvania Warrant, Procter, Master, it would seem that Poor at least met with this lodge. Brother Case offers this comment on the above: "Not a member of any military lodge nor a visitor to American Union, as many of his fellow-officers and fellow New Hampshire men were."

GEORGE READ (DELAWARE)
SIGNER OF THE ARTICLES OF ASSOCIATION, THE DECLARATION OF INDEPENDENCE, AND THE CONSTITUTION OF THE UNITED STATES. Born September 18, 1733, in North East, Cecil County, Maryland. Died September 21, 1798, in New Castle, Delaware. Buried in Immanuel Episcopal Churchyard, New Castle, Delaware.

BIOGRAPHICAL: Studied law, admitted to the bar and practiced in New Castle in 1752. Attorney General for lower Delaware Counties in 1763. Member, Continental Congress, 1774-77. Read refused to vote for the Independence resolution on July 2, 1776, but signed the Declaration later. Judge of the United States Court of Appeals in Admiralty cases in 1782; member, Federal Constitutional Convention in 1787. Prominent state legislator; member, State House of Representatives in 1779 and 1780. The first Senator from Delaware under the new Constitution, March 4, 1789, to September 18, 1793, when he resigned, having been appointed Chief Justice of Delaware, and served in that office until his death.

MASONIC: "Alleged membership very doubtful because of confusion with several others of the same or similar name." (Case) Brother M. E. Vandever, in a memo prepared October 8, 1953, says: "Claimed to be member of St. John's Lodge No. 3, New Castle, Del.—also claimed a member of Lodge No. 3, Philadelphia. However, the Brother of this lodge and the Secretary thereof, signed his name *George Reid."* Brother Charles E. Green, Historian of the Grand Lodge of Delaware, advises that many years of research have failed to uncover any real proof of the Masonic affiliation of the three signers for Delaware. He says, "We reluctantly feel that George Read, the Signer, was not a member of the Fraternity."

JAMES REED (NEW HAMPSHIRE)
GENERAL OFFICER IN THE CONTINENTAL ARMY. Born January 8 (O.S.), 1722, in Woburn, Massachusetts. Died February 13, 1807, in Fitchburg, Massachusetts. Buried in Old Burial Ground, Fitchburg, Massachusetts.

BIOGRAPHICAL: Captain in the Lexington Alarm, April, 1775; Colonel, 3rd New Hampshire, April 23 to December, 1775; Colonel, 2d Continental Infantry, January 1, 1776; Brigadier General, Continental Army, August 9, 1776; became blind and retired from service, September, 1776. Member, Society of the Cincinnati. No information on Masonic membership or activity.

JOSEPH REED (PENNSYLVANIA)
LIENTENANT COLONEL AND MILITARY SECRETARY TO GENERAL WASHINGTON, AND SIGNER OF THE ARTICLES OF CONFEDERATION. Born August 27, 1741, in Trenton, New Jersey. Died March 5, 1785, in Philadelphia, Pennsylvania. Buried in the Arch Street Presbyterian Churchyard Cemetery, Philadelphia, Pennsylvania.

BIOGRAPHICAL: Graduate of College of New Jersey (now Princeton University) in 1757; studied law in the Middle Temple at London. Admitted to the bar; practiced in Trenton in 1767. Took active part in pre-Revolutionary affairs. Member, Continental Congress, 1777-78. Lieutenant Colonel and Military Secretary to General Washington, July 4, 1775, to May 16, 1776; Colonel, Adjutant-General, Continental Army, June 5, 1776; resigned, January 22, 1777; appointed Brigadier General, Continental Army, May 12, 1777, which he declined June 9, 1777. President, Supreme Executive Council of Pennsylvania, 1778-1781. Aided in founding the University of Pennsylvania, and was a Trustee from 1782 to 1785. Appointed the first Chief Justice of Pennsylvania under the new Constitution, but did not serve.

MASONIC: American Lodge of Research *Transactions*, Vol. VI, No. 2, p. 237, shows a Joseph Reed, Pennsylvania, present at festival of St. John the Evangelist in Boston, December 20, 1778. See also *Proceedings of the Grand Lodge of Massachusetts, 1733-1792*, pp. 269-270. This is a meeting of the Grand Lodge of Massachusetts in Ample Form, on December 28, 1778, to celebrate the festival of St. John the Evangelist. Included in the list of those present is a "J. Reed." No other information is available; in the absence of full name or other substantiation, this is too indefinite.

CAESAR RODNEY (DELAWARE)
SIGNER OF THE ARTICLES OF ASSOCIATION AND THE DECLARATION OF INDEPENDENCE. Born October 7, 1728, on his father's farm near Dover, Delaware. Died June 29, 1784, at "Byfield", Dover, Delaware. Buried on his farm, "Byfield", near Dover; reinterred in Christ Episcopal Churchyard in Dover in 1888.

BIOGRAPHICAL: Member, Continental Congress, 1774-76, and again in 1777-78. Re-elected, but before taking his seat was elected President of Delaware, and served from 1778 to 1782, declining re-election. Member of Stamp Act Congress of 1765; Colonel and Brigadier General, Delaware Militia, 1776-77. Rodney's eighty mile ride through the night, in storm and rain, is famous. He arrived just as the roll was being called, and cast his vote for independence, saying: "As I believe the voice of my constituents and of all sensible and honest men is in favor of independence, my own judgment concurs with them. I vote for independence." Prominent in Delaware governmental activities from 1759 to 1777. Associate Justice, Delaware Supreme Court, 1769-1777.

MASONIC: "There is no record of his having been a Mason." (Roth, p. 159) Brother Charles E. Green, Grand Historian of the Grand Lodge of Delaware, adds: "We have never heard or seen any facts that would connect this great man with the Masonic Fraternity. . . . The name has often been confused with that of his nephew, Caesar A. Rodney, who was a member of Washington Lodge No. 1 of Delaware. . . ."

GEORGE ROSS (PENNSYLVANIA)
SIGNER OF THE ARTICLES OF ASSOCIATION AND THE DECLARATION OF INDEPENDENCE. Born May 10, 1730, in New Castle, Delaware. Died July 14, 1779, near Philadelphia, Pennsylvania. Buried in Christ Church Cemetery, Philadelphia, Pennsylvania.

BIOGRAPHICAL: Studied law; admitted to the bar in 1750, and began practice in Lancaster, Pennsylvania. Member, First and Second Continental Congresses, 1774-77. Member of the Colonial Assembly, 1768-1776. Colonel, Pennsylvania Militia, 1775-76. Appointed Judge of Admiralty for Pennsylvania in 1779, and died while serving in that office.

MASONIC: "There is no record of his having been a Mason." (Roth, p. 159) "No information." (Case) A card in the Library of the Grand Lodge of Pennsylvania contains a note: "Masonic record doubtful—no information yet."

EDWARD RUTLEDGE (SOUTH CAROLINA)
SIGNER OF THE ARTICLES OF ASSOCIATION AND THE DECLARATION OF INDEPENDENCE. Born November 23, 1749, in Christ Church Parish, South Carolina. Died January 23, 1800, in Charleston, South Carolina. Buried in St. Philip's Churchyard, Charleston, South Carolina.

BIOGRAPHICAL: A brother of John Rutledge, a signer of the Articles of Association. Studied law at the Middle Temple in London. Returned to South Carolina, admitted to the bar, and began practice in 1773. Member, First and Second Continental Congresses, 1774-77; elected again in 1779, but did not take his seat on account of illness. Lieutenant, South Carolina Artillery in 1775 and a Captain in 1776; taken prisoner at the siege of Charleston, May 12, 1780, and imprisoned at St. Augustine, Florida, until July, 1781, when he was exchanged. Tendered the appointment of Associate Justice of the Supreme Court of the United States by President Washington in 1794, but did not accept. Member, first Board of War, June, 1776, and prominent State legislator after the war. Member, South Carolina legislature, 1782, 1786, 1788, and 1792. Governor of South Carolina, December 6, 1798, and served until his death.

MASONIC: "There is no record of his having been a Mason." (Roth, p. 164) He is mentioned as a Mason in *The Gavel* magazine, Newburgh, New York, April, 1920, p. 60, but proof is lacking. See the *South Carolina Historical Commission Bulletin 1-9* for 1915-1927, in Library of Congress: Rutledge elected to House of Representatives of South Carolina in 1781 and participated in the deliberations of that body "in the Masonic Hall" at Jacksonborough in January and February, 1782.

JOHN RUTLEDGE (SOUTH CAROLINA)
SIGNER OF THE ARTICLES OF ASSOCIATION AND THE CONSTITUTION OF THE UNITED STATES. Born September, 1739, in Christ Church Parish, South Carolina. Died July 18, 1800, in Charleston, South Carolina. Buried in St. Michael's Churchyard, Charleston, South Carolina.

BIOGRAPHICAL: A brother of Edward Rutledge, signer of the Declaration of Independence. Studied law in Charleston and later at the Middle Temple in London; returned to Charleston in 1761 and began the practice of law there. Member, First and Second Continental Congresses, 1774-76, and 1782-83. "Delegate to the Stamp Act Congress in New York City in 1765, and although the youngest member of the Congress, was made Chairman of the Committee that drafted the memorial and petition to the House of Lords." (BDAC, p. 1769) Member of the Federal Constitutional Convention in 1787. Appointed Minister to Holland in 1783, but declined; Associate Justice of the Supreme Court of the United States, 1789-1791. Nominated in 1795 to be Chief Justice of the Supreme Court of the United States, and presided at the August term; but the Senate on December 15, 1795, refused to confirm him. President and Commander in Chief of South Carolina, 1776-78; Chief Justice of South Carolina, 1790-95; Governor of South Carolina, 1779-1782. A card in the Library of the Supreme Council, 33°, Washington, D. C., notes: "referred to as a Mason," with no further information or documentation.

CHARLES SCOTT (VIRGINIA)
GENERAL OFFICER IN THE CONTINENTAL ARMY. Born in 1739 in that part of Goochland County which is now Powhatan County, Virginia. Died October 22, 1813, at "Canewood," Clark County, Kentucky. Place of original burial not known; reinterred, November 8, 1854, in State Cemetery in Frankfort, Kentucky.

BIOGRAPHICAL: Served in the French & Indian War. Lieutenant Colonel, 2nd Virginia, February 13, 1776; Colonel, 5th Virginia, May 7, 1776; Brigadier General, Continental Army, April 1, 1777; taken prisoner at Charleston, May 12, 1780, and was a prisoner on parole to close of war. Brevet Major General, September 30, 1783. Moved to Kentucky at the close of the war, and settled in Woodford County. Governor of Kentucky, 1808-12. One of his last official acts as Governor was to appoint General William Henry Harrison Major General of Kentucky Militia. Member, Society of the Cincinnati. "No record of Masonic connection known." (Case)

NATHANIEL SCUDDER (NEW JERSEY)
SIGNER OF THE ARTICLES OF CONFEDERATION. Born May 10, 1733, in Monmouth Court House, New Jersey. Died October 17, 1781, while resisting an invading party of the British Army at Blacks Point, near Shrewsbury, New Jersey, during the Revolutionary War. Buried in Tennent Church Graveyard, Tennent, New Jersey.

BIOGRAPHICAL: Graduate of Princeton College, 1751, and Trustee of the College, 1778-1781. Studied medicine and practiced in Monmouth County, New Jersey. Member, Continental Congress, 1777-79. Lieutenant Colonel, New Jersey Militia, November 28, 1776, and Colonel in 1781. Member, Committee of Safety, New Jersey; member, Provincial Congress, 1774, and of State General Assembly, serving as Speaker of that body in 1776. No evidence of Masonic membership or activity.

RICHARD SMITH (NEW JERSEY)
SIGNER OF THE ARTICLES OF ASSOCIATION. Born March 22, 1735, in Burlington, New Jersey. Died September 17, 1803, near Natchez, Mississippi. Buried in Natchez Cemetery, Natchez, Mississippi.

BIOGRAPHICAL: Educated by private tutors, and in Friends' school. Studied law, admitted to the bar in 1762, practiced in Philadelphia, and later in Burlington, New Jersey. Member of the First Continental Congress, July 23, 1774, to June 12, 1776, when he resigned. One of the signers of the petition to the King of England, being the last effort of the Colonies to avert an armed conflict. Member, State Council of New Jersey in 1776; elected Treasurer of New Jersey, and served from 1776 to February 15, 1777. No Masonic record.

WILLIAM STEPHENS SMITH (NEW YORK)
LIEUTENANT COLONEL AND AIDE-DE-CAMP TO GENERAL WASHINGTON. Born November 8, 1755, on Long Island, New York. Died June 10, 1816, in Lebanon, New York. Buried in West Hill Cemetery, Sherburne, New York.

BIOGRAPHICAL: Aide-de-Camp to General Washington, July 6, 1781, to December 23, 1781. Princeton graduate, 1774; studied law for a short time. Major and Aide-de-Camp to General Sullivan, August 15, 1776; Lieutenant Colonel of Lee's Additional Continental Regiment, January 1, 1777; transferred to Spencer's Regiment, April 22, 1779; continued as Adjutant and Inspector on staff of General Lafayette, January 1 to July, 1781. He fought in twenty-two engagements in the Revolution. Secretary of the Legation in London in 1784; returned to America in 1788; appointed by President Washington to be United States Marshal for the District of New York in 1789, and later Supervisor of Revenue. Appointed Surveyor of the Port of New York by President John Adams in 1800. "Elected as a Federalist to the Thirteenth Congress (March 4, 1813-March 3, 1815); credentials of his election to the Fourteenth Congress were presented, but he did not qualify, and on December 13, 1815, Westel Willoughby, Jr., successfully contested his election." (BDAC, p. 1837) One of the founders of the Society of the Cincinnati, succeeding his friend von Steuben as President, 1795-97. No evidence of Masonic membership or activity.

RICHARD DOBBS SPAIGHT (NORTH CAROLINA)
SIGNER OF THE CONSTITUTION OF THE UNITED STATES. Born March 25, 1758, in New Bern, North Carolina. Died September 6, 1802, as a result of wound received in a duel with John Stanly, at New Bern, North Carolina. Buried in family sepulcher at "Clermont", near New Bern, North Carolina.

BIOGRAPHICAL: Received his early schooling in Ireland, and attended the University of Glasgow in Scotland; returned home in 1778. Member, Continental Congress, 1782-85; elected as Democrat to the Fifth United States Congress to fill the vacancy caused by the death of Nathan Bryan; re-elected to the Sixth Congress, December 10, 1798, and served to March 3, 1801. Aide-de-Camp to General Caswell in the Revolutionary War, after returning from Scotland. Delegate to the Federal Constitutional Convention in 1787. Governor of North Carolina, 1792-95. Served in North Carolina House of Commons, 1781-83, and in State Senate in 1801 and 1802. A card in the Library of the Supreme Council, A. A. S. R., Southern Masonic Jurisdiction, Washington, D. C., referring to Richard Dobbs Spaight, Jr., says he was the son of the signer of the Constitution, but that the father was not a Mason.

JOSEPH SPENCER (CONNECTICUT)

GENERAL OFFICER IN THE CONTINENTAL ARMY. Born October 3, 1714, in East Haddam, Connecticut. Died January 13, 1789, in East Haddam, Connecticut. Buried in Millington Green Cemetery, but later reinterred in Nathan Hale Park (1904), East Haddam, Connecticut.

BIOGRAPHICAL: Studied law, admitted to the bar, and took up the practice of law. Major in Colonial Army in 1756; served in French & Indian War in 1758. Colonel in the Lexington Alarm, April, 1775; Colonel, 2nd Connecticut, May 1, 1775; Brigadier General, Continental Army, June 22, 1775; Major General, August 9, 1776; resigned, January 13, 1778; Major General, Connecticut Militia, 1779, to close of the war. Member, Continental Congress, 1778-79. Held several local offices; Judge of Probate, 1753. Member, Connecticut Council in 1776, and again in 1780, serving until his death.

MASONIC: There is no evidence of his membership or activity in Freemasonry except this unverified note in *The Master Mason*, Vol. 6, for January, 1929, p. 35: "On December 6, 1776, the British occupied Newport, and after Major General Spencer (a Masonic Brother) had been relieved of the command. . . ." (Brother Harold R. Curtis, *Rhode Island Freemasonry in the Revolution*.)

ADAM STEPHEN (VIRGINIA)

GENERAL OFFICER IN THE CONTINENTAL ARMY. Born about 1730 in Virginia. Died November, 1791, in Virginia. Place of burial is not known.

BIOGRAPHICAL: Colonel, 4th Virginia, February 13, 1776; Brigadier General, Continental Army, September 4, 1776; Major General, February 19, 1777; dismissed, November 20, 1777. "Drunk on duty at Germantown and cashiered." A veteran of the French & Indian War. No information concerning Masonic membership or activity.

THOMAS STONE (MARYLAND)

SIGNER OF THE DECLARATION OF INDEPENDENCE. Born July 1, 1743, at Poynton Manor, Charles County, Maryland. Died October 5, 1787, in Alexandria, Virginia. Buried in "Garden" Cemetery at Havre-de-Venture, Charles County, Maryland.

BIOGRAPHICAL: Studied law, admitted to the bar in 1764, and began practice in Frederick, Maryland. Member, Continental Congress, 1775, 1779, and 1784-85. Member, Maryland State Legislature when not in Congress.

MASONIC: "There is no record of his having been a Mason." (Roth, p. 157) "No information." (Case) The Grand Lodge of Maryland advises on February 11, 1957: "There seems to be no Masonic record in Maryland of Thomas Stone. This, however, does not mean that he was not a Maryland Mason, because our early records are incomplete."

GEORGE TAYLOR (PENNSYLVANIA)

SIGNER OF THE DECLARATION OF INDEPENDENCE. Born July 1, 1716, probably in northern Ireland. Died February 23, 1781, in Easton, Pennsylvania. Buried in St. John's Lutheran Church cemetery; reinterment in Easton Cemetery, Easton, Pennsylvania.

BIOGRAPHICAL: Emigrated to America in 1736, settled at Warwick Furnace, and later at Coventry Forge, Chester County, Pennsylvania; engaged in the manufacture of iron. Member, Second Continental Congress, June, 1776; retired from Congress in 1777 to manage his estates and business in Northampton County. Served in Pennsylvania Provincial Assembly from October 17, 1764, until 1770. Colonel of Pennsylvania Militia in 1775; member, first Supreme Executive Council of Pennsylvania in 1777.

MASONIC: "There is no record of his having been a Mason." (Roth, p. 158) "No information." (Case) A card in the Library of the Grand Lodge of Pennsylvania has this note: "One (of this name) visited Lodge No. 2, Philadelphia, November 23, 1762." Minutes were examined to confirm this, but no further information is available.

EDWARD TELFAIR (GEORGIA)

SIGNER OF THE ARTICLES OF CONFEDERATION. Born in 1737, in "Town Head", in Scotland. (BDAC gives the year as 1735.) Died September 17, 1807, in Savannah, Georgia. Buried in a lot on his plantation, "Sharon", near Savannah; reinterment in Bonaventure Cemetery, Savannah, Georgia.

BIOGRAPHICAL: Educated in Kirkcudbright grammar school, and emigrated to America in 1758, as agent for a commercial house; settled in Virginia, later moving to Halifax, North Carolina, and then to Savannah, Georgia, in 1766. Member, Continental Congress, 1777-79, and 1780-83. Again elected to the Continental Congress in 1785, but declined. Active in pre-Revolutionary movements of 1774; member, Council of Safety of the Provincial Congress, and Committee of Intelligence in 1776. Designated Agent for Georgia to settle the northern boundary of the Commonwealth in February, 1783. Governor of Georgia, 1786 and 1790-93; entertained President Washington at his home near Augusta in May, 1791. No evidence of Masonic membership or activity.

JOHN THOMAS (MASSACHUSETTS)

GENERAL OFFICER IN THE CONTINENTAL ARMY. Born November 9, 1724, in Marshfield, Massachusetts. Died June 2, 1776, of smallpox, in Chambly, Canada. Buried in Chambly, Canada.

BIOGRAPHICAL: Served in the French & Indian War. Colonel of a Massachusetts Regiment, April, 1775; Major General, Massachusetts Militia, June 20, 1775; Lieutenant General, Massachusetts Militia, January, 1776; Brigadier General, Continental Army, June 22, 1775; Major General, March 6, 1776. His earliest commission was from Governor Shirley, dated March 1, 1746, authorizing him to practice "chirurgery and medicine in the Army." "No evidence has been obtained of his membership or activity in Freemasonry." (Case)

MATTHEW THORNTON (NEW HAMPSHIRE)

SIGNER OF THE DECLARATION OF INDEPENDENCE. Born March 3, 1714, in Londonderry, North Ireland. (W. Eugene Rice, in *Masonic Membership of the Signers of the Declaration of Independence*, gives the date as July 1, 1714.) Died June 24, 1803, in Newburyport, Massachusetts. Buried in Thornton's Ferry Cemetery, Merrimack, New Hampshire.

BIOGRAPHICAL: Emigrated to America in 1716 with his father, who settled in Wiscasset, Maine. Studied medicine, and commenced practice in Londonderry, New Hampshire, in 1740; surgeon of New Hampshire troops in the expedition against Cape Breton. Member, Continental Congress in 1776 and 1778. Chairman, Committee of Safety in 1775; Colonel, New Hampshire Militia, 1775 to 1783; prominent state legislator; Chief Justice, Court of Common Pleas; Judge, Superior Court, 1776-1782; member, General Assembly in 1783; State Senator in 1784.

MASONIC: "Alleged connection with the Fraternity wishfully imaginative and not documented." (Case) Brother William L. Boyden states that his Lodge is not known. Traditional and other evidence establishes that he was a Mason. It is claimed he was made one in Louisbourg Military Lodge of the 28th Regiment of Foot, New Hampshire Troops, while a colonial soldier of the Crown. Roth gives this same information, adding date made as January 4, 1746. From the Grand Lodge of Iowa, October 5, 1957: "Is said to have been made a Mason in Louisbourg Military Lodge of the 28th Regiment of Foot, New Hampshire Troops." Two interesting bits of information about higher degrees: *The Masonic Sun,* Toronto, Canada, for April, 1933: "Only one (of the signers of the Declaration of Independence) was of the 32nd Degree—Dr. Matthew Thornton." From the same source, both unverified: "It was at Valley Forge that Baron von Steuben, General Washington's drill master, conferred upon this Irishman the degree of 'Sublime Prince of the Royal Secret', 32°". And again, quoting from an address by Charles Levi Woodbury, delivered at the 150th anniversary of St. John's Lodge No. 1, Portsmouth, New Hampshire, on June 24, 1886: "At this time (1745), as if it were a fore-runner of future events, Dr. Matthew Thornton, then Surgeon of a New Hampshire Regiment, bound on the expedition (to Louisbourg), made his appearance in this town (Portsmouth). He was a *very high Mason* (italics) before he died, perhaps he was then, and doubtless found hospitable brethren here. But none of them were gifted with the second sight to discern that a future signer of the Declaration of Independence of these United States was then partaking of their hospitality."

PETER PRESLEY THORNTON (VIRGINIA)

LIEUTENANT COLONEL AND AIDE-DE-CAMP TO GENERAL WASHINGTON. Born August 10, 1750, at "Northumberland House", St. Stephens' Parish, Northumberland County, Virginia. (*William & Mary Quarterly,* Vol. V, p. 198, 1st Series) Died—place and date unknown, but prior to November 14, 1780. (*Northumberland County, Virginia, Order Book, 1773-1783,* p. 435: "14 November 1780. Daniel McCarty Esq. appointed Guardian of Sally Thornton, orphan of Peter Presley Thornton, deceased".) Buried—place not known.

BIOGRAPHICAL: General Washington wrote this from Germantown on August 5, 1777, to John A. Washington: "I have taken Col. P. P. Thornton into my family as an extra aid. This I dare say, his own merit, as well as the great worth of his father, well entitles him to." Colonel Thornton officially became an extra aide on September 6, 1777. He served for a short time only, presumably resigning on October 6, 1777, preferring line service. Colonel of Regiment of Minute Men in 1775, but resigned to serve as Aide to General Washington. Member Virginia House of Burgesses, 1772-74. No evidence of Masonic membership or activity.

MATTHEW TILGHMAN (MARYLAND)
SIGNER OF THE ARTICLES OF ASSOCIATION. Born February 17, 1718, at "Hermitage", near Centerville, Queen Anne County, Maryland. Died May 4, 1790, at "Rich Neck", Talbot County, Maryland. Buried in the family cemetery at "Rich Neck", Talbot County, Maryland.

BIOGRAPHICAL: Privately educated; Justice of the Peace for Talbot County. Member, Continental Congress, 1774-77. Member of the committee appointed to draw up a protest against the Stamp Act; chairman of the Committee of Correspondence in 1774. "Summoned from his seat in Congress to attend the convention at Annapolis, Maryland, convening June 21, 1776, and served as president of that body, it being during his service in Annapolis that the Declaration of Independence, which he supported, was adopted and signed at Philadelphia." (*BDAC*, p. 1921) Resigned his seat in Congress in 1777, and was elected member of State Senate; was re-elected, but resigned before his term expired. Member, Maryland House of Delegates, 1751-1777, and served as Speaker, 1773-75. President of Revolutionary Convention that directed the affairs of the colony, 1774-77. Chairman of the Committee which prepared the plan of government for the state of Maryland. There is no record of his having been a Mason.

TENCH TILGHMAN (PENNSYLVANIA)
MILITARY SECRETARY AND LIEUTENANT COLONEL AND AIDE-DE-CAMP TO GENERAL WASHINGTON. Born December 25, 1744, at "Fausley", in Talbot County, Maryland, Died April 18, 1786, in Baltimore, Maryland. Buried in St. Paul's Churchyard, Maryland.

BIOGRAPHICAL: On duty as a volunteer at General Washington's headquarters, as Military Secretary from August 8, 1776; Lieutenant Colonel and Aide-de-Camp, and Military Secretary to Washington, April 1, 1777, and served to December 23, 1783. Captain of a Pennsylvania Battalion of the Flying Camp, July, 1776. "His selection to carry to the Continental Congress the announcement of the surrender of Cornwallis was the highest military honor in the gift of the Commander-in-Chief." (DAB) University of Pennsylvania graduate in 1761; a merchant in Philadelphia before the war, he re-entered business with Robert Morris after the war, but the wartime hardship and exertion brought on an early death. Member, Society of the Cincinnati.

MASONIC: One of this name appears in American Lodge of Research *Transactions*, Vol. VI, No. 2, as a member of St. Thomas Lodge, No. 37, Maryland, in 1805 (almost twenty years after Lt. Col. Tilghman's death). Another case of mistaken identity.

JOHN TRUMBULL (CONNECTICUT)
LIEUTENANT COLONEL AND AIDE-DE-CAMP TO GENERAL WASHINGTON. Born June 6, 1756, in Lebanon, New London County, Connecticut. Died November 10, 1843, in Lebanon, New London County, Connecticut. Buried with his wife in crypt beneath Trumbull Art Gallery, Yale University, New Haven, Connecticut; remains removed in 1928 to new Art Gallery. (Case)

BIOGRAPHICAL: Lieutenant Colonel and Aide-de-Camp to General Washington, July 27, 1775, but felt himself unequal to the "elegant duties" of this post, and was thankful when commissioned Major of Brigade to General Spencer, August 15, 1775. Adjutant, 2d Connecticut, May 28, 1775, to July 27, 1775; Deputy Adjutant General, Northern Department, with rank of Colonel under General Gates, June 28, 1776; resigned, April 19, 1777, because of a dispute over date of rank. Aide-de-Camp to General Sullivan in 1778, as volunteer in the Rhode Island campaign. Harvard graduate, 1773. "The patriot-artist of the Revolution." (Case) The son of Governor Jonathan Trumbull, Sr., and a brother of Jonathan, Jr. Member, Society of the Cincinnati. "Not a Mason." (Case)

JONATHAN TRUMBULL, JR. (CONNECTICUT)
LIEUTENANT COLONEL AND MILITARY SECRETARY TO GENERAL WASHINGTON. Born March 26, 1740, in Lebanon, New London County, Connecticut. Died August 7, 1809, in New York, New York. Buried in family vault in Old Cemetery, Lebanon, Connecticut.

BIOGRAPHICAL: Lieutenant Colonel and Military Secretary to General Washington, June 8, 1781, to December 23, 1783, the close of the war. Harvard graduate, 1759. Chosen on July 28, 1775, by the Continental Congress as Paymaster of the forces for the New York Department; resigned, July 29, 1778, and became first Comptroller of the Continental Treasury, November 3, 1778; resigned, April, 1779. Member, First, Second, and Third United States Congresses, March 4, 1789, to March 3, 1795, serving as Speaker in the Second Congress. United States Senator from March 4, 1795, to June 10, 1796, when he resigned. Lieutenant Governor of Connecticut, 1796, and Governor of Connecticut, 1797, until his death, succeeding Oliver Wolcott, Jr. Was re-elected to this office for eleven consecutive terms. "This man was a son of Governor Jonathan Trumbull, Sr., and a brother of John." (Case) Member, Society of the Cincinnati. "Not a Mason." (Case)

NICHOLAS VAN DYKE (DELAWARE)
SIGNER OF THE ARTICLES OF CONFEDERATION. Born September 25, 1738, in New Castle County, Delaware. Died February 19, 1789, in New Castle County, Delaware. Buried in Immanuel Churchyard, New Castle, Delaware.

BIOGRAPHICAL: Studied law in Philadelphia; was admitted to the bar in 1765, and began practice in New Castle County, Delaware. Elected to Continental Congress, February 22, 1777, and served to 1782. Member, Council of Delaware in 1777, serving as Speaker in 1779; appointed Judge of Admiralty, February 21, 1777. President of Delaware, February 1, 1783, to October 27, 1786. No evidence of Masonic membership or activity.

RICHARD VARICK (NEW YORK)
PRIVATE SECRETARY TO GENERAL WASHINGTON. Born March 25, 1753, presumably in Hackensack, New Jersey. Died July 30, 1831, in Jersey City, New Jersey. Buried on the grounds of the Dutch Reformed Church, Hackensack, New Jersey.

BIOGRAPHICAL: Private Secretary, May 25, 1781, to December 23, 1781, to General Washington. Captain, 1st New York, June 28, 1775, to September 24, 1776; Aide-de-Camp and Secretary to General Schuyler, June, 1776; Deputy Mustermaster General, Northern Army, September 25, 1776; Lieutenant Colonel and Deputy Commissary-General of Musters, April 10, 1777, and served to June, 1780; served subsequently as Aide-de-Camp to General Benedict Arnold from August, 1780, until the treason of that officer was known; joined General Washington's staff and served as his private and confidential secretary, May 25, 1781, to December 14, 1799, the date of Washington's death. In 1817, one of the appraisers for the Erie Canal. A founder of the American Bible Society and its President from 1828 until his death. President of the New York Society of the Cincinnati from 1806 until his death. Mayor of New York City from 1791 to 1801. No evidence of Masonic membership or activity.

BENJAMIN WALKER (NEW YORK)
LIEUTENANT COLONEL AND AIDE-DE-CAMP TO GENERAL WASHINGTON. Born ———, 1753, in London, England. Died January 13, 1818, in Utica, New York. Buried in Potters Cemetery; reinterment, June 17, 1875, in Forest Hill Cemetery, Utica, New York.

BIOGRAPHICAL: Lieutenant Colonel and Aide-de-Camp to General Washington, January 25, 1782, to December 23, 1783. Educated in France; emigrated to New York at an early age; settled in New York City; moved to Utica in 1797, and was agent of the landed estate of the Earl of Bath. Second Lieutenant, 1st New York, August, 1773; First Lieutenant, February 24, 1776; Captain, 4th New York, November 21, 1776; Major and Aide-de-Camp to General von Steuben, September 3, 1778. Naval Officer of Customs at the Port of New York from March 21, 1791, to February 20, 1798. Member, United States Congress, March 4, 1801, to March 3, 1803; declined to be a candidate for re-election. A New York merchant; Secretary to the Governor of New York after the Revolutionary War. Member, Society of the Cincinnati. No Masonic record.

JOHN WALTON (GEORGIA)
SIGNER OF THE ARTICLES OF CONFEDERATION. Born in 1743, in Goochland (now Powhatan) County, Virginia. (Georgia Historical Society gives the date of 1738.) Died in May or June, 1783, in New Savannah, Georgia. Buried, presumably, on the family plantation.

BIOGRAPHICAL: Very little information is available on this early American patriot. Strangely enough, his name does not appear in the *Biographical Directory of the American Congress, 1774-1949*. This volume lists (incorrectly) George Walton as a signer of the Articles of Confederation. The Georgia Historical Society makes this information available: John Walton had moved to Savannah, Georgia, by May of 1772. Delegate from Parish of St. Paul in Provincial Congress, meeting in Savannah on July 4, 1775, to approve the "American Bill of Rights"; member, Executive Council in 1777. Commissioned Delegate to Continental Congress by the General Assembly of Georgia, February 26, 1778. His home was in New Savannah, Richmond County. He was a planter, and held office of Surveyor of Richmond County for a number of years. He was a brother of George Walton, signer of the Declaration of Independence. Mrs. (E. A.) Virginia Walton Hayden very kindly furnished this additional information: John Walton was one of the four patriots who on July 4, 1774, signed a notice appearing in *The Georgia Gazette* of that date, condemning the taxes imposed on the colonies by the British Parliament, and calling upon the people of the Province to assembly in Tandee's Tavern in Savannah to formulate plans to redress their grievances. [John Walton was Mrs. Hayden's great-uncle (several times) and double first cousin.] No evidence of Masonic membership or activity.

ARTEMAS WARD (MASSACHUSETTS)
GENERAL OFFICER IN THE CONTINENTAL ARMY. Born November 26, 1727, in Shrewsbury, Massachusetts. Died October 28, 1800, in Shrewsbury, Massachusetts. Buried in Mountain View Cemetery, Shrewsbury, Massachusetts.

BIOGRAPHICAL: Attended the common schools; prepared for college by a private tutor. Harvard graduate, 1748. Colonel of a Massachusetts Regiment, May 23, 1775; Major General, Continental Army, June 17, 1775, (the first Major General commissioned by the Continental Congress); resigned, April 23, 1776, but at the request of George Washington continued on duty to September 20, 1776. He was appointed General and Commander in Chief of the Massachusetts State Forces on May 19, 1775. Member, Continental Congress, January, 1780, to May, 1782, when he resigned. Member, Second and Third Congresses of the United States, March 4, 1791, to March 3, 1795. Justice of the Court of Common Pleas for Worcester County, 1776 and 1777. President of Massachusetts Executive Council, 1777-79. A representative in the Legislature, 1779-1785, serving as Speaker in 1785.

MASONIC: "A bearer at the reinterment of Joseph Warren, but not otherwise shown or known to be a Mason." (Case) Mrs. Muriel D. Taylor, Librarian of the Grand Lodge of Massachusetts, writes: "We have no reliable evidence that he was a Mason." Further, regarding his being a pallbearer at General Warren's reinterment: "This does not prove he was a Mason, as it was a public service."

SAMUEL WARD (RHODE ISLAND)
SIGNER OF THE ARTICLES OF ASSOCIATION. Born May 27, 1725, in Newport, Rhode Island. Died March 26, 1776, in Philadelphia, Pennsylvania. Buried in the Churchyard of the First Baptist Church, Philadelphia, Pennsylvania; reinterment in the Old Cemetery, Newport, Rhode Island, in 1860.

BIOGRAPHICAL: Educated privately. Settled in Westerly, Rhode Island, in 1745, and engaged in farming. Member, Continental Congress, 1774-76. An active patriot, and a friend and correspondent of both Washington and Franklin. Member, General Assembly, 1756-59; Chief Justice of Rhode Island in 1761 and 1762. Governor under the royal charter in 1762, 1763, and 1765-67. One of the founders of Rhode Island College (now Brown University) in 1756, and Trustee from 1764 to 1776. No record of Masonic membership or activity.

JOHN WENTWORTH, JR. (NEW HAMPSHIRE)
SIGNER OF THE ARTICLES OF CONFEDERATION. Born July 17, 1745, in Salmon Falls, New Hampshire. Died January 10, 1787, in Dover, New Hampshire. Buried in Pine Hill Cemetery, Dover, New Hampshire.

BIOGRAPHICAL: Prepared for college by private tutors, and graduated from Harvard College in 1768; studied law, admitted to the bar, and began practice in Dover, New Hampshire, in 1771. Member, Continental Congress, 1778-79. Member, Committee of Correspondence, January 10, 1774; member, State House of Representatives, 1776-1780; State Committee of Safety, 1777-1786; member, State Council, 1780-84; State Senator, 1784-86. No evidence of Masonic membership or activity.

JOHN WILLIAMS (NORTH CAROLINA)

SIGNER OF THE ARTICLES OF CONFEDERATION. Born March 14, 1731, in Hanover County, Virginia. Died October 10, 1799, at Montpelier, near Williamsboro, North Carolina. Buried in the family cemetery at Montpelier, North Carolina.

BIOGRAPHICAL: Moved to North Carolina in 1745 with his parents and settled in Granville County; studied law; admitted to the bar, and began practice in Williamsboro. Donated the land and laid out the town of Williamsboro, North Carolina. Member, Continental Congress, 1778-79. First Lieutenant in 2nd North Carolina Regiment. Deputy Attorney General, 1768; member, State House of Commons, 1777-78, and served as Speaker. Judge of the Supreme Court of North Carolina from 1779 until his death. One of the founders of the University of North Carolina at Chapel Hill.

MASONIC: One John Williams is shown as a member of St. John's Lodge No. 3, New Bern, North Carolina. (ALR, Vol. VI, No. 2) The name of a John Williams appears in the third column of a list of names in the *Proceedings of the Grand Lodge of North Carolina* for 1797, p. 11, but there is no other identification.

WILLIAM WILLIAMS (CONNECTICUT)

SIGNER OF THE DECLARATION OF INDEPENDENCE. Born April 28, 1731, in Lebanon, Connecticut. Died August 2, 1811, in Lebanon, Connecticut. Buried in Old Cemetery, Lebanon, Connecticut.

BIOGRAPHICAL: Harvard graduate, 1751; studied theology for a year. Member, Continental Congress, 1776-78, and 1783-84. A long and distinguished record as a member of the Connecticut legislature, extending over a period of more than fifty years. Colonel, Connecticut Militia in 1775. Judge of the County Court of Windham, 1776-1804; Judge of Probate for the Windham District, 1776-1808.

MASONIC: "There is no record of his having been a Mason." (Roth, p. 157) "Not a Freemason; confused with others who bore this not uncommon name." (Case) From a memorandum prepared by Brother M. E. Vandever, dated October 8, 1933: "Claimed to have been made a Mason during the Revolutionary War, with Arthur Middleton. Several of this name have been connected with the Fraternity in Massachusetts, Connecticut, Pennsylvania, Delaware, and the American Union Military Lodge." There is a Dr. William Williams, a member of the Lodge at Crown Point in 1759, listed on page 77 of the *Proceedings of the Grand Lodge of Massachusetts, 1733-1792*. However, the signer, William Williams, is known to have studied theology, then engaged in mercantile pursuits, and served as town clerk from 1753 to 1796. See *History of American Union Lodge No. 1, F. & A. M. of Ohio*, Charles S. Plumb, 1934, p. 53: "The making of a Freemason of Col. Rufus Putnam of the Massachusetts Line, was begun at a meeting held at the Robinson House at Nelson's Point, on July 26, 1779, when he with Col. William Williams, and Maj. Thomas Byles, of the Third Pennsylvania Regiment, Lieut. Peleg Heath, of the Third Connecticut Regiment, and Mr. Timothy, Quartermaster, at the Garrison of Fort Arold, were severally proposed to be made Masons . . ."

HUGH WILLIAMSON (NORTH CAROLINA)

SIGNER OF THE CONSTITUTION OF THE UNITED STATES. Born December 5, 1735, in West Nottingham Township, Pennsylvania. Died May 22, 1819, in New York,

New York. Buried in the Aphthrop tomb in Trinity Churchyard, New York, New York.

BIOGRAPHICAL: Attended common schools, prepared for college at Newark, Delaware, and was graduated in the first class from the College of Philadelphia (now the University of Pennsylvania) in 1757. Studied theology, and licensed to preach in 1758. Taught mathematics in the College of Philadelphia; studied medicine in Edinburgh, Scotland, and Utrecht, Holland. Returned to Philadelphia and practiced there until 1773. Member, Continental Congress, 1782-85, and 1787-88. Member of the Federal Constitutional Convention in 1787. Member, United States Congress, March 4, 1789, to March 3, 1793. Surgeon General of North Carolina troops, 1779-1782. At the time of the "Boston Tea Party" he was examined in England by the Privy Council regarding it. Member, State House of Commons, 1782. Member, American Philosophical Society, and in 1769 sent abroad on commission to study the transits of Venus and Mercury in 1773. Returned to America in 1776 and settled in Edenton, North Carolina. Moved to New York City in 1793, and spent the remainder of his life there, in literary work. No evidence of Masonic membership or activity.

JAMES WILSON (PENNSYLVANIA)
SIGNER OF THE DECLARATION OF INDEPENDENCE AND THE CONSTITUTION OF THE UNITED STATES. Born September 14, 1742, in Carskerdo, near St. Andrews, Scotland. Died August 28, 1798, in Edenton, North Carolina. Buried in Johnston burial ground on the Hayes plantation near Edenton, North Carolina. Reinterred in Christ Churchyard, Philadelphia, Pennsylvania, in 1906.

BIOGRAPHICAL: Attended Universities of St. Andrews, Glasgow, and Edinburgh. Emigrated to America in 1765, and lived in New York City and Philadelphia. Tutor in College of Philadelphia (now University of Pennsylvania) in 1766; studied law under John Dickinson; admitted to the bar in 1767, practiced in Reading and Carlisle, Pennsylvania, and for a short time during Howe's occupation of Philadelphia, in Annapolis, Maryland; later, in 1778, in Philadelphia. Member, Continental Congress, 1775-76, 1782-83, and 1785-87. Active in pre-Revolutionary movement. Colonel of Fourth Battalion of Associators in 1775; Brigadier General, Pennsylvania Militia, May 24, 1782, to close of the war. Appointed Associate Justice of the Supreme Court of the United States by President Washington, and served from 1789 to 1798. The first Professor of Law at the College of Philadelphia in 1790, and in the University when they were united in 1791. Advocate General for France in America, and guided that country's legal relations to the Confederation. Suggested and outlined the first financial system for the United States in 1780. Member, Federal Constitutional Convention in 1787. A card in the Library of the Grand Lodge of Pennsylvania has this note: "Signer not known to have been a member of the Fraternity."

HENRY WISNER (NEW YORK)
SIGNER OF THE ARTICLES OF ASSOCIATION. Born in 1720, near Florida, Orange County, New York. Died March 4, 1790, in Goshen, New York. Buried in Old Wallkill Cemetery, Philipsburg, New York.

BIOGRAPHICAL: Member of the First and Second Continental Congresses, 1774-76. Voted for the Declaration of Independence but was absent at the time it was signed, attending Provincial Congress in New York, to which he had just been elected. Erected and operated three powder mills near Goshen, New York, and supplied powder to the Continental Army during the Revolutionary War; member of commission to provide for fortifying the Hudson River, which constructed forts at West Point and placed the chain across the river in 1777 and 1778. Served as State Senator, 1777-1782; member of the first Board of Regents of the University of the State of New York, 1784-87. Member of Provincial Congress, 1776-77; one of a committee that framed the first constitution of New York State in 1777; member of state Convention that ratified the Federal Constitution in 1788. No record of membership or activity in the Masonic Fraternity.

OLIVER WOLCOTT (CONNECTICUT)
SIGNER OF THE DECLARATION OF INDEPENDENCE AND THE ARTICLES OF CONFEDERATION. Born December 1, 1726, in Windsor, Connecticut. (W. Eugene Rice, *in Masonic Membership of the Signers of the Declaration of Independence*, gives date of birth as November 26, 1726.) Died December 1, 1797, in Litchfield, Connecticut. Buried in East Cemetery, Litchfield, Connecticut.

BIOGRAPHICAL: Yale graduate, 1747; studied medicine, but did not practice. Member, Continental Congress, 1775-78, and 1780-84. "Commissioned a Captain by the Governor of New York in 1747; raised a company of Volunteers and served on the northwestern frontier until the peace of Aix-la-Chapelle . . . appointed by Continental Congress in 1775 as one of the Commissioners for Indian Affairs for the Northern Department, intrusted with the task of inducing the Iroquois Indians to remain neutral." (BDAC, p. 2037) Commander of the fourteen Connecticut regiments sent for the defense of New York in 1776. Commanded a brigade of militia at Saratoga, at General Burgoyne's defeat, in September, 1777. In July, 1776, on his way home from Philadelphia, he carried off from New York to Litchfield the leaden equestrian statue of George III for the ladies to melt into bullets. (*Oliver Wolcott Papers* in the Library of the Connecticut Historical Society.) Served as Colonel, Brigadier General, and Major General of Connecticut Militia, 1775, to close of the war. Member, State Council, 1774-1786, and at the same time Judge of County Court of Common Pleas. For many years Judge of Probate for the Litchfield District. Lieutenant Governor of Connecticut, 1786-1796, and Governor from 1796 until his death.

MASONIC: "There is no record of his being a Mason, though he is often mentioned as such." (Roth, p. 155) "It has never been shown he was a Freemason. Confused with his son and namesake (1760-1835) who was Grand Master of Connecticut, 1818-1821." (Case) A letter in the Library of the Supreme Council, Washington, D. C., dated August 25, 1932, apparently from St. Paul's Lodge No. 11, A. F. & A. M., Connecticut, states: "He never joined this lodge nor is there any record of his ever visiting the lodge—and our records are quite complete." See *Iowa Grand Lodge Bulletin* for October, 1932, p. 703; stating its Library is in possession of an apron belonging to Wolcott, given him by George Washington, with no other substantiation. This could probably be the apron belonging to Wolcott, Jr., who was Secretary of the Treasury during the latter part of Washington's second term.

GEORGE WYTHE (VIRGINIA)
SIGNER OF THE DECLARATION OF INDEPENDENCE. Born ——, 1726, on his father's plantation near Hampton, Elizabeth City County, Virginia. (Record in Virginia State Library gives only year of 1726; month and day not known.) Died June 8, 1806, in Richmond, Virginia. Buried in St. John's Churchyard, Richmond, Virginia.

BIOGRAPHICAL: Privately educated by his mother; attended the College of William and Mary; studied law, admitted to the bar in 1746, and began practice in Elizabeth City in 1755. Member, Continental Congress, 1775-77. Member of the Federal Constitutional Convention in 1787, but did not sign that document. Appointed Attorney-General of the Colony of Virginia in 1754, the youngest Attorney-General Virginia has ever had. Member, Virginia House of Burgesses, 1758-1768; Clerk of the House of Burgesses, 1768-1775; Chancellor of Virginia in 1778; Judge of the Virginia Chancery Court in 1777. As a member of Committee to review the laws of Virginia in 1777-78, he produced one of the most important reports in the history of American legislation, for it included among other items, the Act which abolished primogeniture. On December 4, 1779, the Board of Visitors of the College of William and Mary established the "Professorship of Law and Police", the first chair of Law in an American College, and Wythe became its incumbent, serving from 1779 to 1791, when he resigned and moved to Richmond. Freed his slaves, and provided for their support until they were able to provide for themselves.

MASONIC: "There is no record of his having been a Mason." (Roth, p. 163) "No information pro or con." (Case) From the Grand Lodge of Iowa, October 5, 1957: "Lodge not known. John Dove, for many years Secretary of the Grand Lodge of Virginia, and an authority on the early Masonic history of the state, says he was a Virginia Mason."

APPENDIX TO THE MASONIC BOOK CLUB EDITION

BY ALPHONSE CERZA

PRESIDENTS OF THE UNITED STATES WHO HAVE BEEN FREEMASONS

George Washington
James Monroe
Andrew Jackson
James K. Polk
James Buchanan
Andrew Johnson
James A. Garfield
William McKinley

Theodore Roosevelt
William Howard Taft
Warren G. Harding
Franklin D. Roosevelt
Harry S. Truman
Lyndon B. Johnson
    (received only the first degree)
Gerald R. Ford

(Thomas Jefferson and James Madison are sometimes claimed to have been Freemasons but the evidence that is available to us today is not adequate to establish their membership.)

VICE PRESIDENTS OF THE UNITED STATES WHO HAVE BEEN FREEMASONS

George Clinton, under Madison
Elbridge Gerry, under Madison
Daniel D. Tompkins, under Monroe
Richard M. Johnson, under Van Buren
George Mifflin Dallas, under Polk
William Rufus King, under Pierce
John C. Breckinridge, under Buchanan
Andrew Johnson, under Lincoln
Schuyler Colfax, under Grant
Adlai E. Stevenson, under Cleveland

Garret A. Hobart, under McKinley
Charles W. Fairbanks, under Theodore Roosevelt
Thomas R. Marshall, under Wilson
Henry A. Wallace, under Franklin D. Roosevelt
Harry S. Truman, under Franklin D. Roosevelt
Hubert Humphrey, under Lyndon B. Johnson
Gerald R. Ford, under Nixon

FAMOUS DOCUMENTS IN UNITED STATES HISTORY

In order to be able to readily identify those of our Founding Fathers who were connected with the Craft and signed certain famous documents the following information is presented.

The Articles of Association, signed on October 7, 1765

Fifty-three men signed this document; ten are definitely known to have been Freemasons; we have some evidence relating to nine signers connecting them with the Craft but not enough at this time to be conclusive; we have no evidence at this time relative to the remaining thirty-four.

The following signers were Freemasons:

Edward Biddle	Charles Humphreys
Richard Caswell	Robert Treat Paine
John Dickinson	Peyton Randolph
Joseph Hewes	John Sullivan
William Hooper	George Washington

The Declaration of Independence, adopted July 4, 1776

Fifty-six men signed the Declaration of Independence; nine are definitely known to have been Freemasons; we have some evidence relating to twenty-three signers connecting them with the Craft but not enough at this time to be conclusive; we have no evidence at this time relative to the remaining twenty-four.

The following signers were Freemasons:

William Ellery	Robert Treat Paine
Benjamin Franklin	Richard Stockton
John Hancock	George Walton
Joseph Hewes	William Whipple
William Hooper	

The Articles of Confederation, adopted July 9, 1778; finally ratified May 5, 1779

Forty-eight men signed the Articles of Confederation; nine are definitely known to have been Freemasons; we have some evidence relating to eight signers connecting them with the Craft but not enough at this time to be conclusive; we have no evidence at this time relative to the remaining thirty-one.

The following signers were Freemasons:

Thomas Adams	Cornelius Harnett
Daniel Carroll	Henry Laurens
John Dickinson	Daniel Roberdeau
William Ellery	Jonathan Bayard Smith
John Hancock	

Constitution of the United States, signed on September 17, 1787

Thirty-nine men signed the Constitution of the United States; thirteen are definitely known to have been Freemasons; we have some evidence relating to seven signers connecting them with the Craft but not enough at this time to be conclusive; we have no evidence at this time relative to the remaining nineteen.

The following signers were Freemasons:

Gunning Bedford, Jr.	Benjamin Franklin
John Blair	Nicholas Gilman
David Brearley	Rufus King
Jacob Broom	James McHenry
Daniel Carroll	William Paterson
Jonathan Dayton	George Washington
John Dickinson	

Related Titles from Westphalia Press

Ancient Mysteries and Modern Masonry: The Collected Writings of Jewel P. Lightfoot, Edited by Billy J. Hamilton Jr.

Jewel P. Lightfoot. Former Attorney General of the State of Texas. Past Grand Master of the Masonic Grand Lodge of Texas. From humble beginnings in rural Arkansas, he worked to become an educated man who excelled in law and Freemasonry. He was a gentleman of his time, well-known as a scholar, public speaker, and Masonic philosopher.

Essay on The Mysteries and the True Object of The Brotherhood of Freemasons
by Jason Williams

This isn't a reprint of a classic. It's a new rendition with new life breathed into it, to be enjoyed both by the layperson trying to understand the Craft and Masonic scholars taking a deeper dive into the fraternity's golden years—when the concepts of liberty and equality were still fresh.

Female Emancipation and Masonic Membership:
An Essential Collection
By Guillermo De Los Reyes Heredia

Female Emancipation and Masonic Membership: An Essential Combination is a collection of essays on Freemasonry and gender that promotes a transatlantic discussion of the study of the history of women and Freemasonry and their contribution in different countries.

Freemasonry, Heir to the Enlightenment
by Cécile Révauger

Modern Freemasonry may have mythical roots in Solomon's time but is really the heir to the Enlightenment. Ever since the early eighteenth century freemasons have endeavored to convey the values of the Enlightenment in the cultural, political and religious fields, in Europe, the American colonies and the emerging United States.

Freemasonry: A French View
by Roger Dachez and Alain Bauer

Perhaps one should speak not of Freemasonry but of Freemasonries in the plural. In each country Masonic historiography has developed uniqueness. Two of the best known French Masonic scholars present their own view of the worldwide evolution and challenging mysteries of the fraternity over the centuries.

Worlds of Print: The Moral Imagination of an Informed Citizenry, 1734 to 1839
by John Slifko

John Slifko argues that freemasonry was representative and played an important role in a larger cultural transformation of literacy and helped articulate the moral imagination of an informed democratic citizenry via fast emerging worlds of print.

Why Thirty-Three?: Searching for Masonic Origins
by S. Brent Morris, PhD

What "high degrees" were in the United States before 1830? What were the activities of the Order of the Royal Secret, the precursor of the Scottish Rite? A complex organization with a lengthy pedigree like Freemasonry has many basic foundational questions waiting to be answered, and that's what this book does: answers questions.

The Great Transformation: Scottish Freemasonry 1725-1810
by Dr. Mark C. Wallace

This book examines Scottish Freemasonry in its wider British and European contexts between the years 1725 and 1810. The Enlightenment effectively crafted the modern mason and propelled Freemasonry into a new era marked by growing membership and the creation of the Grand Lodge of Scotland.

Getting the Third Degree: Fraternalism, Freemasonry and History
Edited by Guillermo De Los Reyes and Paul Rich

As this engaging collection demonstrates, the doors being opened on the subject range from art history to political science to anthropology, as well as gender studies, sociology and more. The organizations discussed may insist on secrecy, but the research into them belies that.

A Place in the Lodge: Dr. Rob Morris, Freemasonry and the Order of the Eastern Star
by Nancy Stearns Theiss, PhD

Ridiculed as "petticoat masonry," critics of the Order of the Eastern Star did not deter Rob Morris' goal to establish a Masonic organization that included women as members. Morris carried the ideals of Freemasonry through a despairing time of American history.

Brought to Light: The Mysterious George Washington Masonic Cave
by Jason Williams MD

The George Washington Masonic Cave near Charles Town, West Virginia, contains a signature carving of George Washington dated 1748. This book painstakingly pieces together the chronicled events and real estate archives related to the cavern in order to sort out fact from fiction.

Dudley Wright: Writer, Truthseeker & Freemason
by John Belton

Dudley Wright (1868-1950) was an Englishman and professional journalist who took a universalist approach to the various great Truths of Life. He travelled though many religions in his life and wrote about them all, but was probably most at home with Islam.

History of the Grand Orient of Italy
Emanuela Locci, Editor

No book in Masonic literature upon the history of Italian Freemasonry has been edited in English up to now. This work consists of eight studies, covering a span from the Eighteenth Century to the end of the WWII, tracing through the story, the events and pursuits related to the Grand Orient of Italy.

westphaliapress.org

Policy Studies Organization

The Policy Studies Organization (PSO) is a publisher of academic journals and book series, sponsor of conferences, and producer of programs.

Policy Studies Organization publishes dozens of journals on a range of topics, such as European Policy Analysis, Journal of Elder Studies, Indian Politics & Polity, Journal of Critical Infrastructure Policy, and Popular Culture Review.

Additionally, Policy Studies Organization hosts numerous conferences. These conferences include the Middle East Dialogue, Space Education and Strategic Applications Conference, International Criminology Conference, Dupont Summit on Science, Technology and Environmental Policy, World Conference on Fraternalism, Freemasonry and History, and the Internet Policy & Politics Conference.

For more information on these projects, access videos of past events, and upcoming events, please visit us at:

www.ipsonet.org

www.ingramcontent.com/pod-product-compliance
Lightning Source LLC
Chambersburg PA
CBHW051545020426
42333CB00016B/2100